The Inextinguishable Symphony

A True Story of Music and Love in Nazi Germany

Martin Goldsmith

John Wiley & Sons, Inc.
New York • Chichester • Weinheim • Brisbane • Singapore • Toronto

Published by John Wiley & Sons, Inc. Published simultaneously in Canada

The following have generously given permission to use quotations from copyrighted works. From the play *Sheppy* by W. Somerset Maugham. Reprinted by permission of A. P. Watt Ltd, on behalf of The Royal Literary Fund. From the poem "September 1, 1939" by W. H. Auden. Copyright 1940 by W. H. Auden. Reprinted by permission of Random House, Inc. and in the British Commonwealth by permission of Faber and Faber Ltd. The poem "It Goes Out" by Heinrich Heine, from *The Complete Poems of Heinrich Heine: A Modern English Version*, translated by Hal Draper. Copyright 1982. Reprinted by permission of Suhrkamp/Insel.

This publication is designed to provide accurate and authoritative information in regard to the subject matter covered. It is sold with the understanding that the publisher is not engaged in rendering professional services. If professional advice or other expert assistance is required, the services of a competent professional person should be sought.

Library of Congress Cataloging-in-Publication Data:
Goldsmith, Martin.
    The inextinguishable symphony: a true story of music and love in Nazi Germany / Martin Goldsmith.
      p. cm.
    Includes bibliographical references (p. 333).
    ISBN 0-471-35097-4 (cloth : alk. paper)
    ISBN 0-471-07864-6 (paper : alk. paper)
    1. Goldsmith, George, 1913– 2. Goldsmith, Rosemary, 1917–1984.
    3. Jewish musicians—Germany—Biography. 4. Holocaust, Jewish (1939–1945)—Biography. I. Title.

ML395.G65 2000
940.53'18'092243—dc21
[B]   00-025955

Printed in the United States of America

10 9 8 7 6 5 4 3 2

To my family

Music is Life, and like Life, inextinguishable.

—Carl Nielsen

The past is never dead. It isn't even past.

—William Faulkner

The oldest hath borne most: we that are young
Shall never see so much, nor live so long.

—William Shakespeare

CONTENTS

1

Prelude

THE FIRST SCENE of the opera *Die Walküre*, the second of the four operas making up Richard Wagner's Ring Cycle, takes place in the house of Hunding, a fierce warlord. The central feature of Hunding's house is a mighty ash tree, its trunk soaring up from the floor, its branches forming a canopy over the roof. Embedded in the massive trunk is a golden sword the god Wotan has left for his son, the hero Siegmund, to find and wield at his hour of need.

In the house where I grew up with my father, my mother, and my brother, there was also an enormous tree growing up through the roof, its great trunk dominating the enclosed space. In many ways we shared a perfectly ordinary family life. My father spoke to my mother. My mother tucked me in at night. My brother and I played with each other, when we weren't fighting.

But none of us ever acknowledged the tree.

The tree wasn't real, of course. But its impact on my family was overwhelming. The effort it required for all of us not to take conscious notice of it was also huge. This enormous presence in our house was the fate of my parents' families—Jews who lived in Germany in the 1930s—and my parents' escape from that fate. Their story, so similar to and yet so different from the six million other stories of that time and place, affected everything these two people did. It was at the root of their lives and grew ever upward as they grew older. And, as in so many other families like ours, it was something we never spoke of.

Not that I was completely unaware of the tree and the shadow it cast on our house. When my friends talked about visiting their grandparents at Thanksgiving or going to the ball game with Uncle Ed,

I knew that something from the past had made similar excursions impossible for me. And returning to our house following an afternoon of playing in the neighborhood, I was often conscious of taking off my own real personality, hanging it up in the closet with my jacket, and donning a sort of internal costume that would enable me to blend in with the emotional scenery. But, again, we never spoke of such things.

Let me hasten to say that such talk was never overtly forbidden. By no means was I or my brother ever shushed when we attempted to steer the conversation in certain directions. We simply never made such attempts. As a family we didn't discuss what had happened in Germany for the same reason that we didn't discuss bauxite mining in Peru. They were both subjects that did not exist for us.

Nor do I want to give the impression of a dark and gloomy household where silence reigned. Not at all. Life revolved around my mother's activities as a musician—a violist—first as a member of the St. Louis Symphony and later as a member of the Cleveland Orchestra, and that meant that there was always music in the house. My parents' friends and colleagues would often come by for after-concert parties, when the house would resound with music and laughter.

But every year the tree grew taller. And as I grew older, I came to be more and more aware of its presence, and of how odd it was that we never spoke of it, since it dominated the landscape. Its leaves turned yellow and drifted to the ground when my mother died in 1984. The tree itself remained, however, casting its prodigious shadow over my relationship with my father. Finally, as we both grew more aware of the ever-quickening passage of time, I decided to do something about it.

In 1992, the year I turned forty, I was traveling in Europe while my father, who was nearly seventy-nine, was also in Europe with his new love, Emily Erwin. We arranged to meet in Oldenburg, my father's hometown. We visited his childhood home, and he told me something of his memories of that long-ago time. He took me to where his father's store had been and told me that Nazi thugs had organized a boycott of the store in April 1933, an action that led to his father's having to sell the family house. He showed me the Pferdemarkt, the Horse Market, where his father had been taken following his arrest in November 1938. Slowly, those shadowy figures, my grandparents, whom

I'd never known, began to take on human form. And for the first time, my father and I began to take notice of the huge tree in our house.

It wasn't a fast process, by any means. A year later, while visiting my father in Tucson, I tried to get him to talk more about his youth. He spoke only briefly, however, and quickly moved the conversation on to something else. It was obvious that he found these trips into the past very painful. But I persisted in my efforts to talk to him about those days, believing that coming to terms with them would somehow benefit both him and our relationship. And that visit to Tucson resulted in something extraordinary: he agreed to come to Washington, D.C., and tour with me the newly opened United States Holocaust Memorial Museum.

A few days before my father's arrival, I happened to mention our plan to Alex Chadwick, a friend at National Public Radio. Alex asked if he could come along with a microphone and record my father's reactions. Both my father and I agreed, and in late January 1994, the three of us visited the museum.

Those hours marked a turning point in my father's life, and in our relationship. At first, I thought I had made a terrible mistake in asking him to come to the museum. To tour the permanent exhibition, you enter an elevator that takes you to the top floor, from which you slowly walk back down to ground level. When we stepped out of the elevator, the first image that met my father's eyes was a huge photograph of General Eisenhower touring a concentration camp after the war, surrounded by the skeletal remains of former prisoners. He gasped and tried to get back into the elevator, but the doors had already closed. Alex and I steadied him and we made our way through the rest of the museum—the names and faces, the piles of shoes and eyeglasses, the cattle car, and an oboe played by the man who sat right next to my father in the Berlin Jüdische Kulturbund orchestra.

My father took it all in and spoke very little. But the next day he came to NPR and recorded an interview with Alex, trying, he said, to explain the unexplainable. Alex prepared a feature for NPR's *Morning Edition*, and suddenly people all over America began calling my father to tell him that they had been moved by his story. He, in turn, was moved by their interest. Having lived in silence with his thoughts and his memories for so long, he had come to feel isolated from other people. Now those people were reaching out to him, and the effect was transforming—for both of us.

He now felt more at ease with his past and with me. I had always felt distanced from him, but now I saw him in a different light: less as someone who had deliberately shut me out and more as someone who had heroically overcome the horrors of the Third Reich to establish a normal and rich life in a foreign land. We became good friends.

And we began to talk about his early years in Germany. The more I learned, the more I respected him, and the more I learned about myself as well. I discovered an important source of my feelings for music. It's beautiful and moving, of course, but music also literally saved my parents' lives. Had they not been members of an all-Jewish orchestra, maintained at the pleasure of Joseph Goebbels's Ministry of Propaganda, they would never have made it out of Germany alive. During their years in Berlin, before their escape, my parents frequently risked everything by defying the Nazi curfews so that they could play chamber music with their friends. As I heard my father tell me his story, I came to realize that somehow I had inherited the knowledge that music can not only enrich your life, it is also something worth risking your life for. I came to see that my chosen profession has been no accident. Maybe, in fact, it chose me.

I learned that the tree growing in our house, like the ash tree in the house of Hunding, also contained a golden sword buried deep within its trunk. My parents' story of music and courage and persistence and luck was no weapon, but it has proven to be a source of great strength and inspiration for me. By sharing his life, my father has enabled me to extract and possess a rich treasure of understanding and hope.

2

Alex and Günther

TUESDAY, NOVEMBER 9, 1999. On a chill and foggy day, my brother and I have come to Sachsenhagen, a small town in Lower Saxony, in search of a cemetery. In the center of the village stands a handsome stone church surrounded by a well-groomed graveyard, its monuments immaculate and garlanded with flowers that seem to glow in the afternoon gloom. But our destination is not here. Around the corner, in a modern annex to the seventeenth-century town hall, we inquire after the location of the town's Jewish cemetery.

Following directions, we drive our rented Volkswagen about a kilometer down the road, keeping a sharp lookout on our right. We pass a few houses, a canal, a clump of trees, a fenced-in yard that encloses a flock of chickens, a small factory, and then find ourselves in the flat German countryside, well beyond the city limits. We return to town and this time ask at the bakery: *"Bitte, wo ist der Jüdische Friedhof?"* We are directed down the same road, with similar results. We see nothing even remotely resembling a cemetery.

We leave the car in the driveway of one of the houses and begin to walk along the road. I spy a path leading off into the clump of trees, a lane made barely discernible by two faint tire tracks. We follow the path for perhaps fifty yards and come upon a low wooden gate, its surfaces covered by a thin layer of dark green moss. To the left of the gate is a narrow pole about seven feet high. To the top of the pole is affixed a small sign, and on it are the words *Jüdischer Friedhof.* We'd found it.

We push open the gate and walk another few yards into the trees. There, beneath the branches, we discover a haphazard arrangement of

My great-grandfather's grave in the ill-kept Jewish cemetery in Sachsenhagen. The circumstances of finding it only added to the thrill of its discovery.

perhaps twenty-five headstones, each of them bearing Hebrew lettering on one side and old German script on the other. The graves are green with the same moss that adorns the gate. The grass is green, tall, and ragged underfoot. The wooden canopy above is green, with flecks of yellow and brown. It is like being under water, or in a dream.

My brother lets out a cry. We rush forward a few paces and stare at the only gravestone fashioned of black marble. It stands directly beneath a tall and graceful spruce tree. We speak, out loud, the words:

"Hier ruht unser lieber Vater Moses Goldschmidt, 18 February, 1835, to 15 April, 1908." Two graves to the left, we read: "Auguste Goldschmidt, born Philipssohn." Moses and Auguste, our great-grandparents.

Four thousand miles from home, on an infamous date in German history, we have found the only memorials to our family that exist anywhere in the world.

ALEX GOLDSCHMIDT, my grandfather, was born in Sachsenhagen on the first day of 1879. Sachsenhagen lies about twenty miles north of a town called Hameln, known to readers of fairy tales as Hamelin, whose inhabitants had a legendary encounter with a mysterious Pied Piper. But it was horses, not rats and mice, that were the chief concern of the Goldschmidt family. My great-grandfather bought and sold them, a profession that was then fairly common among the Jews of the region. He did well for himself, with clients both local and national. Moses also raised children; over a span of sixteen years he and his wife, Auguste, brought five boys and a girl into the world.

Alex was the youngest boy, the only one of the five brothers not to follow his father into the horse trade. The other four continued the family's success, traveling all over Europe to help supply the kaiser's cavalry. But like many a small-town boy, Alex couldn't wait to shake the dust off his shoes and seek his fortune in the big city. So after achieving his *Abitur* degree (roughly equivalent to two years of college) and knocking around north Germany for a few years, Alex moved to the cultural capital of the northwest, a town of thirty-five thousand inhabitants called Oldenburg. A city since 1345, Oldenburg boasted a grand theater and a concert hall, an impressive church dedicated to Saint Lambert, and a seventeenth-century castle that was home to the grand duke of Oldenburg. It was also the capital of the state of Oldenburg. Into this metropolis the twenty-seven-year-old Alex Goldschmidt moved in the spring of 1906. Perhaps with a lingering memory of the family business, he took a room on the city's Pferdemarkt, or Horse Market, where steeds were sold in days of old but where, at the beginning of the twentieth century, automobiles wheezed and chugged. Thirty-two years later, that same Horse Market would be a place of fear and shame for Alex. At the time, though, it provided the young man's window on his new life.

Alex spent little time sitting still. He was a short man, with close-cropped dark hair, a mustache, and rather prominent ears. Full of energy for the task of finding his place in the world, he spent the next year exploring the business possibilities in the vicinity; he made a number of inquiries in Oldenburg and also visited several nearby cities to see what they offered. He spent a few weeks in Hildesheim, a town near his birthplace, and also traveled to the Free Hanseatic City of Bremen, about thirty miles to the east of Oldenburg. His trips to Bremen became more frequent once he'd made the acquaintance of the daughter of Ludwig Behrens, a highly successful importer of coffee. Toni Behrens was nearly nine years younger than Alex and a few inches taller than he was, very slender, with short black hair. She was proud of her hometown, which was also strongly connected to a well-loved German fairy tale, the story of the four animals who became known as the Bremen Town Musicians. It was while Toni was telling Alex how the donkey, the dog, the cat, and the rooster frightened away the robbers that he fell in love with her. They were married in Bremen on March 6, 1908. They took the train back to Oldenburg and moved together into what had been Alex's apartment on the Horse Market. Clearly Alex would have to find larger quarters, particularly after their first child, Bertha, was born in October of 1909.

Fortunately, his various business inquiries had begun to pay off. He had found work in the ladies' garment trade, first as a salesman and then as a buyer. Now he discovered an opportunity to go into business for himself. In January of 1911, Alex bought a building in downtown Oldenburg, a maze of narrow, curving streets paved with cobblestones. At the corner of Schüttingstrasse and Achternstrasse, his property was a building three stories high that gracefully followed the curve formed by the intersection of the two streets. On the ground floor he opened an establishment that featured women's clothes and accessories, a store he called Alex Goldschmidt: *Haus der Mode*, or "House of Fashion." He moved his family into the two floors above the store. And it was there, on November 17, 1913, that my father was born. He was named Günther Ludwig, in honor of Toni's father.

The Goldschmidt family in 1914, a few months before the outbreak of the Great War. From left to right: Bertha, Alex, Toni, and Günther.

I am looking at a picture of the young family. It is the spring of 1914. Alex has recently turned thirty-five. His face is that of a determined businessman, confidant but not cocky, always ready to meet a client halfway but impatient with needless haggling. Is it a completely humorless face, or can I blame his dour expression on the unreasonable demands of the photographer? But no—on his lap he holds my aunt Bertha, who will celebrate her fifth birthday later that year; and in her twinkling expression and her left arm thrown carelessly around Alex's neck I can see only utter ease with the peering shutter and its anonymous operator. Günther, at six months or so, seems in the middle of a speech, or a yawn. And over his right shoulder is the only surviving image of my grandmother Toni. Her short hair, parted neatly in the middle, her thick eyebrows, her strong nose and smallish mouth are all masculine features. This complete stranger, this woman I have never met, nonetheless looks very familiar. Of course—hers is the face my father's will grow into.

Oldenburg's Schüttingstrasse in 1911, the year Grandfather Alex bought his property and opened his store, the Haus der Mode. It was located at the end of the block, on the right, just as the street curves out of sight and intersects with Achternstrasse.

And it was his mother that Günther felt closer to, to whom he turned for emotional support and understanding, for parental companionship. Combining the first two letters of his first and last names, his mother came up with the nickname Gügo for her son. They had common interests where entertainment was concerned; it was Toni who introduced Gügo to theater and music. They went together to the Lamberti Church to hear Bach's *Saint Matthew Passion;* to the Landestheater for Albert Lortzing's opera *Zar und Zimmermann* and Shakespeare's *A Midsummer Night's Dream;* and to the castle of the grand duke to hear Beethoven string quartets and a memorable performance of Beethoven's *Emperor* Concerto featuring a twenty-something pianist named Rudolf Serkin. My father recalls how taken he was with Serkin's beautiful sound and how amazed he was that Serkin played the whole concerto from memory while the members of the orchestra had the music on their stands in front of them. It was during these excursions that Günther developed his lifelong passion for music.

Today the site of the Haus der Mode is owned by the Danish "Tack" chain of shoe stores. My father was born upstairs on November 17, 1913.

Every few weeks or so, he would accompany his mother on her visits home to Bremen. There he would find himself in the charming presence of his grandmother Jeanette. She was short, prim, and proper, with a rule of etiquette handy for any occasion. Her standards for polite behavior have stayed with my father all his life; to this day he is fond of saying things like "As Grandmother Behrens used to tell us, no elbows on the table while we are eating!" Günther looked forward to those train rides to Bremen, his mother at his side.

There were other reasons he felt closer to Toni than to Alex. He remembers his mother as warm, vivacious, aware, very much alive. His father, in the traditional German way, was more remote and less outwardly supportive. The few times Günther came to him for help, Alex reminded his son that the world was a rough place and that one needed to act like a man and fight one's own battles in order to survive.

And, of course, Alex Goldschmidt had fought, and survived, one of the cruelest campaigns in world history. Nine months after Günther was born, World War I exploded across Europe. Alex marched off to join his regiment in Sachsenhagen, leaving Toni in charge of the store in Schüttingstrasse. He fought for more than four years, first on the Belgian front and later on the Russian front, and miraculously, given the unspeakable carnage all around him, was never wounded. What was damaged, however, was his relationship with his son. In January of 1919, two months after the armistice was signed, and just days after his fortieth birthday, Alex returned to the shop on the corner and climbed the stairs to his home.

Gügo, now five, asked his mother, "Who is that man?" The answer came back, "That is your father."

Those lost years formed a gulf that Günther and Alex never bridged. My father remembers that "we never had fights or arguments. But we were never close, either, and never really knew each other."

Knowing about that gulf has helped me come to terms with the difficulty I've felt in establishing a solid relationship with my father. It seems that we do learn best from example, after all, and my father had no strong example of father-son relations from which to learn.

But the war years had been good in one respect: the women of Oldenburg had continued to shop for clothing and accessories, and under Toni's guidance the store had boomed. With the coming of peace, Alex foresaw that many domestic alliances would also be forged soon, and so he added a line of wedding fashions to his offerings. By the autumn of 1919, things were going so well that Alex was able to afford one of the prime plots of real estate in Oldenburg. In October he purchased from Friedrich Otto Graepel, a minister in the new republican government, a large and handsome house at 34 Gartenstrasse. It came equipped with a cook and a housekeeper. By any measure of material success, the young Goldschmidt family had arrived.

Nearby, the palace of the grand duke encompassed enormous royal gardens with carefully tended flower beds, graceful old trees, a placid pond with fish in its depths and ducks on its banks, curving paths to stroll and sturdy benches on which to rest or dream, and overall an atmosphere of peace and tranquility amid the bustle of the city. In 1918, with the coming of republican government to Germany, the duke's private gardens had become a public park. The house on Gar-

The beautiful house at 34 Gartenstrasse, as seen from across the street. Alex's strawberries grew in the back; Günther's chickens thrived in the run on the right.

tenstrasse (Garden Street) was, and still is, just steps away from an entrance to the Schlossgarten (Castle Garden), and my father and his family frequently took advantage of that proximity to walk and play in the park.

The house itself was a thing of beauty. Three stories high, with polished wooden floors, exposed beams on the downstairs ceiling, and a cozy glassed-in veranda, it also boasted gardens in front and back. A gardener came by once a week in spring and summer to take care of the fruit trees, rosebushes, and rhododendrons, and to tend the spacious lawn. There was also a spot in the backyard given over to a strawberry patch. This was the special province of Alex himself; neither the gardener nor any member of the Goldschmidt family was permitted to touch the strawberries or the earth in which they grew until they'd been safely harvested and brought into the house to be eaten. My father remembers once approaching Alex during the preparation of the berry beds in springtime and asking if he could help.

"No," was the short and chilly answer. Günther felt utterly rejected. I remember how sympathetic I felt when he told me about it and how much I thought this simple story revealed about his relationships both with his father and with me, his son. Never having learned the joys of receiving love from the one, it became very hard for him to bestow love on the other.

But if Günther was banned from the strawberry patch, he had his hands full with the chickens. It was his responsibility to take care of the chicken house and run that extended along the north side of the house on Gartenstrasse. His realm included a rooster and a dozen hens. His favorite hen he called Kippkamm; when she was in a broody way, he would bring her into the house and arrange a special nest for her in the attic. The rest of the family knew nothing of this arrangement, or so he thought. But then came the April evening when Günther came home from school, rushed upstairs to the attic, and found an enormous egg in Kippkamm's nest. Proudly he brought it downstairs to show his parents, only to be met with loud laughter. The egg was a goose egg and it had been put in the nest by Alex, in honor of April Fools' Day. Günther, however, found nothing funny in the joke, and still doesn't.

Meanwhile, the family grew. In June of 1920, a second daughter, Eva, was born, followed fifteen months later by a second son, Helmut. Eva came into the world with a club foot and had to undergo surgery, a delicate operation that was performed at the university hospital in Göttingen, about one hundred fifty miles away. Her leg was in a cast for months afterwards, but the operation was a complete success; my father doesn't recall Eva with even the slightest limp. He does remember his younger sister as a quiet and sensitive girl "full of poetry and dreams." I have before me a thin volume of verse by the German poets

Claudius, Goethe, Hölderlin, and Mörike; the anthology is called *Von den treuen Begleitern* (For the Faithful Companion). It was a present from Eva to Günther on his twenty-fourth birthday in 1937. She was then seventeen. She inscribed the book to her brother in the same neat and tiny handwriting she would use five years later when she wrote him her last poignant letters.

Helmut, the youngest of the four Goldschmidt children, apparently didn't make much of an impression on my father. He says his brother has almost completely faded from his memory, though he does say I resembled Helmut a bit when I was younger.

Günther spent most of his time during those happy days on Gartenstrasse with his older sister, Bertha, and her best friend, a girl named Elsa Boschen, who lived more or less permanently in the Goldschmidt household. Elsa's mother was a widow of the Great War, a poor woman who worked occasionally at Alex's store. How it came about my father doesn't recall, but for several years in the mid-1920s, Alex and Toni fed and housed a fifth child. Elsa, Bertha, and Günther played together constantly after school and on weekends, frequently in the nearby Schlossgarten. There they established an imaginary country called the *Anemonen Reich*, or "Anemone Kingdom." One or the other of the children—depending on what day it happened to be—always served as king or queen of the country, issuing decrees, ordering executions, granting pardons, and launching fierce wars against the enemies of the Anemones. These were usually unsuspecting fellow visitors to the park—probably elderly gentlemen who didn't much like children—who found their afternoon snoozes suddenly violently interrupted by three screaming *Kinder* armed with sticks, mud, and frogs from the park's pond. On more than one occasion Alex was visited by customers at his store vowing never to return if the Anemone Kingdom was not instantly and permanently overthrown. My father remembers a lecture on the subject, but one, he says, that was delivered with a smile. So perhaps Alex had a sense of humor, after all.

From September to June, while not terrorizing passersby in the park, Günther attended the Oldenburg Oberrealschule. In addition to studying German literature and history, he took classes in mathematics, biology, French, and English. While he remembers doing reasonably well in those subjects, he didn't really enjoy school very much. There were two main reasons: sports and his religion. Günther never became very accomplished in the art of dribbling or shooting a soccer ball, skills that every German schoolboy needed in his arsenal if he hoped to be widely accepted. And while he could run, and run swiftly, his most painful athletic memory is associated with a track-and-field incident. When he was about twelve, he was assigned to a 110-meter hurdle event. His coach never mentioned the necessity of wearing any kind of supporter, so when Günther didn't quite clear the last hurdle of the race he managed to impart to himself a severe testicular blow that he remembers, wincingly, to this day.

But that pain paled in comparison to the taunts he received on the playground. Günther began to hear the word "Jew" used as an epithet in 1925 or 1926. He would continue to hear it, and see it, and feel its effects, for the next fifteen years.

When it began, the name-calling and other expressions of anti-Semitism came as something of a surprise to him and to the rest of the family. To have their religion (or as the hard-core anti-Semites would have it, their race) singled out as an identifying characteristic was perhaps the biggest surprise of all. As was the case with many Jews in Germany, particularly in the western part of the country, Alex Goldschmidt considered himself a German first and a Jew second. In this land that had only been considered a unified country since Otto von Bismarck formed the Second Reich in 1871, Jews had become thoroughly integrated into mainstream society. More so than in France, Poland, or other European countries, Jews in Germany found their way easily into the arts, the law, the military, business, even government. The German constitution did not exclude Jews when it extended citizenship to all its people.

And Alex had floated easily down that mainstream to his position of prosperity and respectability. He certainly felt that he'd earned his way through hard work and his war service, the duty of a German patriot. When asked, he'd proudly exhibit his reward for four years in the trenches: the Iron Cross, First Class. He would also join in the chorus of voices that denounced the cruel and unfair Treaty of Versailles that the victorious allies had forced Germany to sign at the end of the First World War. But he was no monarchist, pining for the days of blood and iron, empire and glory. On public holidays Alex would un-furl the black, red, and gold flag of the Weimar Republic from a second-story window of the house on Gartenstrasse.

Religious feelings, on the other hand, were a more ambiguous mat-ter in the Goldschmidt family. At school, there was religious instruction every Monday, when a visiting minister led the class in Bible studies. The minister issued frequent reminders that Jesus offered eternal salva-tion, the same Jesus who had been ruthlessly crucified by the Jews. My father remembers feeling quite uncomfortable during those classes, wondering how on earth he could be saved with ancestors such as his. He also remembers walking with Alex through the winding streets of downtown Oldenburg to the synagogue on Peterstrasse for services on the High Holidays. And in December, Hanukkah candles were lit. But like so many German Jews of the time, the Goldschmidts observed German traditions side by side with their Jewish traditions. As the menorah sprouted candles night after night, in another corner of the family living room stood a tall and fragrant *Tannenbaum,* a Christmas tree, its branches decorated with tinsel, ornaments, and more burning candles. On Christmas Eve, after opening presents, my father recalls, he and his family walked hand in hand through the streets of the silent city, admiring the Christmas decorations of their neighbors. And the sweet and lyrical hymns of the holiday, with their pleas for peace on earth, made a great impression on the young Günther, whose ear for music was just then beginning to develop.

So just how Jewish was the Goldschmidt family? Based on my own experiences growing up, not very. When I was very young, our family drove into downtown St. Louis on Sunday mornings to attend talks on nuclear disarmament or world hunger sponsored by the local chapter of the Ethical Society. But I never set foot inside a synagogue until I was nearly twenty. Neither I nor my brother took part in a bar mitzvah cer-emony when we reached our thirteenth birthdays. And at no time were we ever told, either simply or solemnly, that we were Jews. Apparently, whatever Hebraic tendencies there were at home in Oldenburg had not rubbed off on my father.

That is, unless you count music, a talent the Jews seemingly have always had. There was an old Knabe piano in the house on Gartenstrasse, and when he was eleven or twelve, Günther began taking lessons. He loved music, had been inspired by the performance of Rudolf Serkin he'd heard at the ducal castle, but, like many a young boy, he had only a limited tolerance for practicing. His parents never pushed him, so his skills at the keyboard advanced only so far. But Günther and Toni continued to attend performances at the Landestheater, and one day in 1928 the Oldenburg Opera staged the great Romantic opera *Der Freischütz*, by Carl Maria von Weber. There are great passages for the French horn in this music, and Günther left the theater that day determined to learn the horn. But while arrangements were being made to find a horn teacher, mother and son attended another performance at the theater. As fate would have it, this time the company performed Mozart's *Magic Flute*. Seeing Tamino and Pamina walk through trials of fire and water with only the sound of the flute to protect them was enough to change Günther's mind. The flute was now to be his instrument.

I have often wondered whether it is possible for unfulfilled desires to pass down through generations. About thirty-five years later, knowing nothing of my father's original choice of instrument, I began to study the French horn. I actually became pretty good at it for a few years, until the onset of puberty turned my thoughts and desires in other directions.

Alex secured the services of Walter Hoss, the second flutist of the opera orchestra, to teach Günther. And in a little music shop on Baumgartenstrasse, around the corner from his store on Schüttingstrasse, Alex found a wooden flute for his son to play. With the image of Mozart's princely Tamino still fresh in his heart, Günther took to his new instrument with a passion. Even his beloved chickens were relegated to second place in his affections, and he sometimes practiced late into the night. Every week he was well prepared for Herr Hoss, who soon recommended Günther for his Oberrealschule orchestra.

ALL IN ALL, it had been a golden decade for the Goldschmidts, if not for their country. The fledgling Weimar Republic, founded with such good intentions following the defeat of the kaiser in 1918, faced one shock after another in the decade to come. The first was the Treaty of

Versailles, signed in June of 1919, which assigned to Germany full responsibility for starting the Great War and exacted an enormous price. Full reparations were to be determined later, but an initial payment from Germany to the Allies was fixed at five billion dollars in gold marks, to be paid between 1919 and 1921. In addition, there were to be payments in kind, including timber, coal, ships, and cattle. And finally, the map of Europe was to be redrawn, with the Germans making territorial concessions that, among other indignities, granted a corridor of land to Poland, which had the effect of separating the German state of East Prussia from the Fatherland. To most Germans, especially those who had fought in the trenches, the Versailles *Diktat* was nothing short of intolerable. Philipp Scheidemann, the new chancellor of the infant republic, declared angrily, "May the hand wither that signs this treaty!" And no sooner had the signing ceremony taken place in the glittering Hall of Mirrors than a search for scapegoats began, both for the politicians who had caved in to Allied demands and for the "November criminals" who had surrendered on the battlefield, at the eleventh hour on the eleventh day of the eleventh month of 1918.

The country also faced one economic challenge after another in the 1920s, many of them stemming from the severe financial penalties imposed by the peace treaty. The beginning of the decade brought an incredible inflation of the national currency. At war's end, one German mark was essentially equal to one American dollar. But in 1921, the mark's value began to decline. From 10 marks to the dollar, it fell to 75. The next year the slide continued, until one dollar was equal to 400 marks. At the beginning of 1923, the figure was 7,000 marks to the dollar. A month later, it was 18,000. By July the number was 160,000; by late August, unbelievably, a million. In November, it took four *billion* marks to buy a dollar; German currency had become utterly worthless.

The German people were miserable and desperate. The times were ripe for upheaval. On November 9, 1923, a thirty-four-year-old Austrian who had served as a corporal in the German army during the war and who, like Alex Goldschmidt, had been awarded the Iron Cross, First Class, attempted to foment a national revolution from the speaking platform of a beer hall in Munich. The putsch failed, and the

Germany
1919 - 1933

0 Miles 100

Denmark

Baltic Sea

North Sea

Netherlands

Poland

Hamburg

Elbe River

Olden-
burg

Bremen

Weser River

Oranienburg

Oder River

Sachsenhagen

Hannover

Potsdam

Berlin

Sondershausen

Leipzig

Dresden

Düsseldorf

Cologne

Weimar

Belgium

Rhine River

Luxembourg

Frankfurt

Czechoslovakia

Nuremberg

Karlsruhe

France

Munich

Austria

Switzerland

Noah Andre Trudeau

young revolutionary landed in jail, but the world would soon hear more
from Adolf Hitler. His campaign for National Socialism had begun.

The misery of the early 1920s did not bypass Oldenburg. In April
of 1923, still seven months away from his tenth birthday, Günther
attended the annual Easter Market festival held in the square between
the ducal castle and the Lamberti Church. Amid the booths of spring
flowers and woolly lambs from the surrounding fields, he saw another
display that froze his blood: a row of more than a dozen men sitting

on the square's cold cobblestones. They were all missing arms or legs or eyes; some of them were mere torsos with heads. They were veterans of the Great War, and this is how they now made their living: begging at fairs across the country for which they had sacrificed their limbs. Günther reached into his pocket for his fair money, dropped it all into the soldiers' basket, and silently walked home, no longer in the mood for fun.

Inflation and unemployment also visited his hometown. But through it all his father, who might easily have been one of those legless vets in the square, persevered and continued to prosper. The store at the corner of Schüttingstrasse and Achternstrasse remained open for business. Even in the depths of the economic calamity that had befallen them, people needed clothes. And the unbelievable inflation actually helped Alex get out from under the debt he'd been in since the purchase of the store more than a decade earlier. As the face value of money became less and less, owing the bank a thousand marks, for instance, was far less burdensome than it had been. And when the country began to emerge from its economic woes in 1925, business really boomed. On summer weekends, outfitted in colorful clothes and a straw hat, Alex would occasionally hire a horse-drawn carriage to take himself and Toni to the horse races on the edge of town. He was still Moses Goldschmidt's boy after all.

The year 1926 was a banner year for Alex Goldschmidt's store. And in 1927, the year Charles Lindbergh flew the Atlantic and Babe Ruth slugged sixty homers, my grandfather unveiled another first, though one of considerably smaller historic proportion: the first outdoor neon sign the winding streets of Oldenburg had ever seen. It read: "Alex Goldschmidt *Spezialhaus für Damenkonfektion und Kleiderstoffe,*" or "Specialty House for Women's Ready-to-Wear and Dress Material."

The sign formed the basis for an advertisement that Alex took out in the Oldenburg newspaper during the Christmas season of 1927. Business was good, and life must have seemed wonderful to Alex and Toni as they celebrated the season with their four children. But on that same page of newsprint that invited customers to the store, there appeared another announcement informing the citizens of Oldenburg that on Tuesday, December 13, at 8:30 P.M. a meeting of the National

My father as a sensitive, well-dressed young teenager in the mid-1920s.

Socialist party would take place. It would include a discussion on the topic "Left, Right, or Hitler?"

When Alex saw his ad, did he notice the second one, I wonder? And could he possibly have imagined the threat it posed to his life and the lives of his family?

Despite Hitler's arrest in 1923, the National Socialists had maintained their existence during the following years. As the end of the

A mark of success and impending disaster on the same page of newsprint. Detail from the Oldenburger Nachrichten, *December 12, 1927, with advertisements for both Alex Goldschmidt's store (upper left) and an impending Nazi meeting (lower right). The N.S.D.A.P. (the National Socialist German Workers Party) is summed up simply as the "Hitler Movement."*

decade approached and economic turmoil once more gripped Germany in the wake of the stock market crash on Wall Street, the Nazis intensified their efforts to gain political strength. They campaigned extensively in Oldenburg, both city and state. In the city they made themselves known through street demonstrations during which they inveighed against the undue influence of Jews and Communists, and they spoke out in violent opposition to what they termed "degenerate" art at the Landestheater and opera house. Günther attended a performance of the Chamber Music for Piano and Twelve Instruments by Paul Hindemith that was interrupted when a contingent of Brownshirts began throwing eggs and tomatoes at the stage. And in March of 1929, when Günther's beloved opera house in Oldenburg presented the first German staging of Alban Berg's opera *Wozzeck* since its world premiere in Berlin, the Nazis were waiting.

The story of the opera is based on a lurid tale by Georg Büchner about the soldier Johann Franz Wozzeck and his jealous love for Marie, the mother of his bastard child. Driven mad by his suspicions and overcome by hallucinations in which he sees the moon turn blood-red, Wozzeck stabs Marie and then drowns in a pond, leaving their innocent child, now an orphan, playing with his hobbyhorse as the final curtain falls. It's certainly provocative stuff, and the Nazi cultural critics would have none of it. As Berg himself looked on from his box, Brownshirts marched up and down the aisles chanting their slogans until police arrived to clear the theater. Günther, shaken, scared, and outraged by these tactics, rushed home to tell his parents what he'd seen.

Alex just laughed. "These bullies are nothing more than clowns," he reassured Günther. "There's nothing to worry about."

But the clowns began to perform well at the ballot box. In the elections of 1928, the National Socialists had polled just 9.8 percent of the vote in the state of Oldenburg. In the elections of September 1930, the Nazi numbers grew to 27.3 percent. Over the next few months, the party began staging more events in the northwest, appealing directly to farmers, who had been the first in Germany to feel the effects of the worldwide depression.

Flags. Dozens of flags. Flags and banners, red, white, and black, all dominated by the *Hakenkreuz*, the hooked cross, the swastika. That's what my father remembers best about the marches and rallies that began to be a regular part of life in Oldenburg in the winter and spring of 1931. Flags, and men marching, and men shouting, and occasionally men throwing punches—all in a highly charged atmosphere of danger, exaggerated excitement, and belligerence.

IM WUNDERSCHÖNEN *Monat Mai, als alle Knospen sprangen.* "In the beautiful month of May, as all the buds were blooming." Those lines from the poet Heinrich Heine were running through Günther's mind on the warm afternoon of May 5, 1931, as he hurried along Oldenburg's Peterstrasse on the way to a lesson with Herr Hoss. The sun was shining brightly, and everywhere he looked *Knospen* were *sprang*-ing; the borders of the street seemed alive with tulips, daisies, and the flowers of his childhood kingdom, anemones. As Günther reached the corner of Grünestrasse, the street where his teacher lived, he heard a commotion coming from the direction of the Horse Market, where Alex had had his first apartment. Curious, and because he was still a few minutes early for his lesson, Günther kept walking down Peterstrasse to the corner of Brüderstrasse, from which point he could look underneath a railroad overpass and see the market square.

It was, Günther could tell, another Nazi rally. But this one was different somehow. The crowd was bigger, first of all, and the cheers, which burst forth every few minutes, were deep and sustained, like the rumbling of the tympani Günther remembered from the opera house orchestra.

He crossed the street to get a better look and walked right up to the edge of the crowd that ringed a wooden platform that had been set up in the middle of the square. On the platform, clad in a brown shirt with matching brown tie, brown riding breeches, and black boots that reached nearly to his knees, stood a small man haranguing the crowd. His straight brown hair slanted across his forehead from right to left, pointing in the direction of the bright red swastika armband he wore above his left elbow. Over his upper lip perched a neat rectangular mustache. With a start, Günther realized that he was staring at Adolf Hitler, self-proclaimed *Führer,* or leader, of the National Socialists, here in Oldenburg.

Hitler was speaking in a rather relaxed posture, with his weight on one leg and his arms crossed on his chest. He was running through a list of proposals that, he claimed, would bring relief to the people who lived on the farms outside the city limits: cheaper artificial manures, cheaper electricity, higher tariffs on imported corn and wheat, lower taxes. Standing on the ground alongside the platform was a group of

Adolf Hitler, speaking in the Pferdemarkt in Oldenburg on May 5, 1931. The bald man in Nazi uniform behind Hitler is Carl Röver, who one year later would be elected president of the Oldenburg state ministry.

men also dressed in Nazi regalia, and they cheered boisterously each of Hitler's points. But the crowd of civilians, however impressive in numbers, remained largely unmoved.

Then Hitler's demeanor and the sound of his voice changed. Relaxed no more, he stood erect with his weight equally distributed on both feet, his hands clenched into fists in front of him. He seemed to grow, to loom over the crowd at his feet, even to rise above those men and women who hung out of open windows behind and above him.

"Democracy has laid the world in ruins," he thundered. "National Socialism is here to lead the fight against the delirium of democracy and to bring the great German people to the recognition of the necessity of authority and leadership. There is only one right in the world and that right is strength!"

Deep and prolonged cheers, the sound that reminded Günther of the rumble of tympani, echoed through the square.

"What counts on this earth is will," Hitler continued, "and if our will is hard and ruthless enough we can do anything. We Germans are the greatest people on earth. It is not your fault that you were defeated in the war and have suffered so much since. It is because you were betrayed in 1918 and have been exploited ever since by those who are envious of you and hate you; because you have been too honest and too patient. Let Germany awake and renew her strength, let her remember her greatness and recover her old position in the world!"

The tympani rumbled once more, deeper and louder than before.

"My friends and comrades, we are engaged in a great struggle. To this struggle there are only two possible outcomes: either the enemy shall pass over our bodies or we shall pass over theirs, and it is my passionate desire that, if in this struggle I should fall, the swastika banner shall be my winding sheet!"

Pandemonium. The crowd below surged forward, the crowd in the windows seemed to swoop down. The Nazis in their brown uniforms closed protectively around their leader and bore him to the backseat of a convertible automobile nearby. There he stood and reviewed a parade of his followers as they passed by, his upraised right arm returning their salute, their boots ringing out from the pavement of the Horse Market, the whole mesmerizing spectacle a curious combination of calm confidence and bitter resentment.

Günther turned away, now late for his lesson. The sun still shone, but he was suddenly conscious of a chill in the air.

A little more than a year later, on May 29, 1932, 48.4 percent of the voters in the state of Oldenburg cast their ballots for the Nazi party. Though not an absolute majority, that number represented more votes than any other party had achieved. Thus the Nazis were constitutionally mandated to form a government, and the local Gauleiter, or regional leader, a man named Carl Röver, became president of the ministry. Two other Nazis from the city of Oldenburg, Heinz Spangemacher and Julius Pauly, also were appointed ministers of the state government. Oldenburg was the first state in the country to have duly elected Nazi leaders.

ONE FINE EVENING the following autumn, a knock sounded on the door at 34 Gartenstrasse. Alex opened the door to find two men in brown uniforms with swastika armbands standing there. "Yes?" he said.

"Are you the Jew Goldschmidt?" one of the Brownshirts asked.

"My name is Alex Goldschmidt," my grandfather said coldly. "What is it you want?"

"This house," came the reply. "We understand that you bought it from a government minister more than a dozen years ago. Now it is required by Minister Spangemacher."

"Well, I'm terribly sorry, but this house is not for sale, neither to Herr Spangemacher nor to anyone else. Good evening, gentlemen." And with that Alex tried to close the door.

But the Brownshirt placed a polished black boot between the door and its jamb.

"I'm afraid I haven't made myself quite clear. I am not asking you to sell this house. I am telling you to sell it; and sell it quickly. Minister Spangemacher is a busy man."

And with that the Nazi removed his boot from the doorway and he and his companion walked down the front steps and marched smartly away.

Alex closed the door and walked slowly to the living room, where he stood for some time staring into the fire. He was no longer so sure that his adversaries were merely clowns.

Meanwhile Günther watched the two men walk away down Gartenstrasse from his window upstairs, where he was practicing for an Ober-Realschule performance of Mozart's Flute Concerto in G Major. He was nearly nineteen. How appropriate it is that the image of Tamino and Pamina walking safely together through unearthly trials, aided by his magical flute, had been the inspiration for my father to take up that instrument. Soon his own wooden flute would save his young life . . . and that of his life's companion.

3

Julian and Rosemarie

FRIDAY, JULY 6, 1984. El Dorado Hospital, Tucson, Arizona. On a blisteringly hot afternoon, I am sitting by a bed in a darkened, chilled, clammy room whose walls, clearly seeking cheer, are painted orange and blue. In the bed lies my mother, her small frame fighting as best it can a cancer of the bile duct. We are alone in the room, my mother and I.

Since Sunday, summoned by my father, I have watched as my mother has weakened. When the week began, she ate, talked, laughed. Now she lies silently, eyes closed. At irregular intervals, she opens her eyes and slowly turns her head toward a cup of ice chips that rests on the bedside table. This is the signal for me to take a single sliver of ice and place it carefully in her mouth. The acts of eating and drinking now cost more in pain and effort than she can afford. But when the morsels of frozen water touch her tongue, she smiles faintly at me before she once again allows her eyes to close.

Loss, I think. I am at a loss. I do not know what to do, what to say, how to act. I have brought with me a volume of poetry by Emily Dickinson. I don't even know if my mother likes Emily Dickinson, but I have decided that the visions of the great solitary artist will comfort and console both of us. I take up the book and read aloud what Emily has to say about bees and the "narrow Fellow in the grass" and then I read:

> We grow accustomed to the Dark
> When Light is put away
> As when the Neighbor holds the Lamp
> To witness her Goodbye—

I pause and my mother opens her eyes and whispers, "I'm afraid," and I whisper back, "So am I."

I reach to grasp her hand and her grip surprises me with its strength. And, her eyes again closed, she says, my mother says to me, "You're a good son."

The next day, as scheduled, and reassured by a hospital oncologist that I will have the chance to see her again, I fly back east to my home in Washington, D.C. And two days later, on Monday, July 9, my mother dies, at sixty-seven.

ON THAT HOT and endlessly empty day, I was six weeks away from my thirty-second birthday and still about eight years away from my first serious questions about my parents' early lives. I am sure I could have had many wonderful talks with my mother about her memories of long ago; we had grown very close in her last years and we spoke easily with each other. But, like the knight Percival, I failed to ask the question that would have meant so much. And so I am left with only incomplete information about my mother's early years and about the life of her father, Julian Gumpert.

Thanks, though, to some kind and helpful researchers in Germany, and to Hilde Jonas, a harpsichordist and childhood friend of my mother's, I have been able to piece together a few facts and impressions of the Gumperts of Düsseldorf.

My grandfather Julian was born on June 5, 1876, in the town of Deutsch-Eylau in what was then West Prussia but is now Poland. I know nothing of his parents or even if he had any siblings, but one fact stands out: the central interest, avocation, and profession of his life was music. He began studying the violin when he was still a boy; by the time he was nineteen he was already serving as second violinist in a professional string quartet. In the great porcelain city of Dresden, where such musicians as Carl Maria von Weber, Richard Wagner, and Fritz Reiner lived and worked, Julian attended the music conservatory and in 1897 won top prizes for both solo and orchestral performance.

His school days behind him, Julian took up the tools of a traveling musician, securing several notable positions but never staying anywhere for long. At the turn of the century he was making music in Hannover, both playing his violin and serving as conductor of the court orchestra. In 1904 he returned to the East, taking up the post of court concertmaster in the town of Neustrelitz, about eighty miles north of Berlin. Two years later Julian went west once more, again as court concertmaster, this time to the city of Elberfeld, which today is known as Wuppertal. There he seems to have found a situation he liked, for it was nearly a decade until he moved again. When at last he pulled up stakes once more, in the first week of 1915, he didn't travel far; it is only a few miles from Wuppertal to the great city on the River Rhine called Düsseldorf.

Emperor Napoleon called Düsseldorf *"mon petit Paris."* During the wars at the turn of the nineteenth century, when he certainly must have had other things on his mind, Napoleon spent ninety-one thousand francs to ensure that the Hofgarten, Düsseldorf's main public park, was expanded to include wide meadows and new trees. In 1811, the emperor made a triumphant entry into the city. Among those cheering him that day was a thirteen-year-old boy named Heinrich Heine, who would grow up to be one of the great poets of the Romantic era. Heine was only one of many bright artistic lights that have illuminated Düsseldorf. Composer Robert Schumann lived there in the early 1850s as director of the city's orchestra and chorus. And for a few years in the early 1930s, painter Paul Klee served as a professor at the Düsseldorf Academy of Art.

Within months of moving to Düsseldorf, Julian married Else Hayn of Berlin, the widow of a Hamburg physician, and began a twenty-four-year contribution to the cultural life of his adopted city by establishing the Gumpert Conservatory of Music at 10 Ehrenstrasse. There was already one private music school in town, run by two gentlemen named Julius Buths and Otto Neitzel, who had established it in 1902. But as the Buths-Neitzel Conservatory emphasized the instruction of pianists and organists, my grandfather decided that he would concentrate on what he knew best, stringed instruments.

As the Great War raged, the two schools engaged in a more friendly and civilized rivalry than the seemingly pointless one being fought in the trenches. They would occasionally hire teachers away from each other, for example, or schedule faculty and student recitals on the same evening, then compare attendance the next day. Then, in early 1918, Buths and Neitzel initiated negotiations with Julian concerning a possible merger, a possibility that ran into opposition in high places. On January 30 (a date that would take on much more sinister associations fifteen years later), a functionary in the Düsseldorf government wrote to the lord mayor expressing alarm over the proposed merger. A proposal for a city-sponsored conservatory had been introduced, but should these two private schools join forces they would no doubt outstrip the city's best efforts. The lord mayor immediately dispatched letters to both conservatories, expressing his profound admiration, etc., etc., but informing them that it would be in the best interests of all parties concerned if the merger did not take place at that time. The matter was promptly dropped, at least for the time being. Meanwhile, Julian and Else had a more absorbing interest: their infant daughter, Rosemarie.

In August of 1916, his conservatory established, Julian had moved out to the suburbs. He and Else bought a large, rambling house at 8 Preussenstrasse in Hösel, a rural town about fifteen miles away from the conservatory on Ehrenstrasse. And five months later, on the Feast of the Epiphany, January 6, 1917, my mother was born.

I think that to the end of her days she thought of the house in Hösel with love. It was her Howard's End, a place of peace, security, and beauty, with tall, graceful trees, fragrant flowers, and a fish pond in the backyard. One of the very few things she ever said to me about her mother was that she had possessed a fondness for gardening. This fondness, and a very real skill, Rosemarie inherited from Else. Imagining my mother today, if I don't see her making music, she's kneeling in a flower bed, planting marigolds or zinnias, or rocking back on her heels and clapping dirt from her hands as she surveys her handiwork, satisfaction blooming in her eyes.

Rosemarie's most obvious talent, however, she inherited from her father. By the time she could walk she'd already held a violin, and she began taking lessons at the age of three. She began to learn the viola four years later. It was a path that Julian blazed for her, but one she walked down willingly and with joy. She was born to be a musician, and

Proud parents Else and Julian Gumpert flanking infant Rosemarie in front of the lovely house in Hösel, 1917. This is the only picture I have of my handsome grandfather, despite his prominence in Düsseldorf. Apparently, many pictures and artifacts documenting his career were destroyed by the Nazi sympathizer who assumed control of the city's Robert Schumann Hochschule für Musik in 1935.

she seemed aware of that fact and its attendant responsibility from the very beginning. Julian set very high standards and insisted on long periods of practice, often six or seven hours a day, but Rosemarie never rebelled. Her temperament was very much in tune with the discipline her art demanded. (Yet a note of dissent sounds in my memory. Perhaps she accepted her task with less enthusiasm than others remember. When, many years later, it came time for my brother and me to take piano lessons, she didn't insist that we continue for long hours at the keyboard when games of baseball and kick-the-can lured us outside. Maybe our mother was granting us the unfettered childhood she never had.)

But there can be no doubt that Rosemarie, Julian and Else's only child, was the apple of their eye. And if Julian spent considerable time and effort polishing her until her talent shone, I have no evidence that she ever resented it. Her childhood friend Hilde remembers Rosemarie as "born to perform" and deeply committed to music. She confirms another of my vivid memories, that of the vibrant, passionate, emphatic, bobbing-and-weaving manner in which Rosemarie played her fiddle. "Her whole body took part" in her playing, Hilde recalls; apparently, she played that way from the start.

And there was more than long hours of practice in her strict upbringing. Her parents cured her of a tendency toward finicky eating habits by serving her the same food until she finally ate it; if Rosemarie didn't finish what she was served for lunch, she had it again at dinner. And should the food remain unconsumed, it would appear on her plate for breakfast the following morning, and so on. (Again, I think my brother and I benefitted from her memory of this culinary tyranny. She never enforced a similar edict, although our enjoyment of her limited repertory rendered such measures unnecessary.)

Looking at the few pictures I have of Rosemarie as a young girl, I'm struck by the fact that her face changed very little in her sixty-seven years. As a baby lying in her stroller outside the house in Hösel, as a five-year-old holding her instrument, as a teenager, or as an adult, my mother looks more or less the same. It is a serious face, although she had a wonderful sense of humor and laughed a lot, both as a child and in the years I knew her. It is also a face that looks strikingly like mine.

An especially revealing photograph shows Rosemarie hugging Else; there's a bow in the little girl's hair and an expression of deep melancholy on the face of her mother. Else and Julian were fundamentally ill-matched. He was a handsome, outgoing artist, at once flamboyant and absentminded; she was practical and down-to-earth, and neither one understood the other very well. It was a long commute from the conservatory back to Hösel, and often mother and daughter would wait late into the evening for Julian to return. He was occasionally quite late, particularly once he expanded his instruction of female students from the practical to the personal. There were even instances of Julian's bringing "promising" young women home for "private lessons." In light of such liberties, it's no wonder Else looks so sad.

So he was a rat, my grandfather. But Julian was also a very good musician and a superb teacher, able to illustrate both the big picture

A slightly walleyed, melancholy Else holds a two-year-old, beribboned Rosemarie. Neither looks very happy; Julian must be "teaching" late at the Conservatory again.

and the vital details of a piece of music. He was demanding but gentle, given more to inspiration than to enforcement. He was of medium height, very slender, a dapper dresser, and a little bit vain, especially when it came to his long gray hair. He was also adept at the art of making friends and acquaintances; he had time for everyone, from famous musicians to the men who delivered the coal and operated the streetcar. And always, music was the center of Julian's universe. When he played, he traveled somewhere far away. His eyes seemed to turn inward, to gaze into his own heart and the hearts of his listeners. Impractical, dreamy, he left the running of the Hösel household to his wife. He was an artist and took full advantage of it.

When Rosemarie was six years old, Julian enrolled her in a private school known for its selectivity and high standards. The Schuback-Schmidt Lyceum was located on the Hohenzollernstrasse, six blocks from the conservatory. Only about twenty students were admitted to each class by the lyceum's director, a remarkable woman named Trude Heinzmann. She had happened to be in France at the beginning of the Great War; detained as an enemy alien, Frau Heinzmann spent the duration of the war in France, and in those four years she learned to speak and write the language fluently. French was thus a prime subject at Schuback-Schmidt, and Frau Heinzmann taught many of the classes herself. If a student failed to master his or her vocabulary lesson for that week, a common punishment was to be required to report to the director's office for remedial lessons a half-hour before school started.

"Everyone was scared to death" of Frau Heinzmann, recalls Hilde Jonas, but "it was an outstanding school and we learned a lot." Rosemarie was a very good student, serious in her schoolwork as in her music, and quickly won over the school's director. Frau Heinzmann soon learned of Rosemarie's musical gifts, and, when Rosemarie was ten years old, she began performing for the other students at the school. At first, those performances took the form of impromptu, spur-of-the-moment affairs; but within a few years, Rosemarie took part in scheduled recitals. In 1930, when she was thirteen, she joined Hilde and a cellist named Ruth Benrath to play a trio by Haydn. The next year, Rosemarie and Hilde performed a sonata by Handel. My mother's many years on stage had begun.

Between 1930 and 1935, Rosemarie took part in dozens of concerts throughout Düsseldorf. Some of them occurred at the Gumpert Conservatory, which had become one of the centers of the city's music scene; others at the synagogue on Kasernenstrasse under the direction of Rabbi Eschelbacher; and still more in private homes, a well-attended series of events known as House Concerts. In many of them, Rosemarie and Julian played side by side.

Rosemarie at about age seven, when she began to play the viola. Already her expression is deeply serious, her form nearly flawless.

From all I have been able to learn, it seems that Rosemarie walked willingly and joyfully down the musical trail blazed for her by her father. She wanted to be a musician and was determined to make the sacrifices such a commitment required. Julian was her first and in many ways her best teacher, so there developed a close relationship between them. But it was a professional rather than a deeply personal relationship. Rosemarie and Julian saw little of each other outside the practice room. When she wasn't playing her fiddle she would take long walks in the Hofgarten, talking with her friends about school and boys and, above all, music. Rosemarie could confide in her friends, but not in her father, who was there for her as a teacher but for little else. She was an only child, and at times she must have been a lonely child as well.

Moreover, the years of her adolescence coincided with a time in her country's history when Rosemarie's need for comfort and understanding must have been considerable. As the 1930s began and the fortunes of the National Socialists rose in other parts of the country, Düsseldorf resisted longer than many cities. Two groups of its citizens were unusually well established, the Catholics and the Labor Unions, and they provided a breakwater that the Nazi tide couldn't quite overcome, at least at first. But as the hard rain of unemployment and economic misery kept falling, the tide at last swept aside everything in its path. For the Jews of Düsseldorf, the House Concerts and the Gumpert Conservatory would soon become terribly important islands.

4

1933

MAJOR JOSEPH HELL was a German journalist in the 1920s and the beginning of the 1930s. In 1922 he had occasion to interview Adolf Hitler, and he wrote about the experience in his memoirs. Toward the end of his interview Major Hell asked Hitler, "What do you want to do to the Jews once you have full discretionary powers?" Hitler abruptly changed his demeanor, raising his voice and carrying on as if he were addressing an outdoor rally:

> Once I really am in power, my first and foremost task will be the annihilation of the Jews. As soon as I have the power to do so, I will have gallows built in rows—at the Marienplatz in Munich, for example—as many as traffic allows. Then the Jews will be hanged indiscriminately, and they will remain hanging until they stink; they will hang there as long as the principles of hygiene permit. As soon as they have been untied, the next batch will be hung up, and so on down the line, until the last Jew in Munich has been exterminated. Other cities will follow suit, precisely in this fashion, until all Germany has been completely cleansed of Jews.

Eleven years later, on Monday, January 30, 1933, Adolf Hitler, the former Austrian corporal, was sworn in by President Paul von Hindenburg as chancellor of Germany. The next day, Frau Heinzmann, director of Düsseldorf's Schuback-Schmidt Lyceum, delivered flowers to each of the Jewish students in her school. A perceptive woman, she had an inkling of what was to come.

Over the next few months, as the Nazis consolidated their hold on power, they had many items on their agenda, among them the destruction of the Communist Party, the elimination of the trade unions, and the suppression of all civil liberties guaranteed under the constitution of the Weimar Republic. But right from the start, the new regime launched a purge of Jews from Germany's cultural institutions, taking dead aim at the most visible manifestation of what the Nazis termed the "undue influence" of Jews in society, letting them know both forcefully and subtly that they were no longer welcome.

On February 13, within two weeks of the installation of the new chancellor, the distinguished conductor Otto Klemperer presided over a new production of Richard Wagner's opera *Tannhäuser* at the Berlin Staatsoper, or State Opera, an occasion marking the fiftieth anniversary of the composer's death. Then forty-seven years old, Klemperer had been the chief conductor at the State Opera since 1927, following important posts in Hamburg, Bremen, Cologne, and Wiesbaden. But all the dues he had paid meant nothing to the new rulers of Klemperer's country: the conductor was a Jew.

The performance of *Tannhäuser* was attacked the next day by critics seeking to curry favor with the new chancellor, who was known to venerate Wagner and whose close associate Joseph Goebbels had already declared, "the Jew does not understand Wagner's music." Reviewers called the new production an affront to the memory of the great composer and demanded the dismissal of those responsible for this "bastardization." Though the production was scheduled to run for weeks, it had just two more performances before it was closed down. At the end of March, Klemperer learned that his scheduled orchestral concert with the Berlin Staatskapelle had been summarily canceled. These hints were enough for the conductor; a week later Otto Klemperer boarded a train for Switzerland and exile.

Another distinguished Jewish conductor working in Germany was Bruno Walter. Nine years older than Klemperer, Walter also had a long resumé, having conducted in Cologne, Hamburg, and Munich. He had conducted the Berlin Städtische Oper, or City Opera, and the world's oldest symphony orchestra, the Leipzig Gewandhaus Orchestra. He'd also been an assistant to Gustav Mahler and had conducted the world premieres of Mahler's Ninth Symphony and *Das Lied von der Erde* ("The Song of the Earth").

Against Walter, the Nazis employed their old trick of claiming to act on behalf of the general well-being. Arriving at the Gewandhaus for a rehearsal on the morning of March 16, the conductor found the doors to the concert hall padlocked. Walter demanded an explanation and was informed by the Reichskomissar of the state of Saxony that it had become common knowledge that the patrons of the orchestra were extremely unhappy that a Jew was in charge, and that riots were a distinct possibility. He had ordered the concert hall closed and the upcoming concert canceled, he declared, to insure the safety of the musicians and the public. No one was fooled by this transparent ruse.

A week later Bruno Walter was scheduled to conduct the Berlin Philharmonic, and again he found the doors of the concert hall locked against him. This time he was informed directly by the Ministry of Public Enlightenment and Propaganda (headed by the same Joseph Goebbels who had expressed himself about Jews and Wagner) that the hall would be set on fire if he dared to fulfill his commitment to the orchestra. Representatives of the Philharmonic then contacted the Ministry, asking for police protection; they were told that if they wanted the concert to go on as scheduled they should engage the services of an Aryan conductor.

The Philharmonic hastily bowed to the threat and asked the venerable composer Richard Strauss to conduct in Walter's place. The old man agreed, handing the Nazis an early propaganda victory. The compliant press hailed Strauss for stepping in heroically at the last minute "as a salute to the new Germany." The concert, declared another paper, had been met with "overwhelming jubilation" on the part of the audience and the whole evening had been a rousing success, despite the unfortunate arrival at the last minute of "a threatening letter from hateful Jewish Americans." This was a reference to a telegram sent to Adolf Hitler protesting the treatment of Walter and other Jewish musicians. Among the signers of the telegram were the conductors Serge Koussevitzky, Fritz Reiner, and Arturo Toscanini.

Amid all the hubbub, Bruno Walter packed his bags and left Germany, first for Vienna and then for New York. Ironically, born Bruno Schlesinger in 1876, he had changed his name to Walter in honor of the man who wins the singing contest in *Die Meistersinger,* an opera composed by Richard Wagner.

Just a few weeks later, on April 6, a Frankfurt newspaper printed an article by a man who would play a decisive role in the lives of Jewish musicians in the coming years. Hans Hinkel, the new president of the Prussian Theater Commission, explained that Bruno Walter and Otto Klemperer were no longer practicing their art in Germany because there was no way to protect them against the "mood" of a public no longer tolerant of "Jewish artistic liquidators." Thus, Hinkel concluded, it was for their own good that the two conductors had been encouraged to leave.

Other well-known artists were forced to leave Germany as well. It soon became, in the words of one of the emigrés, playwright Bertolt Brecht, "an exodus such as the world had never seen before." As the government became more involved in cultural organizations, the intimidation became more efficient, less haphazard. Reichsminister Hermann Göring, a World War I airman of distinction whom the Nazis had put in charge of the Prussian police, decided to take control of the Prussian Academy of the Arts as well. Göring invited the vice president of the academy's music division, Georg Schumann, for a little talk. The next day Schumann made a speech in which he declared that Jewish influence in the institution had reached unacceptable levels and that it was time that something be done about it. Two months later, the ax fell: the two best-known composition teachers on the faculty—Franz Schreker and Arnold Schoenberg, both Jews—were formally dismissed. Within months, Schoenberg was living in Hollywood. Within a year, Schreker was dead—according to friends, of a broken heart.

In the spring of 1933, the music world prepared to observe the hundredth anniversary of the birth of the great German composer Johannes Brahms, born in Hamburg on May 7, 1833. The centennial would be celebrated all over Germany, nowhere with more enthusiasm, naturally, than in his hometown. In late April, the Hamburg Philharmonic Society published a brochure detailing the extent of its observance of the occasion; the Philharmonic planned to perform all four Brahms symphonies, the violin concerto, and the two piano concertos over the course of a week. The soloist in the piano concertos was to be

Rudolf Serkin, the same marvelous pianist whom Günther had heard playing Beethoven's *Emperor* Concerto in Oldenburg, the musician who, as much as anyone, had inspired Günther to make music his own career.

On May I, word reached the director of the Hamburg Philharmonic Society that an exciting opportunity was at hand. The new chancellor, Adolf Hitler himself, was ready to come to Hamburg as an official patron of the city's tribute to its native son. He would attend the opening concert, make a few remarks, lay a wreath at Hamburg's Brahms memorial. All of this would bring favor and renown to city and orchestra alike. There was just one small problem: the chancellor had noted the participation of a number of Jewish musicians in the printed brochure. Could something perhaps be done to remedy the situation?

The Philharmonic Society acted swiftly: all mention of Jewish artists was removed from the programs. Rudolf Serkin was disinvited.

Music by Brahms was also at the center of an incident involving the violinist Ernst Drucker, the father of Eugene Drucker of the Emerson String Quartet. In the spring of 1933 Ernst Drucker was twenty-four years old and about to graduate from the music conservatory in his native Cologne. As part of his senior exercises he was assigned to perform the Brahms Violin Concerto with the conservatory's student orchestra. In May, shortly after the Brahms Centennial observances in Hamburg, a new administrator with ties to the Nazi Party was installed as director of the Cologne conservatory. He wasted little time putting the new rules into effect; a few days later, Ernst Drucker came into the school to find that his name had been crossed off the list of participants in the next month's graduation concert.

Shocked, Drucker sought out his teacher, the noted Dutch violinist Brahm Eldering, and the two of them made an appointment to see the new director. At the meeting, Eldering courageously declared, "If my student, who has been one of the shining lights of his class, is not permitted to perform the Brahms concerto, I shall resign in protest." The director, clearly taken aback, suggested a compromise: Drucker could perform the lengthy opening movement of the concerto only, and his name would be restored to the printed program. Eldering agreed, probably realizing that this was the best deal he could get under the present circumstances.

On the morning of the performance, Ernst Drucker awoke with a headache and other symptoms of the flu. But he wasn't going to be deterred, either by illness or by the fact that, when he came out to play, the first three rows of the auditorium were filled with Brownshirts. The opening movement of the Brahms concerto begins with a long, noble melody for the orchestra. During those two and a half minutes, Drucker stood with his eyes closed and his arms at his sides, listening to the burnished beauty rising around him. When it was time for his entrance, he was ready, both physically and emotionally. For the next quarter-hour he played as well as he ever had in his life.

At the end of the movement, there was no applause, as all the students who'd come to listen to the graduation concert expected the performance to continue with the concerto's second movement. And for a moment, Drucker thought of breaking his agreement and plunging ahead. But then one of the Brownshirts sitting in the first row jerked his head angrily in the direction of the wings. Drucker straightened his shoulders, bowed, and walked off stage. When the audience members realized that this was to be Drucker's only performance of the afternoon, they began to cheer and stamp their feet, a demonstration of delight that was quickly quelled when several gentlemen in the first three rows stood up and waved their arms for silence.

The next day there was a glowing review of Drucker's performance in the conservatory's student newspaper and another in the Cologne daily paper. But the critic for the *Völkischer Beobachter*, the official Nazi newspaper, had nothing good to say about the performance. He concluded his review with these words: "It is beyond our comprehension how this immortal German concerto could have been entrusted to the Jew Drucker."

Ernst Drucker immediately wrote a letter to the *Beobachter:* "It has obviously escaped your attention that Brahms dedicated his immortal German concerto to the Jew Joseph Joachim." Whether anyone at the paper read the letter is unknown, but luckily there were no reprisals and Drucker began his long career. Within three years, he would be making music with two other young outcasts: Günther Goldschmidt and Rosemarie Gumpert.

Meanwhile, many other musicians in Germany were finding their careers coming under attack, often for the merest suspicion that they were Jewish. It was a suspicion that the accused tried to prove groundless if they could. The city of Lübeck has been an important musical center for more than three hundred years, ever since the great organist and composer Dietrich Buxtehude settled there in the 1660s. In the spring of 1933, the Lübeck daily newspaper reported that a cellist—identified only as John de J.—had been scheduled to give the last concert of the season but was being replaced by a Professor Hofmeier, who offered a piano recital instead. "We are informed," wrote the paper's correspondent, "that it has been established that John de J. is Jewish." Soon thereafter, a telegram arrived from the hapless cellist: "Claim false. Documents perfect."

Not only musicians, but also those who broadcast or wrote about music were the targets of the Nazis' purge. In March of 1933 all of Germany's radio stations became part of Goebbels's ever-expanding Ministry of Propaganda, and dozens of Jews were summarily fired. A short time later, the shadow fell over the country's newspapers as all Jewish music critics lost their jobs. One of the most prominent was Alfred Einstein, the fifty-two-year-old music critic of the Berlin *Tageblatt.* Fortunately, he landed on his feet; leaving Germany, he came to the United States, where he taught at Smith College, Columbia University, and the University of Michigan. He became known as one of the twentieth century's foremost experts on the life and work of Wolfgang Amadeus Mozart; it was he who first updated the Mozart catalogue originally compiled by Ludwig von Köchel.

But of course it was not only Jewish artists who suffered; every Jew in Germany came to feel like an outsider in the first months of 1933. Cities and towns of all sizes began to erect signs at their borders warning Jews that they were not wanted, or proudly proclaiming that here was a village that was *Judenrein,* or "Jew-free." The journalist and writer William L. Shirer reports that he once saw a sign at a sharp bend in the road near Ludwigshafen that read: "Drive Carefully! Sharp Curve! Jews 75 Miles an Hour!"

As debilitating and unnerving and downright unpleasant as all these incidents were, they were still the product of a disorganized and often unruly campaign with no clear direction or official government sanction. But then, within a single week in April, all that changed. The full weight of an empowered National Socialism was brought to bear against the Jews.

In the last days of March, Hitler proposed to his cabinet a one-day boycott of Jewish-owned businesses across the country. Propaganda Minister Joseph Goebbels took up the idea vigorously, promoting it on radio and in the newspapers. On Saturday morning, April 1, Alex Goldschmidt arrived to open his Haus der Mode as usual at nine o'clock, only to find three Storm Troopers already standing outside. They held signs reading "Germans! Defend Yourselves! Don't Buy from Jews!" ("How perverse," thought Alex. "You'd think that the Jews were the attackers rather than the attacked!") Three more Storm Troopers, bearing identical signs, were stationed across Schüttingstrasse in front of Bloom's Apothecary, and three more stood five doors down Achternstrasse where Herr Gross had his delicatessen.

All day long, until Alex closed up shop at four-thirty, the Storm Troopers held their vigil, neither speaking to passersby nor attempting to interfere when the occasional customer entered the store. But their menacing presence did seem to have an effect; business was considerably slower than on most Saturdays. And it wasn't just walk-in trade that took a hit that day. Just before noon, the phone rang; it was Frau Meginnis, who, in a trembling voice, canceled her order for the wedding dress her daughter was going to wear in June. When my grandfather asked her what was wrong, Frau Meginnis told him she'd found a better price in Delmenhorst, a town about fifteen miles away.

Not everyone buckled under the pressure, however. That afternoon Herr Vollmeer, the organist at the Lamberti Church, came in to place an order for a new dress for his wife.

"And what sort of dress did you have in mind?" asked Alex. "Evening wear, spring frock, cocktail dress?"

"Hmm," replied Herr Vollmeer. "I hadn't thought quite that far."

"Fine," said Alex, "What size is your wife, please?"

"Uh, I'm not sure," replied Herr Vollmeer. "Look," he continued hastily, "I don't really care what I buy today. I just know that I want to buy *something*. Anything to show those goons outside that some of us won't be intimidated!"

Alex stood silently for a moment, deeply touched. He then grasped Herr Vollmeer by the hand and said, "I'm very grateful. But go home, find out your wife's dress size and come back on Monday. Our merchandise will still be here then."

But the good Herr Vollmeer wouldn't leave until he'd bought his wife an expensive Italian handbag. "I'm sure this is the right size," he said with a smile. "I'll tell her it's an early birthday present."

"And when is your wife's birthday?" asked Alex.

"July. *Auf wiedersehen*, Herr Goldschmidt," called out the organist, and then he was gone, shouldering his way past the Storm Troopers, his newly bought package held aloft defiantly.

But Herr Vollmeer's act of kindness was not enough to offset a slow day, the first of many that plagued the Haus der Mode through the spring, summer, and fall. The next day's Oldenburg *Nachrichten*, a rightward-leaning newspaper even before January 30, wrote of the boycott in terms it might have used to describe the handling of a fallen tree in the aftermath of an unforeseen thunderstorm; there was no hint of any disapproval of the action itself:

> Yesterday morning, punctually upon the appointed hour, the guarding of Jewish businesses began. The boycott regulations were appropriately and perfectly carried out by representatives of the SA and SS; nevertheless, in some places they were greeted with unfriendly remarks. In a few cases, unruly passersby had to be taken to the police station. But thanks to the discipline of the authorities, no serious incidents occurred outside the boycotted firms. A strong police presence made sure that all transactions went smoothly, especially in the hours before noon with their busy street traffic. A few stores that were targets of the boycott decided not even to open their doors.

The official boycott lasted just that one April day, but it was a powerful signal from the new government of the direction in which it intended to take the country. Alex, worried about business but refusing to believe the worst, began to say to anyone who would listen, "I fought for the kaiser. Hitler can't touch me." It was a belief he would cling to for the next five years.

More devastating than the boycott was what occurred on April 7, the day Hitler's Reichstag passed the Law for the Restoration of Tenure for the Civil Service. The law contained its share of the usual bureaucratic language, but the epicenter of this legal explosion was the paragraph stating that "civil servants who are not of Aryan ancestry" were to be immediately dismissed. A subparagraph defined as "non-Aryan" any person who was descended from a Jewish parent or grandparent.

Here, then, was the legal justification for the expulsion of Jews from government jobs, from police and fire stations, from post offices, from libraries and museums, and from all cultural institutions supported by state or local governments. No more were dismissals to take place on a disorderly ad hoc basis; now there was a law. The response was ruthless and immediate.

In the cultural realm, the effect of the law was most severe where there had once been the most security—the many state-supported theaters, orchestras, and opera companies. Overnight, thousands of Jewish actors and musicians found themselves on the street, with no stage from which to share their hard-won insights into the human spirit with audiences who needed them now more than ever. The list of the suddenly unemployed contained many marvelous lesser known artists, but several prominent names as well: among them, Jascha Horenstein, dismissed from his role as conductor of the Düsseldorf Opera; Hans Wilhelm Steinberg, conductor of the Frankfurt Opera; and Kurt Singer, the deputy director of the Berlin City Opera.

Finally, on April 8, the National Socialist Student Association announced that it was planning "the public burning of destructive Jewish writing" to be carried out in one month's time by university students, ever vigilant in defense of the great German spirit. In a demented echo of Martin Luther's Ninety-five Theses, Nazi students nailed to university doors throughout Germany a list of twelve theses alleging Jewish cultural crimes. Thesis number seven stated: "When the Jew writes in German, he lies. He should be compelled, from now on, to indicate on books he wishes to publish in German: 'translated from the Hebrew.'"

The ritual book burning took place on the evening of Wednesday, May 10. In Berlin, a huge bonfire was lit in the square in front of the Kroll Opera House, and condemned books were wheeled into the square in oxcarts, much as prisoners facing execution during the French Revolution were transported to the guillotine. The student leaders were joined in joyful speeches by Joseph Goebbels, Minister of Public Enlightenment and Propaganda, who shouted, "No to decadence and moral corruption! Yes to decency and morality in family and state! Today I proclaim that the age of a hair-splitting Jewish intellectualism is dead; the past lies in the flames!" After the words were spoken, many more words were burned, as an estimated twenty thousand books were hurled into the bonfire, among them works by Moses Mendelssohn, Albert Einstein, Sigmund Freud, and Franz Kafka, as well as books by non-Jews such as Jack London, Ernest Hemingway, John Dos Passos, Sinclair Lewis, and Helen Keller. Thousands more met similar fates in city after German city. In Heinrich Heine's home town of Düsseldorf, righteous students burned volumes of his poetry. Returning from a House Concert, Grandfather Julian witnessed a bonfire at the base of a hill heading up to the Hofgarten. As he watched the dancing flames illuminate the heated faces of the cultural firemen, Julian thought of Heine's dark warning, issued nearly a century before: "Where men burn books, so shall they burn human beings."

This was the *Stimmung*, the atmosphere, in Germany in the spring of 1933. Jewish businesses and ideas had been targeted for destruction, thousands of Jewish artists were now unemployed. Many Jews responded by packing up and moving away, but many more couldn't, or wouldn't, leave the land of their birth. But what could be done to respond to these spirit-sapping laws and decrees and displays of ugliness? In Berlin, the former opera director Kurt Singer had an idea for an institution that would enable Jewish artists and Jewish audiences to support themselves both monetarily and spiritually, an enterprise that would prove both noble and naive, life-affirming and foolishly risky. It was an idea that would bring joy and hope and laughter to thousands of people who otherwise sought those gifts in vain. And among these virtues, Singer's idea had one more: it would save my parents' lives.

5

The Kubu

June 2, 1933

State Commissioner Hans Hinkel
President, Prussian Theater Commission
Wilhelmplatz 9
Berlin

Your Excellency,

Permit me in all humility, with a sincere request for benevolent treatment, to present to you the enclosed Epic. I remain, with hopes for your most excellent attention,

Your devoted
Dr. Kurt Singer

The Epic that Dr. Singer referred to was a detailed plan for the establishment of a *Kulturbund deutscher Juden*, or Culture Association of German Jews. In the face of political, economic, legal, and social exclusion from daily life, a few leaders of the Jewish community in Germany had decided that the most effective response would be a cultural one.

Those leaders included Leo Baeck, Berlin's chief rabbi; theater critic Julius Bab; conductor Joseph Rosenstock, who had just lost his job in Mannheim as a result of the Civil Service Law of April 7; producer Kurt Baumann; the Dutch-born economist and journalist Werner Levie; and Kurt Singer, a doctor, opera director, and choral conductor.

Shortly after the shock of that first week in April, these six men came together and calculated that there were more than eight thousand Jewish actors, musicians, writers, stagehands, costume designers, and other artists without jobs in Germany. And if, as seemed ever more likely, the segregation of Jews from Aryans continued, there would soon be a considerable audience with fewer and fewer entertainment options. What if, they wondered, Jewish artists organized their own performances for their own public? Wouldn't that solve two major problems at one stroke: the unemployment of the artists and the spiritual hunger of the audience? And wouldn't it also provide an important boost to the morale of the Jews of Germany, at a time when they needed it most?

Baumann, twenty-six years old and a former intern at the Berlin State Opera, volunteered to work up some numbers. Over the next two weeks, he devised a plan that included a budget, artistic personnel, a repertoire list, and a few organizational ground rules. Baumann began by calculating that there were about 150,000 Jews living in Berlin alone, and that every month they spent about 180,000 marks on theater tickets, a figure that didn't take into account money spent on concerts and films. If only 10 percent of the Jewish population (15,000 people) paid 2 marks and 50 pfennigs for a monthly subscription to this new organization, that would mean a base budget of 37,500 marks per month. Then, if a 1,000-seat theater could be found, and individual tickets were sold on a sliding scale from 3 marks for the best seats to 80 pfennigs for the worst, an additional 1,275 marks could be realized from every performance. And if it were possible to stage thirty events every month—including plays, operas, orchestral concerts, chamber concerts, lectures—that would mean a monthly box-office take of 38,250 marks. So the Kulturbund could count on bringing in more than 75,000 marks per month. And that didn't even include what the Bund might be able to attract in donations. Kurt Baumann's calculations indicated that this idea just might work.

But only, everyone quickly realized, with the official permission of the authorities.

To secure that permission, the founding members looked to the forty-seven-year-old Kurt Singer, a remarkable man who would devote his life to the Kulturbund for the next five years. Known for his work as assistant director of the Berlin City Opera (a position he'd lost after April 7), Singer had also made a name for himself as a widely published

Kurt Singer, the Kulterbund's magnetic artistic director. "He had dramatic looks, . . . a wickedly seductive face."

musicologist and a successful psychiatrist. He had a captivating, some would say hypnotic, personality. The writer Mary Lowenthal Felstiner remembers him this way: "He had dramatic looks, with a surge of gray hair rippling back from his forehead, an imposing lithe figure, a wickedly seductive face."

Singer was a strategically sound choice to take on the role of spokesman for the Kulturbund. He had fought in the trenches during the Great War, and, as conductor of the Berlin Doctors' Choir, he had done valuable work researching, collecting, and performing German folk songs. As such, his record as a defender of German art and honor was spotless.

Within a few days, Kurt Singer and Kurt Baumann had revised and refined their original plan, and Singer began the task of finding an attentive ear within the government. After knocking on doors in various ministries and in the offices of the Gestapo, Singer finally found a willing listener in Hans Hinkel, one of the earliest recruits to Adolf Hitler's cause. A Nazi since 1921, able to boast that he possessed Party Number 287, and a participant in the infamous Munich beer-hall putsch of 1923, Hinkel had risen to the rank of Sturmbannführer in the SS. He seems to have had a genuine fondness for music and theater; he also had a real knack for playing the dangerous game of political survival with such veterans of the sport as Hermann Göring and Joseph Goebbels.

Both of those men were on extremely close terms with Hitler, who shrewdly played them off against each other. In the early months of the new regime, Göring and Goebbels jostled for power and position almost daily. Göring, as director of internal affairs of the state of Prussia, claimed authority over the Prussian theaters and opera houses; thus Hinkel, promoted from his humdrum position in the Prussian Ministry of Education to be president of the Prussian Theater Commission, reported to Göring. Yet Goebbels was doing everything in his power to bring all the arts under the rule of his Ministry of Public Enlightenment and Propaganda. Hinkel sensed that Goebbels had the upper hand in this dispute and so smartly kept his head down when the Göring-Goebbels shells started flying. His prudence paid off; that autumn Göring dissolved his Prussian Theater Commission with a promise from Goebbels that he would retain control over the Berlin State Opera. By

Hans Hinkel, the Kulterbund's Nazi overlord. Proud of his long-standing
association with the Nazis, he also fancied himself a cultured man.

then, Hans Hinkel had assumed control of the Kulturbund; within a
short time, his new boss was Joseph Goebbels.

On the day in May 1933 when Kurt Singer came to see him with
his plan for a Jewish cultural association, Hinkel saw the benefits to
himself and his party immediately. First of all, Singer's idea solved the
problem of what to do with all those out-of-work Jewish artists and at
the same time made sure that they wouldn't slip back into mainstream
German artistic life by a back eddy. Hinkel saw immediately that if

Jews had their own theater and orchestra, they wouldn't end up working in some private theater or orchestra that didn't fall under the jurisdiction of the Civil Service Law. After all, the main idea was to further the Nazi aim of a "Jew-free" society and to assist, as Hinkel later declared, in "the construction of a culture of our own blood."

A second reason that Dr. Singer's idea appealed to Herr Hinkel came straight out of the Goebbels book of effective propaganda. In the spring of 1933 there was no assurance (Hitler's blustery claim of a "Thousand-Year Reich" notwithstanding) that the new regime would remain in power. With a large number of unemployed and disaffected Jews in their midst, the new national leaders feared what skillful propaganda from outside their borders might do to internal security. But if the Jews could be mollified by Mozart and Molière, they would be far less likely to rise up in revolution. And to make matters sweeter still, the Nazis could then answer international criticism of their treatment of the Jews by asking plaintively, "But how bad can it really be, after all? Look: they have their own theater, their own orchestra, their own lectures. They are obviously happy and well treated." World leaders, who at this point seemed to require few reasons to limit their efforts on behalf of Germany's Jews, apparently found this line of argument satisfying.

Finally, the ambitious Hans Hinkel saw the nascent organization as an opportunity for his own career advancement. As the organization grew, so too would his responsibilities and realm of influence. And its success would be his success, as well.

So with Dr. Singer and Commissioner Hinkel both seeing opportunity in the other, negotiations began.

Singer's opening move was the letter quoted at the beginning of this chapter, a thoroughly humble missive that accompanied the detailed proposal that the doctor and Kurt Baumann had developed. Five days later, Hinkel's office responded with a brief note to inform Singer that the proposal had arrived and was receiving all due consideration. Suddenly, though, came trouble. Somehow, word of Singer's initiative had reached the ears of Joseph Goebbels. If the propaganda minister decided that the idea was a good one, and approved it, the new organization would likely be placed in the charge of one of his underlings, thus robbing Hinkel of what he saw as an administrative opportunity. Hinkel knew there would be a time to cozy up to Goebbels soon enough, but not right then.

Luckily, the propaganda ministry wrote Hinkel a letter, informing him that Goebbels "is interested in the position taken by the Prussian Theatre Commission in this regard." The commission president took full advantage of the opening. First he dashed off a letter to the propaganda ministry declaring his opposition to Dr. Singer's plan: "Permission should not be granted," he wrote, "because the opportunities for sabotage or other destructive measures are too great, and furthermore because we lack at the present time the resources to maintain the sort of constant controls such an organization would require." Then, having—he hoped—thrown Goebbels off the scent for the time being, Hinkel immediately summoned Singer to his office on Wilhelmplatz. At a noontime meeting on July 6, the two men, allied enemies, hammered out the details and reached an agreement.

On the following day, Dr. Singer sent a letter of understanding to Herr Hinkel.

> I thank you most sincerely for the permission granted yesterday to establish the Kulturbund of German Jews and to lease a theater for closed performances. I hereby guarantee that I will keep the closest watch on the conditions you laid down:
>
> 1. Members must be Jewish, and only Jews will be allowed to attend performances.
> 2. No single-performance tickets may be purchased at the box-office; admission to all events shall be via season subscriptions.
> 3. The programs must be approved by the Prussian Theater Commission or a government office named by the Commission at least one month in advance.
> 4. Each member of the Kulturbund pays the same monthly subscription rate, and no extra charges will be raised for individual events.
> 5. No advertisements or announcements of Kulturbund activities are to be allowed in the general press. They shall be restricted to Jewish newspapers only.

Dr. Singer concluded by asking for speedy confirmation of his understanding so that the business of informing the Jewish public and enlisting artists could begin. But without waiting for an answer, Singer's colleague Julius Bab sent off an exuberant letter that same day to an actor named Fritz Wisten, who had recently been fired from his position as a company member of the theater in Stuttgart:

> Big News! After long and unpleasant negotiations the government declaration arrived yesterday. We have a guarantee that a purely Jewish theater will not only be tolerated but protected. Now our organizational and publicity work begins at a very fast pace. After overcoming this most difficult impediment our theater is at least 90 percent secure, and with that security you can already consider yourself as of today a member of our theater. I cannot send you a contract until the middle of August, but to give you some idea of the fees involved: you would be paid as much as possible under the very limited means that we will have. The maximum amount will scarcely be 6,000 marks a year. Please let me know whether or not we can count on you. Best regards, Julius Bab.

> The reply came quickly:

> Dear, Honored Mr. Bab:

> Hallelujah! Hail to you! I already regard myself as a member of your purely Jewish theater. The question of money should not be an impediment. Do you know what it means to me to be acting again? Warmest regards from Fritz Wisten.

On July 15, Hans Hinkel wrote back to Kurt Singer, confirming his conditions for the formation of the Kulturbund. In addition to the terms Singer had already stated, Hinkel insisted on a measure that would insure that only Jews would attend events sponsored by the new organization: upon joining the Kulturbund and paying the subscription fee, each member would be issued a photo ID card. Admission to all Kulturbund events would require the flashing of the card. In return, Hinkel promised that the Kulturbund would receive police protection; no National Socialist forces would bother either artists or audience members before, during, or after performances.

Fritz Wisten, actor, director, administrator, and one of the first recruits to the Kulturbund.

There remained only an official ceremony in the presence of Minister Göring. By now, Hinkel's ambitions had been realized. Göring had named him to a new position as director and supervisor of Jewish cultural affairs in Prussia. His new duties included the supervision of the Kulturbund. Hinkel, Singer, and Göring met in the minister's office. Years later, Kurt Baumann recalled hearing the details from Dr. Singer. "Göring tried to be amiable and jovial at first," wrote Baumann, but eventually the two Nazis made it very clear that, above all, the Kulturbund must not attempt anything subversive, and that Singer would pay with his head if the rules were not strictly followed. "Göring said something like, 'If you do everything right and do Herr Hinkel's bidding, then things will be fine. But if you get carried away then things will start popping, and you know it.'"

A massive recruitment effort began immediately. Singer, Baumann, Levie, and Bab threw themselves into it with an enthusiasm born of conviction, excitement, and hope. On July 17 they staged the first major publicity event for the Kulturbund—or the Kubu, as it came to be called—at a Berlin synagogue. It was a hot and sticky day, the temple was stifling, yet twenty-five hundred people showed up for a presentation that included a choral performance conducted by Dr. Singer. The show was a smash hit; Baumann recalled that "half of the audience became members on the spot and ninety per cent of the others ten days later, after it had become clear that there would be no disturbances and that police presence would be light." Over the next few weeks more such events were staged, each of them well attended and with similar recruitment success.

Each new member received a membership card, on which appeared his or her photo as well as the Kulturbund's logo, a hand grasping a torch superimposed over the Star of David. Membership also included a printed season program. There was to be one fully staged play or opera each month. Two orchestral performances, two lecture series, and a number of single chamber music concerts or lieder evenings would round out each month's offerings. The subscriber could choose which events to attend on which day, but he or she had to let the box office know in advance; in keeping with the agreement, absolutely no walk-up business on the night of a performance would be allowed.

As autumn approached and the subscription harvest soared, Singer and Bab began the task of attracting artists to the company. Fritz Wisten had already signed on as the Kulturbund's first actor. The first musician was Kurt Sommerfeld, a percussionist who'd lost his job with the Berlin City Opera earlier in the year. When he had gone to the employment office after the dismissal to explain his plight he had been told, "That's not so bad. Go to the Jewish cemetery and become a Jewish gardener." Instead, Sommerfeld had joined a jazz band that played Berlin coffeehouses at night and then, when he heard about the Kulturbund, signed right up. By reviewing the ranks of artists who had recently lost their jobs, by recruiting in those conservatories that still allowed Jews, and by spreading the word in clubs, dives, and bars across the country, Singer and Bab put together a company of twelve actors and forty-three musicians.

Finally the time came to choose a repertoire and stage the first performance. Opening night was set for October 1, in the midst of the High Holidays. The Kubu's directors chose a play because it was less complicated to mount than an opera and a more dramatic opening statement than an orchestra concert. As Kurt Baumann remembered, "There had never been a question which play it should be. There was only *one* work that was suited to depict our new situation." That play was *Nathan the Wise*, by Gotthold Ephraim Lessing.

Written in 1779, *Nathan* was the culmination of the life of the poet and playwright whom Heinrich Heine named "a soldier in the Liberation War of humanity." In the 1740s Lessing had written a play called *Die Juden*, a passionate denunciation of anti-Semitism, and religious tolerance was a theme he returned to often.

Nathan the Wise takes place in Jerusalem during the Crusades, a time and place where Jews, Christians, and Muslims meet on common ground. A man possesses a magic ring that renders those who believe in it pleasing both to God and to all humanity. For generations the ring had been handed down by each father to the son he loved best. This man has three sons whom he loves equally and, not wishing to show favor to any of them, has two identical rings made and gives a ring to each son. After the man's death the three sons argue over which one of them possesses the true ring, just as Jew, Christian, and Muslim have argued over which possesses the true religion. Nathan instructs the audience to believe that only the Last Judgment will reveal which religion is the true one, and that until then it is best for all people to live in a virtuous, peaceful manner. Nathan concludes:

> I bid you, in a thousand thousand years,
> To stand again before this seat. For then
> A wiser man than I will sit as judge
> Upon this bench and speak.

Kurt Katsch in costume as Nathan the Wise, October 1, 1933. "I felt that night more like a priest than an actor."

Kurt Katsch, the actor who played Nathan, wrote in his memoirs how moved he was by that speech and by its reception at the sold-out premiere in the Berliner Theater on Charlottenstrasse. "It wasn't theater anymore," Katsch wrote, "It was an almost religious experience in its intensity. I felt that night more like a priest than an actor, and that I was making a bold statement about freedom."

Perhaps it was a bit too bold. Hans Hinkel was in the audience, along with his staff, and, although there were no incidents and Hinkel went backstage afterward to congratulate the cast, that night was the first and last time that *Nathan the Wise* was performed in Nazi Germany.

October 1933 saw the first monthly newsletter published by the Kulturbund. That initial volume included an essay by the Jewish philosopher Martin Buber entitled "The Name Obliges." Buber examined each word in the organization's name and concluded that with the name came certain responsibilities. "The Kulturbund deutscher Juden has been founded for German Jewish culture," Buber declared, "not as a club or a society but as a federation. A federation means that the members are bound not by interests or activities alone but by life-giving principles and are inextricably bound together." How many of the organization's initial members recognized that bond right away is a matter of speculation, but it was clearly apparent shortly thereafter to an overseas visitor.

Six weeks after *Nathan the Wise*, on November 14, by which time membership in the Kulturbund had grown to more than twenty thousand people, the federation mounted its first opera production, *The Marriage of Figaro* by Wolfgang Amadeus Mozart. Joseph Rosenstock conducted, Kurt Singer directed the stage action, and the cast was headed by Walter Olitzki as Figaro and Fritzi Jokl as Susanna. Again the theater on Charlottenstrasse was sold out, and again Herr Hinkel was in attendance, but there was one important difference. This was one of the very few occasions in the history of the Kulturbund on which a reporter from a foreign newspaper was allowed to attend. Nearly a month later, on Sunday, December 10, Herbert F. Peyser filed this report for the *New York Times:*

One of the most poignant but uplifting by-products of Nazi anti-Semitism is the "Kulturbund deutscher Juden," the "Cultural League of German Jews." This organization [is] a development of only the past few months. Like everything else in the "new" Germany, it exists by the sovereign permission of the Hitler despotism. . . . Reports of its activities are ruthlessly barred from all public prints except a few Jewish journals . . . Its functions may under no circumstances be announced or advertised. . . .

The object of the league . . . is to minister to the spiritual and intellectual necessities of those Jews who still feel that their destinies are inextricably bound up with Germany, who have never ceased to look upon it as their fatherland and who continue to think of its culture as wrought into the living fiber of their being. . . .

The performers must without exception be Jews. So must the stage hands, the ushers, the ticket-takers, the coat-room attendants. Artists who vanished from the theaters, the opera houses and the concert halls of Germany because they were racially suspect may suddenly return to notice under these singular auspices. . . .

"The Marriage of Figaro" took place in the cheery and comfortable old Berliner Theater, a scant three minutes' walk from the Berlin bureau of the New York Times. Like the rest, I was promptly challenged at the entrance to show my credentials, but was admitted without further question on stating that I represented a New York newspaper and upon displaying a tiny American flag on the lapel of my overcoat. . . .

I must resist the temptation to write at length about the "Figaro" I witnessed. . . . Not only was the team-work excellent throughout, but the musical standards of the performance were high and some of the singing compared favorably with the best I have heard in German opera houses. For one thing, I cannot recall how long it is since I last listened to so much faultless intonation in the course of a single evening.

The little orchestra—about equal in size to what Mozart had at his disposal—played capitally, though Herr Rosenstock's tempi were sometimes damagingly fast. . . . Perhaps the humors of the piece were not as sharply defined as they can be; perhaps the key of the whole representation was pitched a little low. No doubt there were psychological grounds for these rather muted overtones.

The spirit of the performance found its counterpart in the demeanor of the audience. There was true cordiality, and scarcely an aria went unrewarded with applause. Yet something in the manner and in the tranquil dignity with which that gathering listened to the unfoldment of Mozart's divine comedy presently became inexplicably but incredibly affecting—something of a spirit that somehow called to mind a congregation of early Christians at worship in the catacombs. And when the opera ended and one emerged on the street, the sight of the crooked cross and the thud of the Storm Troopers' boots seemed more than ever odious.

Mr. Peyser captured something important, and hinted at a fundamental ambiguity, in his perceptive piece. For the better part of the next eight years the Kulturbund would offer performances of the highest caliber to an audience that craved them. But the walls of the Kulturbund theaters would never be stout enough to keep out the intrusive thud of the terror that lurked outside. Patrons who entered the sanctuary, clutching their photo IDs, had to pass a gauntlet of SS men who ranged around the entrance and regarded the incoming crowd with ill-disguised contempt. Inside, the seats were always full, and a festive feeling reigned; but the attendance was always boosted by at least a couple of agents from the Gestapo, there at Hinkel's orders to make sure that nothing untoward happened. The programs, which patrons could purchase for ten pfennigs each, would often contain gentle but urgent reminders, such as this one from the opening night of *Nathan:* "We ask our members to bear in mind that we are a community in need when you consider how to behave. We do not want to give the people around us any reason to become displeased. In that spirit, we hope our members will avoid political discussions of any kind while attending performances." After the show, audience members were forbidden to go backstage to see the artists. As the lights came up, the people would file slowly and no doubt reluctantly outside, there once again to avoid the stony expressions of the SS and, as the number of restaurants that served Jews dwindled, to hurry home through the increasingly dangerous streets.

More than one member of the Kulturbund would speak of the organization as an island of serenity in the midst of the ever-rising Nazi flood. But the image itself is ambiguous: an island is a place of both refuge and isolation. As the Kulturbund began to expand and to offer its members a wider variety of entertainment, those members embraced their isolation from the rest of German society ever more tightly. The anti-Semitic architects of the National Socialists, those who wanted above all else to render the Jews invisible, to establish a "Jew-free" Germany, thus found unwitting allies in the Kubu's leaders. In the words of author Lucy Dawidowicz, "the walls of an invisible ghetto began to rise up around the Jewish community."

And yet, accustomed as they were to attending concerts, plays, cabarets, and lectures, how could the members of that community turn away from the only performances available to them, especially performances of such high quality? In December of 1933 the Kulturbund presented its second play, William Shakespeare's *Othello*, in a production featuring the actor Fritz Wisten. By the end of the year the Kulturbund orchestra, conducted by Joseph Rosenstock and Michael Taube, had offered concerts of music by Mozart, Haydn, Beethoven, Schubert, Marcello, Pergolesi, and Chopin. There had been string quartet evenings, piano recitals, violin recitals, evenings of song and cabaret, choral concerts, a Strauss festival a few nights before New Year's Eve. And on October 16, the first Kulturbund outside of Berlin—the Jüdischer Kulturbund Rhein-Ruhr, with its headquarters in Cologne—announced its formation. It would be the first of many offspring.

By now, the Ministry of Propaganda had begun to use the existence of these all-Jewish organizations as a shield to blunt international disapproval of the still-new Reich. "The leadership of the Kulturbund has repeatedly assured us," claimed Hans Hinkel, "that the measure we have taken is a humane one, for Jewish artists and for the cultivation of Jewish art." If the Jews themselves were happy with conditions in Germany, what was there to criticize?

In December, as the year that forever altered the history of the Jews in Europe came to a close, the new Cologne Kulturbund published a statement of intent for its initial subscribers. "The goal of our stage," it read in part, "is to bring to all people the joy and courage to face life by letting them participate in the eternal values of poetry or by discussing the problems of our time, but also by showing lighthearted pieces. We intend to keep the connection with the German Homeland and to form at the same time a connecting link with our great Jewish past and with a future that is worth living for."

Such hope. It breaks your heart.

6

The Mask

SONDERSHAUSEN is a small town in the lovely hills of Thuringia. About fifty miles to the southeast lies Weimar, the city of Goethe and Liszt and the birthplace of the failed fourteen-year Republic. Sondershausen lies on a bluff overlooking the Wipper River. The ruins of a medieval castle guard the southern approach to the town, although for several centuries now its crumbling walls have been the site of nothing fiercer than lovers' quarrels. On the first day of October 1933, as the Kulturbund deutsche Juden took its first bows in Berlin, Günther arrived in Sondershausen to begin his studies at the music academy.

He had earned his *Abitur* degree in Oldenburg during the ugly days of April, when springtime tulips and Nazi decrees bloomed with equal ardor. Sondershausen had enjoyed a reputation as a good music school for over a century. A strong recommendation from his teacher, Herr Hoss, and a successful audition for an academy representative had earned Günther a place in the fall semester's class. In September, two months shy of his twentieth birthday, he prepared to leave home for the first time.

But two shocks, in quick succession, marred his departure. His mother, Toni, developed a glandular dysfunction; she lost a great deal of weight and took to spending long days in bed. And then his father gathered the family together to announce some terrible news: since the boycott, business at the Haus der Mode had fallen so sharply that he'd come to the painful decision to sell their beautiful house on Gartenstrasse. Although Alex had managed to avoid selling to Nazi Minister Spangemacher, he was now forced by the authorities to sell his beloved house for far less than it was worth.

In the last week of September, the family prepared to move into a small apartment at 35 Wurzburgerstrasse, near the railroad tracks a little bit west and north of the Pferdemarkt. Cleaning out the Gartenstrasse house was agony for Günther. Leaving behind the roses and rhododendrons—even the strawberries—was a blow to his soul, and nothing matched the misery of having to part with his chickens. There was no room for them in the new apartment. Alex found a farmer from the nearby countryside to come with a van to take them away.

Having sold much of their furniture and dismissed the cook, the housekeeper, and the gardener, the Goldschmidts moved into the Wurzburgerstrasse apartment on the last day of September. Alex was deeply depressed, Toni was too weak to leave her bed, and Günther, anxious as he was about leaving Oldenburg, actually welcomed the opportunity to leave the gloom of his new home. The next morning, only Alex and Eva accompanied Günther to the station to see him off. As the conductor blew the whistle announcing the departure of his train, Günther hugged his sister, then turned to his father. There was an awkward pause. Alex shook Günther's hand vigorously, then slipped a small package into his son's coat pocket before turning silently away and trudging off. Eva waved and hurried after her father.

A few minutes later, as his train chugged slowly down the tracks, Günther took the little package from his pocket. It was a box of condoms, Alex's not-so-tender way of saying, "Be careful." In Bremen, where Günther transferred to a southbound train, he dropped the package into a trash can.

The next six months were a time of music and melancholy for my father. He practiced diligently and appeared on stage a few times, including one concert in which he played first flute in a performance of Chopin's Second Piano Concerto. But to be in a small town in Germany in those days meant coming face-to-face with intolerance on an almost daily basis. The mayor was an unabashed Nazi, the market square was festooned with swastika flags, and the small city park soon sprouted signs that read "No dogs or Jews allowed." Günther quickly realized that he was the only Jew in his class, and as his fellow students made the same discovery they snubbed him one by one. He took to spending long hours walking along the river. On more than one occasion, rather than use the practice rooms at the academy, Günther took his flute to the ruins of the old castle, there to play mournful Bach sarabandes amid the echoing stones and falling leaves.

One day in late March of 1934, just as the first crocuses were blooming, a brief letter appeared in Günther's mailbox, informing him that, while his attendance and musicianship had been exemplary, the Sondershausen Music Academy regretted to inform him that, due to "racial reasons," his place the following semester would be offered to another student. Günther felt a mixture of pain and relief, the indignity of his expulsion soothed somewhat by the prospect of the end of his isolation. It was time to move on, but where would he go?

All around him, the cultural life of the country was moving on—in a direction designed to leave him and his kind far behind. In September of 1933, as the Kulturbund was rehearsing its premiere production of *Nathan the Wise,* Propaganda Minister Joseph Goebbels had unveiled a mammoth new organization called the Reichskulturkammer, the Reich Culture Chamber, or RKK for short. An important outpost in Goebbels's expanding empire, the RKK was established "to promote German culture on behalf of the German *Reich* and *Volk*" and "to regulate the economic and social affairs of the culture professions." The RKK was subdivided into separate chambers for music, theater, the visual arts, literature, film, radio, and the press. The point of the enterprise was to dictate what could and could not be created, performed, or exhibited, and who would be allowed to do the creating, performing, and exhibiting. It was plain from the start who *wouldn't* be allowed to do much of anything.

In the manner of a newly elected American president announcing his cabinet choices over a period of weeks, Goebbels unveiled the make-up of the various culture chambers throughout the autumn of 1933. On November 15, with great fanfare, Goebbels presented the new president of the Reichsmusikkammer (the RMK): the distinguished Richard Strauss, composer of the great tone poems *A Hero's Life* and *Death and Transfiguration* and the operas *Salome* and *Der Rosenkavalier.* Strauss had already come to the aid of the Reich back in April, when he substituted for Bruno Walter at the Berlin Philharmonic. Now he provided the Nazis with another important propaganda coup. Strauss has been sharply criticized for accepting the post. However, it seems fair to conclude that he sincerely believed that he could exert a positive influence on German musical life from this new position. In his opening remarks at the November 15 ceremony, he stated his intention to restore an active affinity between German composers and German listeners, recreating the relationship he believed had existed in the days of Buxtehude and Bach. There is no evidence that Richard Strauss was in any meaningful way a Nazi; nevertheless, his acceptance of the presidency of the RMK lent a credibility to the enterprise that it would otherwise not have had.

If there was any doubt what further effect the establishment of the music chamber would have on Germany's Jews, it was quickly dispelled by the RMK's membership guidelines. You could join only if you could prove that you were "politically and racially reliable." And you could perform or teach music professionally only if you were a member of the RMK. Thus if you were Jewish or "unreliable" in any way, you could forget about making music your profession in the new Germany. Unless—

Unless you joined the ever-expanding ranks of the Kulturbund. Encouraged by the success of the original in Berlin and the second Kulturbund in Cologne, Jewish culture associations were beginning to bloom throughout the country. In March and April of 1934, as Günther was absorbing his dismissal from Sondershausen, the newest branch blossomed in Frankfurt.

Although the Frankfurt, or Rhein-Main, regional Kulturbund also maintained a theater, a cabaret, and a lecture series, its main strength was its music. The source of that strength was the character of conductor Hans Wilhelm Steinberg, who had been relieved of his duties as music director of the Frankfurt Opera in the days following the decree of April 7, 1933. In his early thirties, Steinberg had established enough of a reputation that he easily could have found work abroad and enjoyed the inevitable upswing of his career. He eventually did emigrate to the United States, where he would be known as William Steinberg and conduct the orchestras of Pittsburgh, Buffalo, and Boston. Yet he chose to stay in Frankfurt and lend his prestige and artistic vision to the founding of the new Kulturbund.

Steinberg began recruiting musicians for his Jewish orchestra in March. On April 17 he was introduced as artistic director at the official ceremony that marked the establishment of the Rhein-Main Kulturbund. The leaders, who included Chairman Albert Ettlinger, Finance Director Walter Sulzbach, and Rabbi Georg Salzburger, pledged to work together with the entire Jewish community of Frankfurt. "It is only through the cooperation of both artists and audiences," their statement read, "that we all can bring about this endeavor and share likewise in its consolation and joy." Nearly six weeks later, on May 28, the new orchestra made its debut. With Steinberg conducting, the ensemble offered a program of Schubert's Fifth Symphony, Mendelssohn's Violin Concerto (with Hans Bassermann playing the fiddle), and Beethoven's First Symphony. The musicians performed in the Vereinshaus, a concert hall on a street in central Frankfurt called Eschersheimer Landstrasse, and, as had been the case with the Berlin Kulturbund on *its* opening night, the house was packed.

As this musical ferment was going on in Frankfurt, Günther passed through town, oblivious to how his destiny would one day draw him back. But now, in the spring of 1934, Günther was on his way to further his flute studies at the Music Academy of Karlsruhe, about 125 miles south of Frankfurt. The capital of the state of Baden and the former seat of the grand duke of Baden, Karlsruhe was a much bigger and more cosmopolitan town than Sondershausen, and overt anti-Semitism had yet to seep much below the upper strata of the city's social order. Best of all, Günther had a good friend already living there—his old Anemone-*ami* Elsa Boschen, who was enrolled in the Karlsruhe Art Academy.

For the first time in his life, Günther threw himself into his studies wholeheartedly. His teacher, Franz Spittel, who had been officially honored with the old imperial title of Kammervirtuoso, was vibrant and inspirational, able to pass on his knowledge of the mysteries of technique and musicality with humor and passion. Under Professor Spittel's guidance, Günther delved more deeply into the inexhaustible charms of Mozart, the composer whose *Magic Flute* had spurred him to take up the flute in the first place. He worked on both of the concertos Mozart composed for that instrument, as well as Mozart's marvelously lyrical concerto for flute and harp. Here Günther's heart was stirred by more than the music. The harpist was an attractive young woman with lustrous long brown hair; her name was Maria Himmelsbach, which means "heavenly brook." During their practice sessions together, Günther found himself increasingly attracted to her. Alas, she seemed unmoved. At last, Günther resolved to ask Professor Spittel if it would compromise their music making for him to ask Maria out for a bite after a rehearsal. Gently, the Herr Professor advised him to fish in other waters.

"Her father is Heinz Himmelsbach, a local Nazi Gauleiter in the region around Kassel. I cannot imagine that he would allow her to be seen in public with you, much less grant his permission for anything further to develop. I am sorry, Günther, but in the long run your heart—and the rest of you—will be better off if you concentrate on Mozart and forget Maria."

He took his teacher's advice in one respect, but my father has never, to this day, forgotten that "heavenly brook."

Luckily, he had Elsa and her wide circle of friends to console him. Among those friends were the brother and sister Henry and Herta Maas, whose father served in the city government of Karlsruhe. Oberregierungsrat Maas had a thick slice of ham in him; on many a night the young people gathered at his feet to hear him read the poems and stories of Edgar Allan Poe by candlelight as the wind whimpered outside.

And then there was Andre, a dashing young art student, reserve officer in the French army, and Elsa's lover. Andre embodied a French cliché: he wore a beret, affected a pencil-thin moustache, smoked Gauloises cupped in his left hand, preferred the strongest and most aromatic of French cheeses, and owned a Persian cat. He called his cat Wusche, a name my father found so appealing that, a few years later, he adopted it as a pet name for my mother. Andre could be counted on to suggest midnight bicycle rides to a nearby lake, there to argue art and aesthetics until dawn. Freedom was his credo: an artist must always be free, in body and mind. Günther and his friends found Andre immensely appealing for his wit, his energy, his passion, his unbridled enthusiasm for life.

One day Andre invited Günther to the academy so that he could construct a mask of his face. Günther agreed readily. In his studio Andre inserted small rubber hoses into his subject's nostrils so he could breathe and then applied a heavy layer of wet gypsum to Günther's face. While the plaster dried, Andre spun breathtaking tales of his amorous conquests and also declared that Günther's face revealed a deep and serious character that should serve him well in his own romantic pursuits.

"You'll see what I mean," enthused Andre, "when the mask is ready. Plaster always reveals what the brain tries to conceal. The plaster will make your face transparent so that your soul can shine through. If you then take the time to study the mask, it will tell you secrets that will render all women slaves to your every desire. I am doing you an immense favor, my friend, an immense favor. I trust you will not forget me when it comes time for thanks and gratitude."

With Maria Himmelsbach and other heavenly visions dancing in his head, Günther waited eagerly for the time when Andre would stop talking and remove the mask. After smoking nearly a full pack of Gauloises, Andre pronounced the plaster sufficiently hard. But try as he might, Andre could not pull the mask from Günther's face. He had evidently not applied enough lubricant to his subject's forehead, cheeks, and chin. For more than two hours, Andre pulled and tugged, while Günther hollered in pain and called Andre every foul name he could think of. At last the plaster released Günther's face, taking with it most of his eyebrows and lashes. He was the Academy laughingstock for weeks to come. And although no love slaves emerged from the ordeal's aftermath, Günther indeed never forgot Andre.

But Andre stayed in my father's memory for another reason as well. Shortly after the incident of the mask, Elsa became pregnant. Abortions were illegal. Unmarried motherhood was enough of a challenge, of course, but the situation was doubly difficult because the Nazi authorities frowned on liasons between German women and representatives of the archenemy, the French. Whether he was aware of that aspect of the situation, or whether he was just, in his mind, being true to his credo of freedom, Andre immediately left Karlsruhe and skipped home to Grenoble.

Some months later, when Elsa's daughter was born, she moved to a little town in the Black Forest to be with her mother. Shortly thereafter, in August of 1935, she arranged for an interview at the local school, where she hoped to become an art teacher. When she walked into the office of the school's principal, she was confronted instead by three members of the Gestapo. They charged her with carrying on two highly undesirable relationships: one with a French officer, which had resulted in the birth of a bastard child, and the other with a Jewish family in Oldenburg, the Goldschmidts. It was obviously too late, she was told, to do anything about the first relationship—and luckily it was no more—but Elsa's correspondence with the Jews must stop at once. Was that unmistakably clear?

Elsa said simply, "These people are my oldest friends. No, they are my family. I have lived with them, played with them. They took me into their home. I can no more sever my relationship with them than I could sever my right arm. I'm sorry, but I must refuse."

Again came the order to break off ties with the Goldschmidts, as well as an order to join the local chapter of the Nazi women's organization. Elsa quietly said no to both.

Five years later, her resistance would have resulted in immediate death. But now Elsa Boschen paid simply with her sinews and sweat. Without being allowed to see her mother or daughter, she was taken immediately to a labor camp in the Rhine valley, there to assist in Chancellor Hitler's preparations for war. For the next twenty-seven months, Elsa worked in cement, helping to construct the immense tank obstacles that would play such a crucial role when Hitler launched his *Blitzkrieg*.

Years later, when next she and Günther spoke, he asked her if, during that time in the labor camp, she ever regretted her loyalty to his family.

"Oh, Günther!" she exclaimed, her eyes shining. "I was, am, and always will be a faithful subject of the Anemone Kingdom. You know nothing could ever make me forget that. In fact," she continued, "I used to imagine that I'd just been temporarily captured by an enemy kingdom. I spent hours and hours plotting my escape. Those fantasies probably kept me alive."

Officer Andre was less lucky. In May of 1940, just after the German army, aided by Elsa's efforts, swept into France, he was shot while riding his bicycle on the outskirts of Grenoble. He was not in uniform at the time. Today, a small plaster plaque marks the spot where he fell—the first person of his city killed by the invader.

DURING THE WINTER and spring of 1934–1935, as Elsa's pregnancy progressed, Günther continued his studies with Professor Spittel at the Karlsruhe Academy. And throughout Germany, the Kulturbund deutsche Juden continued to flourish. In the eighteen months since the curtain first went up on *Nathan the Wise*, the Berlin Kulturbund offered a rich array of performances. In March of 1934, the orchestra and chorus performed Felix Mendelssohn's oratorio *Elijah* with the Ukrainian-American bass Alexander Kipnis in the title role. In May of 1934 Kulturbund audiences attended, in the same week, Handel's oratorio *Judas Maccabeus* conducted by Kurt Singer and William Shakespeare's *Twelfth Night* with incidental music by Engelbert Humperdinck. In November came Beethoven's opera *Fidelio* conducted by Joseph Rosenstock and staged by Singer; the two artists collaborated again two months later with *The Bartered Bride* by Bedřich Smetana. In the spring of 1935 the theater company offered George Bernard Shaw's *Candida* and one of the first German productions of *Six Characters in Search of an Author* by Luigi Pirandello.

Singer and Rosenstock came perilously close to running afoul of their censors when they staged the first-ever German production of Giuseppe Verdi's *Nabucco* in April of 1935. Probably the most famous moment in the opera is the third-act chorus of Hebrews lamenting their enslavement, yet Commissioner Hinkel and his staff apparently saw nothing objectionable in this dramatic reflection of conditions outside the theater. Two months later, however, Hinkel did exercise his authority. Again Singer and Rosenstock collaborated, this time on a production of the frothy operetta *Die Fledermaus* by Johann Strauss Jr. On June 20, Singer wrote to Hinkel:

The Court Music Director Johann Strauss, the nephew of the noted composer, has expressed his desire to visit one of our performances of his uncle's work. Thus I ask for your permission to allow Mr. Strauss and his wife to attend the performance of *Die Fledermaus* on Monday, June 24.

During its first two years, the Berlin Kulturbund operated primarily out of the Berliner Theater on Charlottenstrasse. In 1935, the Kubu moved into new headquarters at 57 Kommandantenstrasse. This promotional flyer for the new theater proudly proclaims "good seats for everyone," but goes on to warn that there are only eight hundred seats to be had. The implication was "reserve your seat today!"

The answer, with no explanation, appeared the next day.

> In response to your letter of the 20th of this month, permission cannot be granted to the Court Music Director Johann Strauss to attend a performance of your *Fledermaus*. Hinkel.

In Frankfurt, the Kulturbund's achievements were mainly musical, with Hans Wilhelm Steinberg leading the way. In July of 1934, the members of the orchestra were joined by violinist Ernst Drucker—a little more than a year removed from his graduation concert encounter with Brownshirts—playing the solo part in Mendelssohn's Violin Concerto. He soon became the Frankfurt orchestra's concertmaster. In October, Steinberg gave a series of Arnold Schoenberg concerts in honor of the composer's sixtieth birthday. Public acceptance of this inventor of the twelve-tone method of composition has never been warm or wide, and the Frankfurt audience proved to be no exception. Demonstrating that religious solidarity only goes so far, attendance at the Schoenberg Festival was light. In January of 1935, however, Steinberg and the orchestra gave one of their most significant and popular performances when they offered the world premiere of the Second Piano Concerto (called *Symphony for Piano and Orchestra*) by the Austrian Jewish composer Ernst Toch. Steinberg led a fully staged production of Mozart's opera *The Abduction from the Seraglio* in April. And the orchestra continued playing to full houses, not only at Frankfurt's Vereinshaus but also on tour in such cities as Hamburg, Bremen, Kassel, and Hannover.

And indeed the news about these all-Jewish artistic endeavors had been spreading to more and more cities throughout Germany. By the spring of 1935, there were the "Big Four" Kulturbünde in Berlin, Cologne, Frankfurt, and Hamburg, as well as Cultural Associations in Munich, Mannheim, Leipzig, Stuttgart, Dresden, Bonn, and dozens of smaller towns. Membership in these many organizations exceeded fifty thousand.

There would eventually be a Kulturbund in Düsseldorf as well. But with the one in Cologne, just a few miles away, doing so well, the cultural leaders in Düsseldorf established something similar called the Bildungsausschuss, or Education Committee. Its aims and ambitions were much the same as those of the Kulturbünde in other cities: to provide cultural opportunites for artists and audiences adversely affected by the Nazi threat. The Gumpert Conservatory became an even more important source of concerts, as Jews were forbidden to attend events at "Aryan" theaters. And soon the conservatory became the headquarters of a new ensemble: the Jewish Chamber Orchestra, conducted by Julian Gumpert. Not surprisingly, a frequent soloist with the orchestra was the conductor's daughter, Rosemarie.

Across the country, Kurt Singer, Julius Bab, Werner Levie, Fritz Wisten, Leo Baeck, Hans Wilhelm Steinberg, and other Kulturbund leaders were very happy with what they had accomplished. In Berlin alone, the Kubu employed about one hundred fifty musicians, actors, dancers, stage-hands, costumers, and box office personnel—people who had all been out of work two years earlier. Performances in Kubu cities were greeted by full houses and critical cheers, though only in the officially sanctioned Jewish newspapers, of course. And Hans Hinkel was happy; as he had hoped, the success of "his" Jewish artists had become his personal success as well. In a public display of satisfaction with how matters were proceding, Joseph Goebbels moved him to the Ministry of Public Enlightenment and Propaganda in early 1935 to become one of the three supervisors of the RKK. And soon afterward, Hinkel could add a new title to his resume. Germans have always been enamored of long and cumbersome honorifics and Hinkel would have needed an extra-large business card to fit all the verbiage of his new title: Special Commissioner for the Supervision and Monitoring of the Cultural and Intellectual Activity of All Non-Aryans Living in the Territory of the German Reich.

But the Gestapo (a contraction of the words *Geheime Staatspolizei*, or Secret State Police) was not happy. The police objected to the official name of the Kulturbund on ideological grounds. "Kulturbund deutsche Juden"—"Culture Association of German Jews"—rankled because the words implied that there was such a thing as a German Jew, or a French Jew, a Polish Jew—or an American Jew, for that matter. To the dyed-in-the-wool anti-Semite, Jews were outside the sphere of national consideration; they were simply an international abomination. So early in 1935, at the insistence of the Gestapo, the name was changed to Jüdische Kulturbund—Jewish Culture Association.

Soon the secret police thought of another improvement, one that fell in quite neatly with the designs and desires of both Hans Hinkel and Kurt Singer. The ever-increasing number of Kulturbünde made supervision more and more problematic, and different rules and regulations had been established in each city. The obvious solution was to bring all the disparate enterprises under one roof and create a super-organization that would render policy decisions straight from Berlin. Hinkel was sure to agree, as this single organization would only increase his power and influence with his boss, Dr. Goebbels. And Kurt Singer, who also relished the increased prestige such a consolidation could bring him, was eager to represent the Jewish artists. To clinch the deal, Hinkel called a meeting of delegates from all the local Kulturbünde, to be held in his (newly expanded) office in Berlin on April 27 and 28, 1935. The Gestapo was invited, too.

During the meeting, Special Commissioner Hinkel was polite, even charming, asking about recent productions and inquiring after the wives of several local leaders. He also left no doubt that a single unified organization was what he wanted and what he expected. According to the official Gestapo report, Hinkel told his audience that he was speaking to them "in confidence," and that if word about this gathering should ever get out, only "unpleasantness" would be the result. It was, of course, up to the delegates to decide, but surely they could see the advantage of a single body. At this point, Hinkel turned matters over to Dr. Singer, who pointed out to his colleagues all the structural advantages unity would bring. There being no strong objection, Singer declared at the end of the meeting, "I hereby make the official announcement to the Special Commissioner and to the gentlemen of the State Police that the creation of an umbrella organization of the Jewish Kulturbünde in the Reich was unanimously agreed upon by the delegates present here."

The next day Hinkel didn't even bother to attend. Singer and his colleagues hashed out a few details and the meeting adjourned, with all the delegates believing that they had accomplished something important: they'd ironed out a few organizational and procedural wrinkles that would lead to a more smoothly run system, and they'd once again demonstrated their willingness to cooperate with their Nazi bosses. Surely, they thought, this would only help them in the future.

What was really on the minds of the Nazis in the room can be gleaned from the official Gestapo report: "The establishment of a Reich Organization of Jewish Kulturbünde has taken place in order to allow smoother control and surveillance of all the Jewish cultural associations." All Jewish cultural associations that were not a part of the new national organization were henceforth banned. From now on, the strings would be just a little easier to pull.

7

Pathétique

JULIAN GUMPERT was late. He had a full day ahead of him at the conservatory on Ehrenstrasse, with lessons to give, meetings to run, and, in the evening, a recital to perform—Bach, Debussy, Bartók, and Brahms. He had scheduled his first student, a charming young woman from Dortmund who was working on Beethoven's *Kreutzer* Sonata, for ten o'clock in the morning, and here it was already a quarter past nine. It was a good ten-minute walk to the streetcar stop in Hösel, and this eighth day of August was not conducive to moving briskly; warm and muggy, the weather threatened thunderstorms that afternoon.

Julian hurried down the stairs, grasping his violin case in one hand and his forest-green umbrella in the other. He pushed open the door with his shoulder and nearly bowled over Herr Gruber, the postman. Waving his umbrella apologetically, Julian was already several steps down the sidewalk when Herr Gruber called out, "Herr Gumpert! I think you should see this—it looks official."

Turning back impatiently, Julian could see that the envelope the postman was holding out to him bore more than the usual number of swastika insignias. It was from Berlin. Julian set down his fiddle case, hooked his umbrella over his left wrist, and tore open the envelope. The letter informed him that, as of August 5, 1935, Herr Julian Gumpert had been officially ruled out as a candidate for membership in the Reichskulturkammer and the Reichsmusikkammer.

Nodding to Herr Gruber, Julian stuffed the letter back into its envelope and buried it in the inside breast pocket of his suit jacket. He then picked up his fiddle and set off once again. But he could not so easily dispose of the letter's insidious contents. Julian's thoughts matched the hurried tempo of his footsteps as he considered his options. On the one hand, this notice was in no way unexpected; the whole purpose of the Culture and Music Chambers was to prevent Jews from joining. Putting Julian's exclusion in writing changed nothing; its only purpose was his humiliation. On the other hand, it was yet another unpleasant reminder of the perilousness of his position—and of his daughter's. If Rosemarie was to find work commensurate with her talent, he had better act fast. So Julian resolved to add another item to his busy day: a telephone call to Hans Wilhelm Steinberg.

Unbeknownst to Julian, Steinberg and two other musicians who would soon enter his daughter's life had received similar notices that day. He was right: the RKK and the RMK existed solely to winnow Jewish artists out of German life. The chambers' leaders had spent considerable time and effort expelling artists who had managed to join despite their religion, and launching preemptive strikes against known Jews before they had a chance to apply. And in the first week of August 1935, the RKK had officially notified not only Julian Gumpert but also Ernst Drucker, Hans Wilhelm Steinberg, and another conductor— the Viennese-born Rudolf Schwarz—that they were not among the elect.

Shortly before noon, after his lesson with Fräulein Dortmund— Julian resolved to learn her name one of these days—he placed the call to Frankfurt. He'd met Herr Steinberg on two occasions when the younger man had conducted in Düsseldorf, and he felt no compunction about using his position on behalf of his daughter. Steinberg required a bit of convincing, but when Julian hung up the phone he had arranged an audition. Rosemarie would play for the conductor, and a chance to join the Frankfurt Kulturbund Orchestra, in ten days.

Like many a talented artist, Rosemarie loathed auditions. Performing, communicating with audiences, that was the compelling part of her life's work. But being asked to display her talent as if she were hawking a rug in a marketplace, and, what was worse, knowing that only if she succeeded at selling herself would she be allowed to perform as she truly wanted to, was nothing short of a waking nightmare. With such pressure came all the awful symptoms: a racing heart, clammy palms, a mind and memory that refused to perform to their usual standard, a dull yet persistent headache. The symptoms were all in full flower as Rosemarie and Julian, each carrying their instruments, walked up to Frankfurt's Vereinshaus on Sunday afternoon, August 18, for her appointment with Hans Wilhelm Steinberg.

It was a few minutes before two o'clock, the appointed hour. Julian looked at his watch, turned to his daughter, noticed her pained expression, and smiled compassionately.

"Don't think of it as an audition. Just imagine that it's early Sunday morning and you and I are playing together, just the two of us, as we have for so many years. You play beautifully and Herr Steinberg would have to be totally deaf not to notice."

Rosemarie tried to smile back, but just the left side of her mouth turned up, weakly, only to fall back down an instant later.

"I think I have to visit the bathroom. Do you think there's one in there? Or a place I could get a drink of water? Or maybe lie down for a few minutes?" And then, "Oh, Father, do you really think this is a good idea?"

Julian grinned broadly. He took Rosemarie's viola from her, set it down next to his fiddle, and hugged her tightly. He whispered into her ear, "I think it's the best idea I've had in years. Now," he instructed, backing away from her, "stand up straight. Let your arms hang down. Close your eyes. Breathe in deeply. Good. Now exhale."

Rosemarie stood with her eyes closed. She could hear the nearby song of a thrush and wished she could climb up into the tree with him and stay there the rest of the afternoon.

"All right," commanded Julian gently, "walk in there and show Herr Steinberg what you can do. And remember that I'll be right there with you, at least in spirit. Go on, then. Don't forget the instruments." And handing her both violin and viola, he gave her a firm push toward the door.

Somehow, Rosemarie found her way to the stage of the dimly lit hall. There were chairs and music stands and a single floor lamp with a naked bulb emitting a few weak watts, but there was no sign of human life. Just as she was starting to hope that there had been some mistake, a voice from the audience called out, "Fräulein Gumpert?"

"Yes?" Peering into the auditorium, Rosemarie could barely make out a bald head and two keen eyes about two thirds of the way toward the back.

"Good afternoon. Thank you for coming. I'm Herr Steinberg. I see you've brought two cases. Good. Your father mentioned that you play both violin and viola. Shall we begin with the violin? Good. Do you have some Bach, some Paganini? Good."

And for the next forty minutes, as Steinberg barked out commands from his half-hidden position among the velvet-covered seats, my mother stood on the stage and played and played, and played some more. A movement of a Bach partita. One of the Paganini caprices. The slow movement of a Mozart sonata. The opening of the Mendelssohn concerto. Then, on her viola, Wagner's devilishly difficult *Ride of the Valkyries;* a movement of one of the Brahms sextets; the finale of the sonata for flute, viola, and harp by Debussy; the Shrove-Tide Fair tableau from Stravinsky's *Petrouchka.*

It was incredibly demanding, but once she drew forth the first notes with her bow, Rosemarie felt completely at ease. This was all music she had worked on before, all music she loved (except for the Wagner, which was just *so* tricky), and the more she played the more confident she became. She was actually starting to enjoy herself when Steinberg called out.

"All right, Fräulein Gumpert. Since you are from Düsseldorf, I presume you like Schumann?"

"Yes, very much."

"Good. On the stands behind you, you will find the parts for Schumann Two. If you would, please, sit down in the viola section and begin with the second movement."

The second movement of Schumann's Second Symphony is a pell-mell scherzo, an expression of sheer exuberance that never falters till finally the music simply stops. When Rosemarie reached the end of the movement, she was perspiring mightily but sharing Schumann's high spirits.

"Good, Fräulein Gumpert, very good," came the voice from the auditorium. "You seemed to be enjoying yourself."

"I was. Schumann has always been one of my favorite composers."

"Good, good," came the reply. "As it happens, you'll be playing that very symphony when we give our first concert of the season next month. First rehearsal on the tenth. Congratulations."

And with that, Herr Steinberg pushed himself out of his seat and strode off into the shadows, leaving Rosemarie in great glee on stage.

She flung her fiddles into their cases and raced outside to find her father. By his huge grin, she knew that he had already heard the good news.

"I got the job! Steinberg offered me the job! I can't believe it!" Rosemarie crowed.

"Of course you got the job," Julian told her, pride welling up like tears in his eyes. "I sneaked in to listen. You played like an angel."

So on September 10, 1935, my mother began her first professional job, as a violinist and part-time violist of the Frankfurt Kulturbund Orchestra. The season lasted nine months and she was paid 150 Reichsmarks a month. The program of her very first concert, conducted by Steinberg, included the incidental music to Goethe's *Egmont* by Beethoven, the exuberant Schumann Second, and a much darker work by Schumann, his Cello Concerto in A minor, one of the last pieces he wrote before madness drew the curtain on his composing career. The soloist in the concerto was the brilliant young cellist Emanuel Feuermann, whose playing would flash across the international musical sky for only a brief period before he died in 1942, a few months shy of his fortieth birthday.

Herr Steinberg found Rosemarie a place to live, in the home of an elderly doctor who was also a major patron of the orchestra. His house was just a few doors away from Steinberg's, on a quiet street called Im Trutz, a few minutes' walk from the Vereinshaus. Rosemarie was eighteen years old, and she was about to embark on a new path in her life's journey. The lives of her fellow German Jews were about to change as well, but for the worse.

Since the spring of 1933, and the initial spasm of anti-Jewish laws, decrees, and regulations, subsequent measures had been announced more slowly. In August 1933, Jews had been banned from swimming in Wannsee Lake just outside Berlin; in September of 1934, Jewish youth groups had been forbidden to wear uniforms or carry banners or hike

Rosemarie at eighteen, about the time she landed her first professional job as a member of the Frankfurt Kulturbund Orchestra.

together; in July of 1935, Jews had been denied entry to all public pools and baths throughout Germany. But now a heavier blow by far was about to fall.

On September 11, 1935, the day after Rosemarie's first rehearsal with the Frankfurt Kulturbund Orchestra, the Nazis opened their annual party conference in Nuremberg. There were five days of high-decibel speeches and the nighttime torchlight parades made known to the world by the spectacular films of Leni Riefenstahl. For the grand finale on September 15, Adolf Hitler journeyed to Nuremberg in a special train, accompanied by members of the national government. At eight o'clock that evening, the first meeting of the Reichstag to be held in Nuremberg since the sixteenth century was called to order. Clearly, something out of the ordinary was at hand.

After a few preliminaries, the chancellor stepped forward and began to speak. Europe was becoming unstable, Hitler declared, pointing to recent events in Lithuania as proof of increased activities that could be traced to international communism and, of course, to the Jews. While it was not possible for Germany to control provocative Jewish conduct all over the globe, Hitler vowed that the Fatherland could, and would, see to it that such activities would not be allowed within German borders.

The German people, in righteous outrage against these cowardly tactics, continued the chancellor, were ready to rise up and physically defend themselves against the Jews. In order to prevent such understandable but potentially unfortunate confrontations from occurring, and in order for the German *Volk* to be able to enjoy "tolerable relations with the Jewish people," Hitler declared that it was time for a "singular momentous measure," a "legislative solution" to this vexing problem.

With that, Hitler turned the microphone over to Hermann Göring to announce this new measure, which remains among the most abhorrent actions of that repulsive regime. The "legislative solution" announced that night consisted of three decrees that came to be known simply as the Nuremberg Laws.

The first law was the Reich Flag Law. It proclaimed that the official German colors were black, red, and white; that the swastika flag was the national flag; and that Jews were forbidden to display those colors. Why? Well, for that you had to refer to the second law, the Citizenship Law. Only Germans, you see, could fly the German flag, and the Citizenship Law drew a major distinction between Germans and Jews. From now on, there were to be "citizens of the Reich," who enjoyed full political and civic rights, and "subjects of the Reich," who would be entitled to none of those rights. To be a "citizen" you had to prove that German blood flowed through your veins. And with that came the preamble to the third of the Nuremberg Laws:

"Fully aware that the purity of German blood is the condition for the survival of the German *Volk*, and animated by the unwavering will to secure the German nation forever, the Reichstag has unanimously decided upon the following, which is hereby proclaimed." What followed was the Law for the Defense of German Blood and Honor. It prohibited marriage and extramarital sex between Jews and Germans, and also protected the flower of German female purity by making it illegal for any Jewish home to employ as a housekeeper, nanny, or maid a German woman under the age of forty-five.

To further codify the Nazi concept of Judaism as a "race," the Nuremberg Laws categorized Jews according to their parentage, much as breeders in Kentucky might judge horses by the quality of their bloodlines. Charts and graphs appeared, explaining the difference between a *Deutschblütiger*, or a person of "German" blood, and a Jew, and thus introducing the concept of the *Mischling*, someone of mixed blood—a mongrel. You were a "German" if you had four "German" grandparents. If you had one Jewish grandparent, you were a *Mischling* of the Second Degree. If you had two Jewish grandparents, you were a *Mischling* of the First Degree. If you had three Jewish grandparents, you were considered a Jew. And finally, if you had four Jewish grandparents, you were not only a Jew but a *Volljude*, a "Full Jew."

Thus, on the fifteenth of September, 1935, the Jews of Germany were officially decreed The Other, Them. No longer citizens of the country they had served long and well, Jews were legalized strangers in what had become a very strange land. I cannot imagine the shame, humiliation, and disbelief with which German Jews read the newspapers the next morning. Günther, sitting at a cafe within sight of the old ducal castle in Karlsruhe, its columns swathed in now officially sanctioned swastika flags, felt a mixture of fear and naive hope. "Maybe now the people will realize what swine these Nazis are," he thought, "and get rid of them." It was a foolish hope, born of the utterly unexpected nature of the decrees. Günther, along with so many German Jews, was in shock. And who among them could see what lay ahead?

But that very morning, as Hitler and other party members entrained for Berlin, Propaganda Minister Joseph Goebbels stayed behind in Nuremberg to address his staff. His words reveal his contempt for Germany's new "subjects," and also offer a chilling hint of a later, more drastic Nazi solution to "the Jewish problem":

> We have absolutely no interest in compelling the Jews to spend their money outside Germany. They should spend it here. One should not let them into every public swimming resort, but we should say: We have up there on the Baltic Sea, let's say, one hundred resorts, and into one of them will go the Jews; there they should have their waiters and their business directors and their resort directors and there they can read their Jewish newspapers, of all of which we want to know nothing. It should not be the nicest resort, but maybe the worst of those we have, *that* we will give them [laughter from the audience], and in the others we'll be among ourselves. That I consider right. We cannot push the Jews away. They are here. We do not have any island to which we can transport them. We have to take this into account.

A LITTLE MORE than two months later, just after Günther's twenty-second birthday, he was summoned to the office of his teacher, Professor Spittel. He immediately noticed that the Herr Professor was extremely agitated and upset. His face was pale, and he hadn't shaved.

"Ah, Günther, thank you so much for coming to see me," he said. "Please, sit."

Günther sat and waited as Professor Spittel paced around his office, obviously searching for words. At last he stopped by the window and, looking out at the leaden sky, began to speak in a low voice he had to fight to control.

"You have been with us here at the academy for about a year and a half, isn't that so? Yes, and in all that time you have been a good student, a very good and attentive student. You have applied my few little suggestions to your playing, which has become . . . " and here his voice trembled a little, " . . . simply marvelous, very sweet and sensitive and musical. You are due to graduate in the spring, and it would have been my pleasure, my great pleasure, to sign your degree and to recommend you to any orchestra or opera company in all of Europe."

At that the professor turned to face Günther, stared at him a moment, and then closed his eyes.

"But you will not graduate. Yesterday afternoon, I was informed in no uncertain terms that you must leave the academy. Now, and without a degree." He opened his eyes and stared woodenly at Günther. "I am sorry. I am so very sorry."

Perhaps twenty seconds passed as the news sank in. Günther felt overwhelmed and short of breath, as though he had been kicked in the stomach.

"And there's nothing I can do? Nothing you can do?"

Professor Spittel turned away and moved back to the safety of his window. "I am in a very bad way, you see. My wife . . . one of her parents is Jewish, and . . . " His already low voice trailed away to silence.

Truth, when it emerges, pierces painfully.

"Yes," said Günther after a moment, regarding the old man with unblinking eyes. "One of those nasty first-degree *Mischlinge* difficulties. Yes, well, I can see how that could present a problem for you, Professor. Well, don't worry—I won't be another one. I'll just go."

Before he reached the door, Professor Spittel called out, "Please, Günther. Please know how sorry I am. Please remember that."

Günther stopped, then walked across the room to shake his teacher's hand.

"I will, Herr Professor. I will remember all I've learned from you, and your many kindnesses. I will remember everything."

Günther walked back to his apartment in a daze. But by the time he was back in his room, he had decided what to do. With the humiliation of the Nuremberg Laws in the recent past, with the jolt of this second expulsion in the present, and with no assurances that even greater ordeals didn't lie ahead, he could find no good reason to stay in the country of his birth. On that late November afternoon, as an early dusk descended on Karlsruhe, my father resolved to leave Germany. He would find a neighboring country that would take him in, and remain there until the German people came to their senses and evicted Chancellor Hitler. Then Günther would return. Or, he concluded sadly, he would never return. But his homeland was no home to him now.

Over the next three months, he investigated the possibilities with the help of an acquaintance from Elsa's old circle, a woman named Ursula who worked in a shop that sold maps and globes. Günther had always liked the idea of north, so he decided that Sweden, across the Baltic Sea, would be his new home. With Ursula's contacts, and after writing a few letters, he found himself a small apartment situated above a milk bar in central Stockholm. At Christmas 1935, Günther went home to Oldenburg to tell his family of his decision.

By then there had been another change of address for the Goldschmidt family, and an act of betrayal. In the last days of the 1920s, as business boomed at the Haus der Mode, Alex had made arrangements with another businessman in the clothing trade, Magnus Sander, to open a shop one flight up from the Haus, in the apartment where Alex and Toni had lived before the move to Gartenstrasse. Herr Sander promoted his establishment as being *Klein Preis, Etage,* or "Discounts, Upstairs." For a time both stores did well, as shoppers found it convenient to obtain their fine merchandise and accessories at the Haus der Mode, and then to climb the stairs for an additional bargain or two.

But then came the April Boycott of 1933 and the subsequent downturn in Alex's fortunes that had forced the move to Wurzburgerstrasse. For a time he did his best to keep his store afloat, working fifteen-hour days and cutting prices on his quality apparel, hoping to make up in volume what he lost on individual sales. But nothing seemed to help; business was just draining away. Some of Alex's most reliable customers cut off their trade, and others, such as the loyal Herr Vollmeer, moved out of town.

In January of 1934, after a crushingly disappointing holiday season, Magnus Sander came down the stairs with a proposition. Since Alex had cut his prices so severely, Herr Sander pointed out, their two stores were more similar than they once had been. If Alex was willing to sell, Sander would consolidate both stores into one and assume the risks as sole proprietor.

Alex did not take long to think it over. In March the sale went through, and the Haus der Mode ceased to exist. Magnus Sander took over the whole operation, although Alex remained owner of the property. Alex called upon some of his colleagues from early in his career and found a job as a buyer for a department store with headquarters in Bremen. In May, his income reduced once more even with the profits from the sale of his store, Alex was forced to move his family into yet another apartment, this one located at 53 Ofenerstrasse.

But insult was added to financial injury when Alex opened his newspaper one day in June 1934 and read the advertisement placed there by the man he had welcomed into his business. The ad proudly proclaimed that "the Jew Goldschmidt" was no longer in trade at the corner of Achternstrasse and Schüttingstrasse and that customers were invited to visit the fine and wholesome establishment now operated solely by Magnus Sander.

Eighteen months later, when Günther visited the Ofenerstrasse apartment to tell his family of his intention to move to Stockholm, his father was still seething with anger and resentment. Alex did not object when Günther revealed his plan, but when he somewhat timidly suggested that his father also consider pulling up stakes, Alex would have none of it.

"Where would I go? What would I do? I'm nearly fifty-seven years old. And besides, I fought for the kaiser; Hitler can't touch me. And neither can that Sander-*Schwein*, who I'm going to give such a *potch* one of these days. . . . "

When Günther left Oldenburg for Karlsruhe a few days after Christmas, he assumed that the next time he would see his parents he would be well on his way to becoming a Swedish citizen.

That same Christmas week saw Rosemarie at home in Düsseldorf, regaling her parents with tales of her first season as a member of the

Frankfurt Kulturbund. After the opening concert of Beethoven and Schumann, there had been a program of cantatas by Bach and Kuhnau and psalm settings by the Jewish composers Bernhard Sekles and Solomon Rosowsky; another concert conducted by Hans Wilhelm Steinberg with music by Gluck and Mozart and the heaven-storming Symphony No. I by Gustav Mahler; and, for Hanukkah, a performance of Handel's *Judas Maccabeus* conducted by Nathan Ehrenreich. After a few days at home, Rosemarie was expected back in Frankfurt for a gala New Year's concert, conducted by Steinberg, of scenes from operas by Offenbach.

"And how is His Eminence treating you?" her father wanted to know.

"Herr Steinberg? Very well. He hasn't said very much to me, but he seems pleased with my work."

"He should be. He should bless the day I called him up and told him about you!"

"I only have one question," said her mother. "Are you happy?"

"Oh, yes!" Rosemarie responded. "I've never been happier. I'm making music with some very talented people, I'm busy all the time, and they're even paying me!"

In the next two months, she would enjoy three more series of concerts with His Eminence. The music included arias by Haydn and Mozart, Mendelssohn's *Scottish* Symphony, Chopin's Piano Concerto No. 2, the violin concertos by Brahms and Dvořák featuring solo performances by Ernst Drucker, and music by Jewish composers Karol Rathaus and Berthold Goldschmidt. Berthold was no relation to the Oldenburg Goldschmidts, but his presence on the program was a signal coincidence in light of the crucial crossing of paths that was about to take place.

All this time, Günther had been occupied with his emigration to Sweden. On a mild evening in the second week of March 1936, as he busied himself with the task of placing books in boxes in his Karlsruhe apartment, the telephone rang, and, quite simply and naturally, Günther picked it up and said, "Hello?"

How, I wonder, could my father ever again answer the phone without an elevated pulse? I can imagine him, for the next sixty years, always half-expecting that another thunderbolt would strike him through the wire, and then hanging up the receiver with an inward quizzical smile when it didn't. For here was a call straight out of fiction, quite literally a moment when my father's life was utterly altered.

Not that he knew it instantly. The voice on the other end merely explained that the Kulturbund Orchestra of Frankfurt needed a flutist for two concerts in Frankfurt and Hamburg. The orchestra's principal flutist had come down with a bad cold and was unable to play. And somehow the Kulturbund officials had heard of this young man's talents.

Günther weighed the offer for a few minutes. On the one hand, here was an opportunity, a real job, his first chance to play his flute professionally. And with his imminent move, the money would certainly come in handy. On the other hand was the move itself. Awash in boxes, his life turned upside down, he wasn't sure what future this job promised in the long run. But in the end, the prospect of actually playing in an orchestra won him over. Günther said yes.

The only remaining rehearsal was at two o'clock the next afternoon in Frankfurt. So the next morning, Günther threw a few things into a suitcase, including his wooden flute and his favorite bright blue sweater, and boarded the train for the two-hour journey to Frankfurt.

As a sort of good-luck charm, to ward off nerves and to steady his fingering, Günther decided to wear his blue sweater to the rehearsal. He arrived at the Vereinshaus early, hoping to meet some musicians who would let him know what to expect. While scanning the bulletin board for the schedule, flute case in hand, he felt a tap on his shoulder and a voice asked him, "You the new flutist?"

He turned to see a man who appeared to be in his early thirties, with long, prematurely gray hair, holding a violin.

"Yes, I am. My name is Günther Goldschmidt. I've just arrived from Karlsruhe. I'm afraid I have no idea where I should be or what I should be doing now."

"Well, then, let me be the first to welcome you. I'm Walter Liebling, and as you can see I play the violin in our little band."

"How long have you been a member?"

"For about four months. I used to build houses for a living, but one day last December I ran into an acquaintance from my fiddling days and he recommended that I give this a try. And I'm glad I did. Sitting in a chair a few hours a day sure beats working all day on a building site. I think you'll find a few of us in this orchestra who used to do something else. Now this is what's available, and you won't find many complainers."

"What should I know about the conductor, Herr Steinberg?"

"The Old Man? Well, he runs a tight ship, very picky, extremely sharp ears. He also has a bit of a chip on his shoulder, if you ask me. You know, he used to be an assistant to Otto Klemperer at the Opera in Berlin before they ran him out. I also think he's planning to be on the first boat he can book passage on. But all in all, he's as good as we can expect. After all, he's a conductor. You know the difference between an orchestra and a bull, don't you?"

"No, I don't."

"A bull has the horns in the front and the asshole in the back. Get it?" And Herr Liebling began to laugh uproariously.

Günther smiled politely and turned back to the bulletin board. To his relief, the violinist had begun to walk, still chuckling, out onto the stage. And to his great pleasure he saw that the featured work on these programs he would play in Frankfurt and Hamburg was the Symphony No. 6, the *Pathétique* Symphony, by Tchaikovsky. The great Russian composer had poured out his soul in this, his very last work, a blatantly autobiographical symphony full of all the exultant highs and tragic lows this deeply emotional artist was capable of expressing. As such, it appealed to Günther's romantic sensibilities completely. It also has some great flute parts.

At two o'clock precisely Hans Wilhelm Steinberg strode briskly onto the stage and mounted the podium. "All here? Good, good. All right. Let's work on the symphony."

And for the next hour and a half, Günther found himself in direct contact with the heart and soul of Pyotr Ilich Tchaikovsky as the orchestra rehearsed the *Pathétique*. First they ran through the piece from beginning to end, experiencing the emotional explosions of the opening movement; the crooked waltz of the second; the soaring, marching exuberance of the third; and the utter defeat and gloom of the last movement. And then Steinberg turned their attentions fully to the finale, from the heartbroken cry that begins it, through the anguish of the middle section, to the very end, where, its strength spent at last, it lurches fitfully into the grave.

When Steinberg at last put down his baton and announced a fifteen-minute break, Günther sat rooted to his chair, his face wet with a mixture of sweat and tears. The stage had nearly emptied, and he still sat, staring at his score, his flute in his hand, when he noticed a young woman standing beside him, chestnut-brown hair cascading over her shoulders, her round face illuminated by deep brown eyes. She carried a viola. "Hello," she said. "My name is Rosemarie Gumpert. You're new, aren't you?"

It's a moment that, for my father and mother, should have been marked by some extraordinary sign, by the sounding of bells or the falling of a star. That moment may well have saved my mother's life. It certainly assured my father's lack of a Swedish passport in years to come, not to mention my very existence. Two lives, brought into coincidental contact through institutional hatred, were about to become one, bound together by loneliness, fear, love, and music.

Let me tenderly imagine their first encounter, as Rosemarie, moved by the tears on the young flutist's face, remarks that his sweater is her favorite color. He, embarrassed by those same tears, blows his nose, hurriedly disassembles his instrument and bends down to put it back in its case, straightens up and knocks over his music stand, sending the Tchaikovsky score flying. By the time the two of them retrieve the scattered pages and stand facing each other, they are both laughing.

This image, their first encounter, these two young people meeting for the first time on a crowded stage in Frankfurt, rehearsing the tortured, exalted music of Tchaikovsky under the watchful eyes of their enemies, fills me with uncomprehending awe.

After the rehearsal Günther and Rosemarie strolled across the street to a small cafe to drink hot chocolate, eat sponge cake, and talk. The following night, after the concert, they returned to the cafe for more chocolate, more cake, and lots more talk. The next week, on March 24, two days before my father's departure for Sweden, they met again in Hamburg for the second concert. This time there would be no opportunity for a late evening. The members of the orchestra took the night

JÜDISCHER KULTURBUND HAMBURG

Dienstag, den 24. März 1936, 20.15 Uhr
Tempel, Oberstr. 120

Das verstärkte Orchester des
Jüdischen Kulturbundes Rhein-Main

Leitung: Generalmusikdirektor HANS WILHELM STEINBERG
Solistin: HERTHA KAHN (Violine)

Robert Müller-Hartmann .. .. Suite
                               Ouverture
                               Lento
                               Finale

Ludwig van Beethoven .. .. Konzert für Orchester und
                               Violine op. 61 D-dur
                               Allegro ma non troppo
                               Larghetto
                               Rondo (Allegro)

Peter Tschaikowsky .. .. 6. Symphonie (Pathétique)
                               op. 74 h-moll
                               Adagio
                               Allegro con gracia
                               Allegro molto vivace
                               Adagio lamentoso (Finale)

MÄRZ	Conventgarten, Theatersaal, 16 und 20.15 Uhr
30. Montag Die für den 12. Febr. gelösten Karten haben Gültigkeit	Auf vielfachen Wunsch wiederholt **Komödie der Irrungen** von Shakespeare Regie: Hans Buxbaum Bühnenbild: Anny Gowa Kostüme: Käte Friedheim Musik: Kurt Behrens Tänze: Erika Michelson (Milee)
31. Dienstag Die für den 13. Febr. gelösten Karten haben Gültigkeit	PREISE: Nachmittagsvorstellung RM. 0.50 (Karten nur in beschränkter Anzahl) Abendvorstellung RM. 3.50, 2.70, 1.90, 1.40

Because the first flutist of the Rhein-Main (Frankfurt) Kulturbund Orchestra caught a cold, Günther joined the orchestra for this concert . . . and met Rosemarie. This is the program from the second of their two concerts together in which they played the Pathétique *Symphony.*

train back to Frankfurt, while my father headed off to his home in Oldenburg to say his goodbyes to his family. But the two new friends were able to share a few minutes together at the Hamburg railroad station, no doubt with steam escaping from the engines and a light rain falling, talking and laughing until they had to follow the orders of a different kind of conductor and board their respective trains.

What drew them together? Certainly there was a shared love of music, their common experience of making music under restricted circumstances, and their youth. But I'm sure that Günther and Rosemarie were also attracted by the mutual hope that, finally, they had found someone to understand their loneliness, their feelings of not belonging. She was an only child whose father inspired her but kept her at arm's length. He never really knew his father, a lack that was probably at the root of his lifelong sense of himself as a stranger.

So as the two trains pulled away from Hamburg that March night in 1936, the two quickening hearts yearned for each other in mingled sadness and newly kindled joy.

The next day, just hours before leaving for Sweden, Günther mailed Rosemarie a copy of Rainer Maria Rilke's *Letters to a Young Poet*. I have the little volume before me now, a precious relic. On the first page is the following inscription, in German, naturally: "Rosemarie Gumpert— A small memento of two concerts—Tchaikovsky—in Frankfurt and Hamburg in March 1936. G.G." I wonder which of Rilke's gentle and profound observations made the greatest impression on the sender and on the recipient. More than sixty years later, two in particular strike me. "Destiny is like a wonderful wide tapestry in which every thread is guided by an unspeakably tender hand, placed beside another thread, and held and carried by a hundred others." And "It is always my wish that you might find enough patience within yourself to endure, and enough innocence to have faith. Believe me, life is right in all cases."

A few days later, Günther was thrilled to receive a return envelope from Frankfurt. Inside he found an enthusiastic letter from Rosemarie, thanking him for the book and expressing her happiness at having met him. But she had addressed the letter to Gustav Goldschmidt, apparently confusing him with the king of Sweden. It must have been a wee bit exasperating for Günther to think that he had made so little an impression upon the object of his affection that she couldn't even remember his name. But having inherited my mother's occasional difficulties with such matters, I can only smile with love and indulgence. What, indeed, is in a name?

Thus began an ardent correspondence between Frankfurt and Stockholm. Rosemarie kept Günther informed about the latest doings in the orchestra, and he told her of his attempts to learn a new language. He mentioned the long afternoons he spent downstairs in the milk bar, drinking tall glasses of milk and now and then eating a bowl of vanilla ice cream while studying Swedish grammar and trying to advance his vocabulary by eavesdropping on nearby conversations. But in deference to what he hoped were her growing feelings for him, he left out an important detail. There was a young woman with a baby carriage whom he met for strolls in a nearby park and who quizzed him on the latest words and phrases he had mastered. Today, very little of what he learned that summer remains, except for *tak*, Swedish for "thank you."

Believing, as did Rilke, in a beautifully woven destiny, and in the rightness of life, Günther, after spending six months in the white night safety of Sweden and engaging in a regular and intense correspondence with Rosemarie, decided to go back to Germany to be near her. The opportunity presented itself when the same flutist who'd caught cold in March fled to Palestine in August. Foolishly or romantically—or both—my father accepted the position of principal flutist of the Frankfurt Kulturbund Orchestra.

Would I have done the same thing? Whatever my answer, I have the advantage of hindsight, of knowing the terrors of the next ten years. But still, even in the late summer of 1936, my father must have known what a damn-fool thing he was doing: deliberately, and with all his faculties intact, voluntarily going back to Nazi Germany, to the country whose leader had vowed to eradicate his kind from the earth forever. And for what? Ah, for love. For music and for love. I don't know if I would have done it. But I do know that I love and admire him for it. I think it's the most wonderful story I know.

8

La Vie Bohème

THE OPENING ACTS of Giacomo Puccini's opera *La Bohème* sing the praises of young love, and of the power of youthful ardor and fulfilling work to overcome the curse of poverty. Rodolfo the poet, Marcello the painter, Schaunard the musician, Colline the philosopher, and Mimi the seamstress are cold, hungry, and destitute, but they take joy in their work and their infinite hopes.

For two years, beginning in the autumn of 1936, Günther Goldschmidt and Rosemarie Gumpert were similarly sustained by the potent forces of young love and gratifying work. Even though they were outcasts, despite the constant flow of propaganda and frequent exhibitions of Nazi force, Günther and Rosemarie were probably happier in those years than at any other time of their lives. Their work and love fulfilled them and, in the spirit of Puccini, they were living *la vie bohème*.

It began around the middle of September, when Günther said goodbye to the young woman with the baby carriage, had a last dish of ice cream in the milk bar downstairs, and left hospitable Sweden for Nazi Germany. Günther found an apartment directly across from Rosemarie's, on the street called Im Trutz. It was a neighborhood in which many musicians lived, only a few minutes' walk from the Vereinshaus, the main Kulturbund concert hall on Eschersheimer Landstrasse.

Today the street is narrow, quiet, and peaceful, with two- and three-story houses rising on either side—much as it was in the middle 1930s, despite heavy bomb damage during the war. At the bottom of Im Trutz, the street empties into a small park, with a curving pond framed by graceful willow trees. Günther and Rosemarie spent hours and hours in the park walking, sitting at the edge of the pond, eating sandwiches, feeding the crumbs to the gabbling ducks, occasionally spreading out a blanket and losing themselves in sleep in the sun. The western end of the park borders a square in which stands the venerable Old Opera House. They would often include the square in their walks, although, of course, attending a performance at the opera was impossible for them; as Jews, they were forbidden.

On days when there were no rehearsals or performances, the two young people often would wander through Frankfurt's museums, or take a streetcar a few miles north to the city's splendid Palmengarten, an elaborate park filled with exotic plants and strutting peacocks. Or they might borrow bicycles and mount an all-day excursion to the hills and valleys of the Taunus region to the west, their baskets full of crusty bread, cheese, and flavorful little sausages for a noontime repast. As autumn gave way to the rain and chill of winter, they would retreat to each other's rooms to read and snuggle. By the end of the year, they had become inseparable.

They made no effort to hide their budding romance from their colleagues in the orchestra, and indeed it was the subject of no little merriment among their fellow musicians. A cellist named Wolfgang Brettschneider fancied himself a poet and wrote a lot of amusing doggerel to keep himself and his stand partner diverted during long rehearsals. Three Brettschneider verses have survived, all of them concerned with the foibles or identifying characteristics of the members of the orchestra, and all of them remarking on the closeness of a certain flutist and his pretty violist.

In one, the poet remarks how curious it is that, while the two sit next to each other in a normal fashion on a bus in daylight, once darkness falls they cast but a single shadow. In another, in which he runs through the alphabet listing each member of the orchestra by the letter of his or her last name, he says that since it is impossible to separate Goldschmidt-Gumpert, he must name them together, and he hopes they will not mind that violinist Max Greenbaum is listed here in the G's as well.

In his third bit of humorous verse, Herr Brettschneider declares that since Fräulein Gumpert and Herr Goldschmidt are inseparable on Earth, they should not be parted even after death. He then hints at something that seems very familiar to me, even though he is writing fifteen years before I was born. In the poem, Günther hangs a cage in his room and Rosemarie, like a bright and cheerful canary, hops willingly inside, there to listen to her friend playing sweetly on his flute. It's a caricature, of course, but my father always was a bit possessive of my mother as I was growing up, preferring that they stay at home together rather than go out with friends, as my mom would have liked. If Herr Brettschneider is to be believed, this was a dynamic that must have been in place from the very beginning.

But the schedule of rehearsals, concerts, friends' concerts, and leisure activities left little time for Rosemarie to stay in her cage, no matter how accurate a portrait the poem may be. Since these were their first jobs in an orchestra, there was always new music to learn. The first concert of the season took place on October 20. The program included the "Calm Sea and Prosperous Voyage" concert overture by Mendelssohn, Mozart's Symphony No. 34 in C Major, and Beethoven's Symphony No. 2. Günther and Rosemarie had not played any of these pieces before, and what a marvelous discovery they must have been. Günther in particular was thrilled by the opportunity to play his first Beethoven symphony, although he also felt a bit intimidated by the symphony's last movement. Once famously described by a purple-prosed critic as "a hideous dragon that beats about with its tail erect," the Second's finale leaves the flute exposed to launch the rollicking tune and then pipe above the whole orchestra as the symphony romps to its conclusion. Günther practiced long and hard, and at the end of the concert, with the Vereinshaus audience on its feet, he was rewarded with his first solo bow.

By the beginning of Günther's first season with the orchestra, Hans Wilhelm Steinberg had left Frankfurt for Palestine, there to conduct the new Palestine Symphony, an ensemble put together by Bronislav Hubermann with the encouragement of Arturo Toscanini. The new music director of the Frankfurt Kulturbund Orchestra was Julius Prüwer, and although today he is not as well known as Steinberg, he was a very accomplished musician. In 1936, Prüwer was sixty-two years old. He had studied with Johannes Brahms and the noted conductor Hans Richter in Vienna, held important conducting posts in Cologne and

Günther with his wooden flute.

Breslau, and then from 1924 to 1933 taught at the Berlin Hochschule and was on the conducting staff of the Berlin Philharmonic. All of that counted for nothing with the new authorities, of course; Prüwer's high-profile career had abruptly ended after the passage of the Civil Service Law of April 7, 1933. Luckily for him and for his fellow Jews in the Rhein-Main Kulturbund, however, he found a home in Frankfurt.

As gratifying as it was for Günther to make his debut with the orchestra in the prominent position of principal flute in the Beethoven Second, he was even more excited by his next opportunity; on November 11 the Kulturbund gave a complete performance of Mozart's opera *The Magic Flute,* the work that had inspired him to take up his instrument in the first place. Now, instead of watching from the audience, Günther played the flute from the orchestra pit as Tamino led Pamina through their trials on stage. After the performance, Günther was too keyed up to sleep, so he and Rosemarie took a trolley down to the River Main. As the two young musicians walked back and forth across a pedestrian bridge that spanned the river, with the moon playing its silver scales on the lapping water beneath them, Günther told Rosemarie how Mozart's magical music had brought them together across the miles and years that had conspired, futilely, to keep them apart.

"Just think," he said, "I learn to play the flute because of Mozart, then we're brought together because I play the flute and that other fellow gets sick, and tonight, together, you and I, we perform that same opera. It's fate. No, it's our destiny, the tapestry of our destiny, as Rilke would say. And what a beautiful tapestry it is—and you are."

Rosemarie, moved, gazed at Günther for a moment and then seized him by the lapels of his overcoat and kissed him, with enough force to break his rimless glasses. A fragment of glass cut his cheek; at the sight of blood Rosemarie began to laugh and cry and apologize, but Günther happily clasped her in his arms, looked over her shoulder at the moon and smiled. The next night, when Günther walked into the Vereinshaus, he was wearing a small bandage and his prescription sunglasses. I would not be at all surprised to learn that his appearance inspired Wolfgang Brettschneider to write another snappy verse, but if it did, the poetry hasn't survived.

At the intermission of the opera that night, a message arrived with disturbing news from Leipzig. Felix Mendelssohn had been the most famous conductor of the Leipzig Gewandhaus Orchestra, and shortly after his death in 1847 the city had erected a statue in his honor. Now, in November of 1936, the musicians of the Kulturbund learned that the statue had been pulled down on orders from the authorities. In the midst of the merriment of Mozart's fairy-tale opera, Günther and Rosemarie were reminded of the ugly reality of their lives.

Coincidentally, the Kulturbund's next big production was Mendelssohn's oratorio *Elijah*, presented on December 17 by orchestra, chorus, and soloists. Then on January 6, 1937, Rosemarie's twentieth birthday, the Kulturbund greeted the New Year by performing Beethoven's Seventh Symphony, the Mendelssohn Violin Concerto, two new choral pieces by a Jewish composer from Frankfurt named Max Kowalski, and the waltz "Roses from the South" by Johann Strauss Jr., in a jaunty arrangement for chorus and orchestra by assistant conductor Richard Karp.

After the concert there was a party in honor of Max Kowalski, and Günther insisted that he and Rosemarie attend. This was a bit out of character for Günther, who usually preferred that the two of them go off by themselves. Rosemarie was pleased, and also a bit mystified, until she arrived and realized that Günther, with Kowalski's hearty cooperation, had planned a surprise birthday party to coincide with the celebration of the premieres. He led a toast in her honor with a glass of wine, and then presented her with a new scarf, which he produced with a flourish from his pocket. The orchestra members roared their approval, and Rosemarie blushed deeply.

Both Rosemarie and Günther had chosen to spend the Christmas and New Year's holidays with each other rather than traveling home. They wrote to their families about the press of orchestra business, claiming that they were just too busy to leave Frankfurt for even a few days. But they also let slip a bit of the real reason for their decision by telling their parents of their new acquaintances. Rosemarie wrote to Julian of Günther's skills as a flutist; Günther went further, telling his parents that his new violist friend was the most extraordinary musician he had ever met.

The rest of the 1936–1937 Kulturbund season continued as it had begun—with music, friendship, and laughter. Is it possible that my father looks back and sees only the fun and ignores the obvious dangers of being Jewish in Germany in the 1930s? Perhaps. But I must remind myself that he and Rosemarie were twenty-three and twenty years old, respectively, during those months, and living away from homes that had been restrictive, each in its own way. Even the Nazi dictatorship couldn't entirely legislate away the pleasures of youth. And the Kulturbund offered them an opportunity to learn new music and make new friends, as well as the enormous satisfaction of bringing to life all that beauty for an audience sorely in need of it. The joys of young love and the healing power of music must have made it easier for Günther and Rosemarie to live with the Nazi menace, at least during those years in Frankfurt.

The orchestra season ended in late March, when Julius Prüwer conducted a program of another Mendelssohn concert overture, "The Fair Melusine"; the Beethoven Violin Concerto, with Ernst Drucker taking the solo part; and the great Symphony No. 9 by Franz Schubert. In early April, the members of the orchestra lent their talents to a benefit concert for the Kulturbund. Professor Prüwer brought back a number of the ensemble's hits from the past season, including the Bloch Concerto Grosso, Tchaikovsky's Serenade for Strings, and dances and rhapsodies by Antonin Dvořák and Franz Liszt. At the end of the concert, the noted contralto Paula Salomon-Lindberg, who performed regularly with the Berlin Kulturbund, took the stage to perform a set of songs by Modest Mussorgsky.

The benefit was a huge success. The concert hall was sold out and each piece was met with a loud ovation. Rosemarie and Günther attended a big party at Ernst Drucker's home after the concert, a bash that finally ended at dawn. Walking home through the green and gold of a springtime morning, the two of them felt very happy and content with their lives.

Knowing they would be back together in Frankfurt in the fall made it easier to say goodbye and travel to their respective hometowns for the summer. But after about six weeks in the cramped gloom of the apartment on Ofenerstrasse, Günther concocted an urgent need to rehearse some chamber music with Rosemarie and caught the next train for Düsseldorf.

In November of 1936, Julian and Else had left their home in Hösel and moved into the city, to an apartment at 17 Boltensternstrasse, across the railroad tracks from the Gumpert Conservatory. For a week in May 1937, after his unexpected arrival, Günther lived with the Gumperts, accompanying Julian to school in the mornings and to concerts in the evenings. He nervously played his flute for the older man on several occasions, hoping to assure Herr Gumpert that his daughter had not taken up with an inferior musician. At the end of the week, just before Günther was to return to Oldenburg, Julian delighted both young people by presenting them with the manuscript for a one-movement fantasy for flute and viola he had composed expressly for them. Günther and Rosemarie now had a piece of music that was truly "their song."

The two young people met again in Frankfurt in the fall, eager to resume their careers. Over the summer, more than a dozen members of the orchestra had left Germany, as had a number of Kulturbund subscribers. In the face of a smaller ensemble and dwindling attendance, the organization's leadership, including Rabbi Salzburger and Professor Prüwer, decided to reduce the number of orchestral concerts in the upcoming season.

The summer had seen another significant development as well. Those two Beethoven symphonies, numbers Two and Seven, that Günther and Rosemarie had so enjoyed playing, would be the last ones they would perform in Germany. Word had come down from Hans Hinkel's office that all composers born in Germany would henceforth be declared off-limits for the Kulturbund. It had always gone without saying that Wagner and Strauss were forbidden; now Brahms and Beethoven, Bach and Schumann had been added to the list as well. To ensure compliance with this new edict, a pair of men from the Gestapo would attend every rehearsal and every concert. What level of musical expertise these gentlemen possessed, or whether they could tell a Beethoven symphony from a Tchaikovsky concerto, was an open question, but their mere presence was an effective deterrent; nobody felt brave, or foolish, enough to find out.

With the opening orchestral concert delayed until November 11, the first two months of the Kulturbund's 1937–1938 season consisted of chamber music evenings, song recitals, and lectures about music, art, and religion. Günther and Rosemarie often attended these evenings as interested spectators and supportive colleagues, but on the night of November 6, Günther was one of the featured musicians, joining violinist Margot Stern and pianist Martha Sommer in a program of duets and trios by Baroque composers. Rehearsing and performing that concert was musically stimulating for him, of course, and it was personally gratifying as well. From the very beginning of their relationship he had been convinced that, of the two of them, Rosemarie was the better musician. (Fortunately, this would remain only a minor issue between them, at least for the next few years.) But for this one night, at least, he was the one who had been asked to step forward and perform, and it did his confidence a world of good. After the concert, Rosemarie beamed her compliments and Günther felt more of an equal.

The next week both of them took their places on the stage of the Vereinshaus as members of the orchestra. Julius Prüwer conducted a program that consisted of the *Holberg Suite* by Edvard Grieg, an arrangement of the *Devil's Trill* sonata by Giuseppe Tartini, and the *Rustic Wedding* symphony by the Hungarian-born Jewish composer Karl Goldmark. The festive atmosphere of the packed hall and the jollity of Goldmark's portrait of pastoral joy were tempered by an incident at intermission. One of the Gestapo men who sat together in the first row of the balcony had invited two guests without informing anyone in the Kulturbund box office. The guests arrived just as the orchestra was returning to the stage to begin the symphony. Because room had to be made for them, an elderly couple was rudely and roughly evicted from their seats. As the glorious cacophony of the musicians tuning their instruments filled the Vereinshaus, Günther and Rosemarie witnessed the white-haired man and woman being shoved and kicked up the aisle to the exit. Try as it might, Günther thought, the Kulturbund could never wholly succeed in keeping ugly reality in its proper place out on the street.

Walking back to Im Trutz after the concert, Günther and Rosemarie talked about the brutality they had seen. Unsettling as the violence had been, Rosemarie remembered in particular how the two old people had each done their best to shield the other from the blows of the thugs. Their obvious devotion had lent a glimpse of beauty to the ugliness of the moment. It was, she said, an inspiration. Günther agreed. Before going into their separate houses for the night, the two young people pledged that they, too, would protect each other from whatever evil forces might try to do them harm.

The next morning they saw each other in a new light. Having declared their devotion, they felt a new closeness, and, with it, a desire to seal that intimacy with their first night together. And rather than choose just any night, they decided to wait another six weeks and usher in the New Year at an inn in their beloved Taunus hills.

As they were counting down the days to the end of the old year, they learned of the loss of an important member of the Kulturbund Orchestra, and for an entirely unexpected reason. Franz Calvelli-Adorno, a forty-year-old native of Frankfurt, was the principal of the ensemble's second violin section. In mid-December, Calvelli-Adorno was summoned to Gestapo headquarters and informed that the authorities, looking into his background, had discovered that two of his grandparents were of "Aryan" descent. His "racial" classification had thus been altered from Full Jew to Half Jew, and as such he was no longer qualified to retain his position in the Kulturbund. He was summarily dismissed.

Shocked, his friends and colleagues in the orchestra decided to present him with a gift to mark his departure. They bought Calvelli-Adorno a copy of *Das Atlantisbuch der Musik,* a collection of essays about music by such notable figures as Edwin Fischer, Wilhelm Furtwängler, and Georg Kulenkampff, with an introduction by Richard Strauss. As New Year's Eve approached, conductor Julius Prüwer and thirty-one members of the orchestra, including Günther and Rosemarie, signed their names to the book's first page in a fond expression of farewell. Today that list of autographs is a haunting reminder of an unbelievable and absurd occasion.

But on that last weekend of the year, Günther and Rosemarie were determined to leave the senseless world behind them. On Friday morning, December 31, they boarded a train in the Frankfurt Hauptbahnhof to begin their intimate journey. In the town of Taunusstein they caught a bus that took them to a carriage that clip-clopped its way to a tiny inn on a forested hillside. There was no electricity in the inn; the rooms were lighted by candles and warmed by fireplaces. Snow began to swirl as dusk fell, and by midnight the world was white in the darkness beyond the inn's walls. Embraced by the stillness of their little room, Günther and Rosemarie lay locked together beneath down blankets, lost in love and sleep.

They spent the first day of 1938, a year that would inflict so much pain on their families and on so many of their fellow German Jews, immersed in pleasure. When they awoke, it was nearly noon. Günther dressed and made his way downstairs, where he convinced the landlord, with a few winks and expressions of "you know how it is," to let him take a basket of rolls and fruitcake up to his "wife." After they'd eaten, they made love again and then slept until dark. Rosemarie shyly accompanied Günther downstairs for a New Year's repast of roast goose, new potatoes, sauerkraut, and a winsome Rhine wine. After a walk in the woods, the two young lovers returned to their downy bed. When they departed the inn on Sunday morning they felt more grown up, more secure—and more deeply happy—than at any time they could remember.

Their blissful mood remained largely intact through the coming of spring. The first week back in Frankfurt included the Kulturbund's next concert: music by Mendelssohn, Mozart, and Liszt conducted by Julius Prüwer. Another concert in early February featured familiar music by Rossini and Schubert sharing the bill with contemporary Jewish composers Jakob Schoenberg, Max Wolff, and Richard Fuchs. The Kulturbund mounted its last big production in March, offering two performances of Handel's oratorio *Belsazar*, with Nathan Ehrenreich conducting the orchestra, two choruses, and four soloists.

Those performances would have consequences. The oratorio tells the biblical story of Belshazzar, king of Babylon, who was punished by God for worshipping idols and persecuting his Jewish subjects. At its climax, the piece relates the chilling moment when the king sees the handwriting on the wall telling him that he has been "weighed in the balance and found wanting." In performing this compelling tale, the Kulturbund was making a powerful and heroic statement of defiance to all who would listen. One who apparently did listen was Reichskommissar Hans Hinkel, who acted swiftly to forbid future performances of Handel's music. Despite his German birth, Handel had not been on the list of banned composers issued in 1937. The Nazi authorities apparently took Handel's interest in such Old Testament themes as Belshazzar's feast and Judas Maccabeus as evidence that the composer must be Jewish. Consequently, the Rhein-Main Kulturbund had had no trouble securing permission for its performances of *Belsazar*. Soon after the concerts, however, word came down from Berlin that Handel was henceforth off-limits.

The last orchestral concert of the 1937–1938 season, and the concert that would prove to be the very last the orchestra of the Frankfurt Kulturbund would perform, took place on Wednesday evening, the seventh of April, five years to the day after the passage of the Civil Service Law that had been instrumental in the creation of the Kulturbund. The program included an overture by the German Jewish composer Giacomo Meyerbeer (whose real name was Jakob Liebmann Beer), the *Symphonie Espagnole* for violin and orchestra by Eduard Lalo, the Symphony No. 5 by Tchaikovsky, and four songs for baritone and orchestra by Max Kowalski, who had so generously shared the spotlight with Rosemarie on the occasion of his opening-night party and her twentieth birthday more than a year earlier.

Although no official announcement had yet been made, the Kulturbund's active rumor mill had churned out the news that the orchestra would be shut down, due to a lack of funds and the increase in musician emigration. So it was with an extra measure of pleasure, sadness, and nostalgia that Günther and Rosemarie savored this last evening in the company of their colleagues. The program held special significance for them both. Rosemarie had played the opening movement of the Lalo with her friend Hilde Klestadt at the Gumpert Conservatory in 1934, a year before she joined the Kulturbund. For Günther, any Tchaikovsky symphony immediately reminded him of the Sixth, the piece that had, in effect, introduced him to Rosemarie in March of 1936. And their affection for Max Kowalski made any performance of his music a special event.

When Julius Prüwer strode onto the stage to begin the concert, he helped fuel speculation that something was up by turning to the audience and making a little speech.

"My friends," he said, "I have seen much and heard much in my life in music. I have listened to the great Johannes Brahms play the piano and I have had the pleasure of conducting perhaps the finest orchestra in the world, the Berlin Philharmonic. But nothing in my life can compare with what I have experienced with these wonderful musicians and with you. Together, we as a community have approached the altar of music humbly and with the deepest veneration. And we have been rewarded with a blessing that I trust will last our whole lives. For that I thank God, I thank music, I thank this orchestra, and I thank you. Tonight, my heart is very full."

As one, the members of the audience rose to their feet and gave Professor Prüwer an ovation that lasted for three minutes. When the conductor asked the orchestra to stand, concertmaster Ernst Drucker refused to leave his seat, directing the applause solely to the podium. Rosemarie, tears in her eyes, tapped her music stand with her bow in the string musicians' universal sign of respect. And Günther clapped loudly along with the audience.

With that, the concert took off and never really came back to Earth. Something extra-musical was at work on stage, some mysterious force that every performer has encountered at one time or another. The weight of the here and now dropped away, leaving each musician light and free to soar to the highest reaches of imagination. From this height, the mind relinquished its hold over the human apparatus and left the heart and soul in command. The printed notes on the scores were no longer the merest black dots on white paper but cairns on the path of a wonderful journey of discovery shared by musicians and listeners alike. For Günther, the climax came in the finale of the Tchaikovsky Fifth, when the great striding melody seemed to lead the way to a victory that not even Caesar or Napoleon could have imagined, a triumphant expression of the human spirit that a million brown-shirted men bearing hooked-cross flags could never hope to extinguish.

The concert closed with Max Kowalski's four songs, all settings of poems by Heinrich Heine, the poet from Düsseldorf. As if he had known in advance that this would be the Frankfurt Kulturbund's final performance, Kowalski ended his cycle with a Heine verse called "It Goes Out":

The curtain falls, the play is through,
The gentlefolk go home on cue.
And did they like the play, I wonder?
I think I heard the bravos thunder.
A much-respected public clapped
Its thanks to the poet for the play.
But now the house is silence-wrapped,
Laughter and lights have dimmed away.

But hark, a sound rings dull and thin
From somewhere near the empty stage:
Perhaps a string has snapped within
A violin decayed with age.
A rat emerges from its hole,
The last lamp sputters low in doubt,
It groans despair, and it goes out.
That last poor light was my own soul.

Kowalski's orchestration complemented Heine's imagery. As the baritone, Wilhelm Guttmann, sang the last line, the instruments of the orchestra stopped playing one by one, each an extinguished light. Finally, only five instruments remained: double bass, cello, viola, violin, and Günther's flute. The strings dropped out in turn until only Günther, sustaining a high C, was left. Kowalski's score instructed him to play until his breath gave out, and my father, his eyes closed, blew gently as if coaxing a flickering ember to blossom into flame. At last his lungs were empty and what bloomed was silence, a deep and profound quiet that echoed throughout the hall. No one moved.

After a few moments, Max Kowalski walked out on stage. He was fifty-five years old, slim, with a bald head, bushy gray beard, and bright blue eyes behind rimless spectacles. As he approached Prüwer's podium, several people in the audience began to clap, but Kowalski, smiling, held up his hands.

"No," he said, "no thundering bravos, please."

Muted laughter sounded from scattered seats. Kowalski swept his eyes over the hall and continued.

"I think if Herr Heine were with us now, he would write a different poem. I sense many a soul shining brightly in this place tonight, none brighter or warmer than the soul of this magnificent organization, this Kulturbund, which has sustained us all these last four years. But now, no applause, and certainly no tears. Let us go in peace."

Kowalski took the hand of Julius Prüwer and the two of them, followed closely by concertmaster Ernst Drucker and the rest of the orchestra, filed silently off stage. Behind them, the members of the audience gathered hats, coats, and scarves and walked slowly out into the early spring chill. No one uttered a word.

Backstage, first Rosemarie, then Günther, embraced Max Kowalski.

"Thank you for your music tonight," said Rosemarie. "And thank you for your friendship these last months."

"Thank *you*," replied Kowalski. "And thanks, Günther, for your lovely playing tonight. Wasn't this a very special evening?"

"It was. It really was," Günther said. "Tell me, Max, is it true what some of us have heard? Is the orchestra folding?"

Kowalski closed his eyes for a moment.

"I think so. You'll hear more in a few days. But what a magnificent concert this was, if it should prove to be the finale."

He pumped Günther's hand, kissed Rosemarie, reached into his pocket for a handkerchief, blew his nose vigorously, and then walked off. It was the last time they saw him.

The following Wednesday an identical letter arrived at both their houses, informing them that the Rhein-Main Kulturbund Orchestra would not reconvene for the autumn season. However, they were both asked to join the orchestra of the Berlin Kulturbund, an exciting opportunity that did much to take the sting out of the letter's announcement. They were expected in the German capital in early September to begin rehearsals for the first opera of the new season, Giuseppe Verdi's *Rigoletto*.

Günther and Rosemarie stayed in Frankfurt through June, playing chamber music with friends, walking in the park, taking occasional trips into the countryside—in short, continuing their happy and innocent *vie bohème*. They both spent the month of July and most of August with their families, but joyfully reunited for an excursion on the Rhine on August 28. Günther came to Düsseldorf, and there they boarded a boat that wound up the river toward Frankfurt, slowly passing the craggy hills and ancient ruined castles and active vineyards with their heavy harvest of grapes, a timeless scene that renders the Rhine one of the most romantic waterways in the world.

A few miles above Frankfurt, just before the Rhine splits off from the River Main, their craft floated by an enormous jagged stone that loomed overhead and cast an immense shadow upon the rolling waters. It was the legendary resting place of the Lorelei, a beautiful maiden who lured unsuspecting sailors to their deaths while combing her long blond hair. She had been immortalized in another memorable poem by Heinrich Heine.

As they passed into the shadow of the Lorelei rock, Günther and Rosemarie leaned against the rail and gazed upwards. Günther slipped his arm around her waist and murmured the opening lines of Heine's verse into her ear: "*Ich weiss nicht was soll es bedeuten, dass ich so traurig bin*" ("I do not know what it means that I should be so sad").

"Are you sad, Günther?" asked Rosemarie, pulling away so that she could look into his eyes.

"No, Wusche. I'm just the opposite. Today I'm so happy that I cannot begin to understand what Brother Heinrich is talking about."

The young lovers laughed as their boat swept out from under the shadow of the rock and continued their gently rocking journey.

They spent three days in Frankfurt saying goodbye to friends, packing up their few belongings, and cleaning out their rooms. On September 5 they boarded a train for Berlin. After several days' search, they found a place to live, two rooms in the house of a lawyer named Otto Hoffmann, who lived on Alte Jakobstrasse not too far from the Brandenburg Gate and a five-minute walk from the Kulturbund's theater on Kommandantenstrasse.

The first rehearsal with their new colleagues was scheduled for Thursday, September 15. They walked into the imposing courtyard of 57 Kommandantenstrasse, through the theater's foyer with its twin curving staircases leading up to the balcony, and into the theater itself. It was much grander than the Vereinshaus in Frankfurt, and both Rosemarie and Günther felt as if they had arrived at the top of their profession.

That afternoon they met the dynamic leader of the Kulturbund, Dr. Kurt Singer, who would direct the production of *Rigoletto;* the music director, Rudolf Schwarz; and the scenic and costume designer, Heinz Condell. After a few opening remarks from Dr. Singer, Schwarz and the orchestra set to work on Verdi's dark and dramatic telling of Victor Hugo's tragic tale of jealousy, passion, and betrayal.

A few days before the premiere the singers joined the orchestra, and Günther and Rosemarie were pleased to discover that the title role was to be sung by baritone Wilhelm Guttmann, who had performed the Heine songs by Max Kowalski at the final Frankfurt concert back in April. After the first dress rehearsal, they sought out the singer backstage. Expecting a hearty welcome, Günther and Rosemarie were surprised to encounter a grim-faced Guttmann, who almost snapped at them when they knocked at the door to his dressing room.

"You kids still here? I heard you'd got out already. Well, what're you doing in this lunatic asylum?"

"We're both in the orchestra," explained Günther. "Is anything the matter?"

Guttmann sighed heavily. "I don't know. I'm just not myself these days. It's harder and harder for me to leave my work here in the theater when I go home at night. Maybe it's this damn curse."

In the opening act of Verdi's opera, the jester Rigoletto torments an aged courtier, Monterone, whose daughter has been seduced by Rigoletto's employer, the duke of Mantua. As he is being hauled off to prison, Monterone curses Rigoletto with a father's curse. As the drama plays itself out, the duke seduces Rigoletto's daughter, Gilda, and the jester conspires to have the duke killed by the assassin Sparafucile, only to discover, to his horror, that Gilda, in love with the duke, has sacrificed herself to save his life. At the very end of the opera Gilda dies in her father's arms and all Rigoletto can do is howl to the heavens, *"Ah, la maledizione!"* ("Ah, it is the curse!")

"For some reason," continued Guttmann, "I've been more affected by this old man"—and here he shook his jester's bells—"than anything I've done in the past five years. I can't seem to shake the feeling that something terrible is about to happen."

On Saturday night, October 1, the Kulturbund premiered its production of *Rigoletto,* and it was clear to Günther and Rosemarie that Wilhelm Guttmann's ill feelings of impending doom had foretold nothing about the performance. Audience, artists, and the critic from the Jewish newspaper who came to review the production all agreed that they had just witnessed one of the high points in the history of the Kulturbund. Even Guttmann himself, after savoring seven solo curtain calls, managed a smile when Günther sought him out to congratulate him.

"Yes, everything seemed to come together tonight. I still have a funny feeling, though. Well, who cares about a curse, anyway? Let's all go out and get drunk!"

The next afternoon Günther and Rosemarie took the subway across town to the zoo. They bought two cheese sandwiches and a bottle of buttermilk from a vendor and strolled down the curving paths in search of their favorite animals. When they reached the polar bears, they sat on a bench facing the rocks and water and enormous off-white beasts, ate their sandwiches and drank their milk, then threw their crumbs to some waiting ducks. The sun peered down through the branches of the now golden trees. Rosemarie stretched out on the bench with her head in Günther's lap.

"Are you glad we've come here?" she murmured, nearly asleep. "Was it a good idea?"

"Yes, Wusche, it was a good idea," Günther whispered back. "It's a bigger theater, a bigger orchestra. And besides, we're together." He bent down and kissed her. "Where we belong." Rosemarie smiled, her eyes closed.

But Günther, his mind still haunted by the power of the previous night's performance, gazed over the tops of the trees towards the buildings of downtown Berlin. A red, white, and black flag flapping in the soft autumn breeze caught his eye, and he remembered Verdi's cruel final chords to the dagger-sharp words, *"Ah, la maledizione!"*

9

Kurt Singer

THE ENSEMBLE Günther and Rosemarie had just joined, the Jüdische Kulturbund of Berlin, was the nerve center of the Reichsverband, the umbrella organization of all the Jewish culture associations that had been allowed to emerge in Hitler's Germany. During the years Günther and Rosemarie had lived their relatively happy bohemian lives in Frankfurt, the Berlin Kubu had undergone several significant transformations as it scaled the heights of artistic achievement and then slowly and painfully began its descent.

Back in October of 1935, a month after the appearance of the noxious Nuremberg Laws, the Kulturbund had staged a celebration. The occasion was the fiftieth birthday of the Kubu's founder and leader, Kurt Singer, who had been born on October 11, 1885, in West Prussia, the son of Rabbi Moritz Singer. Though trained as a neurologist and psychiatrist, Kurt Singer also had a background as a violinist and conductor. He had founded the Berlin Doctors' Choir in the 1920s before assuming the position of assistant director of the Berlin City Opera. Dr. Singer also wrote extensively about music, and, ironically, two of his special areas of study concerned composers held dear by the Third Reich. In 1913 he published a paper about Richard Wagner and ten years later a book about the choral music of Anton Bruckner. Within a week of the Bruckner book's publication, noted conductor Wilhelm Furtwängler penned Dr. Singer a note congratulating him on it.

Kurt Singer's fiftieth birthday occasioned many tributes saluting the man who had brought forth the Jüdische Kulturbund and continued to captain the organization through the always choppy waters of sanctions and official decrees. The Jewish press published full-page advertisements.

On October 11, Werner Levie, the Kubu's administrative director, presented Singer with an immense birthday card embossed in gold and featuring twin laurel wreaths. The members of the Kulturbund pooled their resources and bought him a complete coffee service with the initials *KS* engraved on each plate, cup, and saucer. That night, the Kubu's theater director, Julius Bab, delivered a speech in which he praised Dr. Singer's courage, first evoking the poet Goethe's description of courage as that quality without which a human being "would be better off never having been born."

"This is not the courage of tensed muscles and a clouded brain," Bab went on. "It is the courage that stems from the deepest realms of human consciousness. Only he who appreciates every day deeply, both the joys and worries that each day offers, and is able to remove himself from them, who truly gives himself fully to the most elevated aspects of life, only he can possess the courage to live a life which transcends the personal. You will continue to experience trials and hard work but you will also have the great comfort of living a life in the service of God. Not despite the despair of the times but precisely because of the neediness of these times, we want and need to cultivate all the beautiful arts and we want to sustain our spirits by staying in touch with the noblest and most sustaining of life's offerings. Dear Dr. Singer, we thank you."

And then, as a climax to the observances, Kurt Singer himself conducted three vocal soloists, his own Doctors' Choir, and the Berlin Kulturbund Orchestra in a gala concert that included a Bach cantata, the "Song of Destiny" by Johannes Brahms, and a music drama by Felix Mendelssohn called *Die erste Walpurgisnacht.* There was standing room only, and prolonged ovations greeted the massed ensembles at the concert's close. The applause not only acknowledged a well-performed evening of great music but also expressed the audience's gratitude to Singer for providing more than two years' worth of entertainment and escapism in highly trying times. None of it would have been possible without the courageous efforts of this singular, charismatic personality.

Over the next three years, Kurt Singer would continue to oversee the Kulturbund and maintain an all-consuming, exhausting schedule: planning programs, directing opera productions, conducting orchestral and choral concerts, attending rehearsals, developing budgets, writing

Kurt Singer in charge.

and delivering fund-raising appeals, exhorting his colleagues toward ever higher standards and more ambitious projects, and all the while smoothing things over with Hans Hinkel and the Ministry of Propaganda. Kurt Singer saw the Kulturbund as his life's work, and he threw himself into it with a seemingly bottomless supply of energy and devotion.

As is true of many an intense, energetic artist, Kurt Singer often struck those around him as arrogant, abrasive, and absolute. He would stride through the offices of the Kulturbund speaking only to those he deemed worth his time and ignoring others. Dancer and choreographer Hannah Kroner admits today that she and her fellow dancers were afraid of him and stayed out of his way as much as possible. But she and other Kubu artists also acknowledged his deep and broad intelligence and realized that his strict, exacting standards were largely in the service of his work and were only occasionally unleashed to support and soothe his well-developed ego.

Singer's efforts, as well as those of the many artists, stagehands, and administrators who made up the Jüdische Kulturbund, were rewarded with an ever-increasing subscription base. At its peak in 1936, there were seventy thousand members attending performances in forty-nine different cities across Germany, with twenty thousand members in Berlin alone. Jewish merchants supported the effort by filling the Kulturbund's programs with advertisements, to the extent that one observer noted that the Kubu was helping to counteract the Nazi boycott slogan, "Never buy from Jews."

The Kulturbund employed nearly two thousand artists, none of whom could have worked anywhere else in Germany. And the range of performances put on by those artists was extraordinary. Here's just a partial list of activities that took place in Berlin alone. In the same month he celebrated his fiftieth birthday, Singer directed a production of Rossini's *Barber of Seville*, and he followed that up with directing *Samson and Delilah* by Camille Saint-Saens and *Vienna Blood* by Johann Strauss in the first six months of 1936. Other Singer-directed operas in the next two years included *A Masked Ball* by Giuseppe Verdi, *The Merry Wives of Windsor* by Otto Nicolai, and Tchaikovsky's *Eugene Onegin*. Some dramatic highlights of that period were George Bernard Shaw's *You Never Can Tell*, Sophocles' *Antigone*, *Ghosts* by Henrik Ibsen, and Shakespeare's *Much Ado About Nothing* and *A Midsummer Night's Dream*, featuring the complete incidental music by Felix Mendelssohn conducted by Kurt Singer. And the orchestra of the Berlin Kulturbund, under the direction of Joseph Rosenstock, Rudolf Schwarz, and Hans Wilhelm Steinberg, performed music from Bach and Pergolesi to Mahler and Bloch.

Every repertory item, of course, had to be approved by Hans Hinkel. Occasional difficult negotiations with the Reich Commissioner ate up valuable hours of Dr. Singer's time and consumed untold quantities of his energy. Questions of musical censorship were fairly straightforward, as slowly but surely more composers were added to the banned list. But the Hinkel office also insisted that the word "blond" be stricken from a play by Ferenc Molnar on the grounds that such an important Aryan trait would be sullied in a Jewish context. And while permission was granted to stage Shakespeare's *Hamlet*, its most famous soliloquy was suppressed. The Nazi censors apparently believed that in the middle of the "To be or not to be" speech, the lines "For who would bear the whips and scorns of time, the oppressor's wrong, . . . the law's delay, the insolence of office" might incite the audience to violence. To err on the side of caution, Hinkel simply expunged the entire speech.

And then there were other matters that arose, such as the case of the Nine Allisons. This troupe of German acrobats had achieved an international reputation by the fall of 1935. But the passage of the Nuremberg Laws brought to light the fact that the Allisons were made up of eight "Aryans" and one Jew, a man by the name of Arthur Cohn. The authorities ruled that Cohn could no longer perform with the Allisons, despite the group's testimony that every member of the troupe was necessary if their complex routines—the stunts that had made them famous in the first place—were to remain part of their repertoire. Arthur Cohn finally wrote to Kurt Singer, asking him to intervene with the Ministry of Propaganda. Singer wrote to Hinkel, pointing out that Cohn had been with the Allisons for twenty years, that his father and brother had both fought in the World War, that his brother had been awarded the Iron Cross, Second Class, and that here was an extraordinary case that would most likely not come up again. Hinkel never answered the letter, however, and the Nine Allisons passed into acrobatic history.

A more serious debate with Hinkel, one that directly affected the very nature of the Kulturbund, involved the organization's offerings. The Kubu's artists wanted to perform the best works of the standard repertory, and these were the works that their audiences wanted to see and hear. After all, most of the artists who joined the Kulturbund in the aftermath of the purges of early 1933 had been employed by the major German theaters, orchestras, and opera companies, and the audience members who bought subscriptions to the Kulturbund had been subscribers of those same mainstream organizations prior to 1933.

And yet, as the months went by and the authorities' attitudes evolved, the Nazis decided that only "authentic Jewish art" was appropriate for the Kulturbund to perform. One of the leading National Socialist idealogues, Alfred Rosenberg, attended a Kulturbund play as a guest of Hans Hinkel and afterwards complained, "These are performances by Jews for Jews but they perform nothing Jewish." Rosenberg wanted a cleaner, more definitive break between the "German" and the "Jewish"—in other words, artistic segregation to mirror Germany's increased social segregation. After all, reasoned Rosenberg, wasn't that the whole point of the purges of 1933, to limit the baleful effects of Jewish control over German art?

In his public statements, Hinkel began to emphasize the separation of Jews and non-Jews in German cultural life. "Jewish artists are working for Jews," he pointed out in a speech he gave in 1936. "They may work unhindered so long as they restrict themselves to the cultivation of Jewish artistic and cultural life, and so long as they do not attempt, openly, secretly, or deceitfully, to influence our culture." The paranoid fear that a Jew might try to foil German cultural security and pass as an Aryan, thereby undermining all Nazi efforts at purity, was the subject of another Hinkel address:

> We know that time and again Jews work in disguise; we know that some deception is still unsolved. We view changing this situation, wherever it still exists, as our most important task. We will hold the guilty accountable, not just the Jews, but all those who want to smuggle their way through the back door. This will come to an end. What we want is pure separation. Just as anonymity is undesirable, so too is Goynymity.

Shortly thereafter, Hinkel gave an interview to a newspaper in Frankfurt and declared, "If among the offerings of the Jewish community there are works by Beethoven, Goethe, and Mozart, then that is not the point of the exercise. It is much more about giving Jews the opportunity to develop within their own spiritual and creative borders. If this development is less than satisfactory for them, then they can better understand why we don't want them to be masters of our cultural life."

This line of reasoning, of course, was nothing more than further manipulation by the forces in power of their utterly weak but hopeful subjects. Kurt Singer and his fellow artists naively continued to think that the "point of the exercise" of staging plays and operas and concerts was the spiritual uplift of their community. For the Nazis, however, the "point" was, first, to maintain their campaign to drive the Jews as far away as possible from "German" society and, second, to score the occasional advantage in their great "racial" debate. It wasn't enough that the artists of the Kulturbund were forced to practice their craft off by themselves, for limited audiences, away from the bright lights and publicity of Berlin's theater district or Philharmonie. The thought that Jewish artists might perform music composed by Beethoven or Brahms or that a Jewish mouth might speak the words of Goethe seemed the very definition of artistic defilement in the minds of the Nazi keepers of culture.

If there was to be a "Jewish cultural organization," went this reasoning, let such an organization stage strictly "Jewish art"—by which Rosenberg, Goebbels, and Hinkel meant music performed on harps and shofars and plays that concerned themselves with petty daily life in the shtetls of Russia or Poland. By making this argument, the Nazis actually found themselves in ironic agreement with the Zionist critics of the Kulturbund, who also found the doings on Kommandantenstrasse a bit too comfortably middle-class for their tastes. "The fact is," wrote one critic, "that the Kulturbünde in the Reich are much more reflective of the old German theaters than of specifically Jewish ones. They perform the classics: Shakespeare, Lessing, Goethe, the Greeks, plus Shaw, Ibsen, Wilde, etc. Furthermore, the manner of performance is completely identical with the old theaters. Is a repetition of this sort a good reason for a Jewish stage? The question must be objectively answered with a simple 'No!'"

Kurt Singer may or may not have agreed with the Zionists, but he had no choice but to agree with the Nazis. So, ever the pragmatist and also, at least publically, embracing his heritage as the son of a rabbi, Dr. Singer decided to turn this newest necessity into a virtue. He announced that the 1936 season of theatrical offerings would open on September I with a play by Yitzhak Leib Perez called *The Golden Necklace.* He also agreed to a three-day conference, attended by Hinkel and members of the Gestapo, to discuss the future programming of the Kulturbund. The meeting began the same week *The Golden Necklace* opened.

This was the season of Hitler's greatest propaganda coup, the staging of the summer Olympic Games in Berlin. During the summer and early fall, in deference to the sensibilities of the foreign journalists who would be visiting German soil, the Nazis relaxed a number of anti-Jewish ordinances, removed some of the more overt anti-Semitic signs and billboards that had dotted the countryside, and did all they could to showcase a happy, well-functioning society.

Among the changes to official policy trotted out for the Games was a relaxation of strictures forbidding the mainstream German press to attend Kulturbund performances. A critic for the *Berliner Tagesblatt*, described by a Kulturbund historian as "the newspaper for educated Nazis," attended the opening-night performance of *The Golden Necklace* and described it with all the condescending wonder of an American plantation owner marveling at the "natural rhythm" of his darkies:

> The title of the piece, as well as its entire contents, have a symbolic character. In the course of the evening we see the victory of traditional Eastern customs, borne of blood relations and a Jewish religion of the soul not to be understood by our Western rationalism. How incredibly strange this world must seem to our foreign visitors; most of them will probably not be able to enter it.

The critic concluded, however, by voicing approval for this sort of repertoire for a Jewish theater operated by and for Jews. "The Kulturbund is going in the right direction," he concluded, "and is showing with this production that this is the way, the only way."

In this atmosphere, the three-day Kulturbund conference opened on September 5. As Hinkel and Gestapo representatives looked on approvingly, Kurt Singer pledged to establish an office in the Kommandantenstrasse complex that would house an expert in Hebrew and one in Yiddish, that he would see to it that his artists would be educated in "Jewishness," and that his audiences would be prepared for a more Jewish repertoire by way of lectures and brochures. Dr. Singer concluded,

> All of us who are Jews in Germany have pledged, with firm handshakes, to seek the same ideals with the same Jewish cultural composure. We recognize the character of these times.

And we will embrace them, not be overtaken or surprised by them. We shall reclaim a new spiritual land for ourselves. But we will not just view this new Jewish culture in Germany from afar. No, we shall seek it out and greet it, with a Jewish melody in our hearts, steadfast in character, driven by love, and always supported by the honesty of our deeds.

He then announced that the 1936–1937 theater season would offer—in addition to pieces by Shakespeare, Ibsen, and Hugo von Hoffmannsthal—*Amcha* by Shalom Aleichem and *Schabbathai Z'wi* by Nathan Bistritzky; and that the upcoming music season would open with a new setting of the Friday evening Sabbath service by an American composer named Jacob Weinberg.

After the conference, Dr. Singer called his colleagues together and told them that this latest turn in their relations with the Nazis, while seemingly yet another restriction on their freedom of expression, was in reality a marvelous opportunity to look inward and backward, a chance to learn about and cultivate a great tradition while continuing to inspire their audiences. "Who knows," he enthused, "one day we just might succeed in putting on the same play twice, first in German and afterwards in Hebrew, and reach out to the source of all literary tradition: language itself. A road of a hundred years lies before us; it ends where all Jewish culture must begin: in Eretz Israel."

Others weren't quite so enthusiastic. It bears repeating that the majority of German Jews, particularly those in metropolitan centers, had long since assimilated into German society and considered themselves Germans first and Jews second. Many of them had very little sense of either religious or cultural identity. Most of the Kulturbund actors knew little or no Hebrew or Yiddish, and the thought of appearing on stage and having to speak those languages was as daunting—and unappealing—as mounting a play in French or Russian. (To date, all productions had been presented in German translations.) And musicians who had trained all their lives in the musical language of Mozart and Beethoven weren't eager to, as one of them whispered, "restrict ourselves to lutes and timbrels and all those other Old Testament instruments."

Even Rabbi Joachim Prinz, who had taken part in the conference, had his doubts about the wisdom of this new enterprise. He pointed out that in the past three years, more than ninety thousand German Jews had fled the country; those who were left, he said, were probably less eager to begin exploring their cultural roots than they were to learn the intricacies of visas and passports. "These days," Rabbi Prinz declared, "the most important music we can hear is the whistle of locomotives and the bellow of ships."

But Kurt Singer persisted in his conviction that the arts were vital not only to the spiritual well-being of the Jews but also to a peaceful coexistence with the Nazis. He so deeply believed in the civilizing power of culture that he felt certain that, eventually, his tormentors would recognize the inherent worth of the Jews and allow them to live in peace. Each new decree, he felt certain, would be the last, and stability would doubtless follow. The fact that Hans Hinkel seemed so interested in the details of the Kulturbund was one more piece of evidence that the Nazis were paying attention to his efforts. It was an illusion, of course, but one in which Dr. Singer very much wanted—and needed—to believe. And even if there was to be no reconciliation between Nazi and Jew, the opportunities were still immense—to create a new German-Jewish culture that would outlast the Thousand-Year Reich.

So the Jüdische Kulturbund set off on its journey to become more Jewish. But the results were disappointing, at least at the box office. During the 1936–1937 season, the most popular of the Kubu's offerings was its production of Shakespeare's *A Midsummer Night's Dream* with the Mendelssohn incidental music. Next came the Nicolai opera based on Shakespeare, *The Merry Wives of Windsor,* and Verdi's opera *A Masked Ball.* Sidney Kingsley's hospital drama *Men in White* was next in order of popularity, and only then came the first of the strictly Jewish offerings, the Nathan Bistritzky play *Schabbathai Z'wi.* At that production, and at the other offerings in which Jewish themes were sounded clearly, the audience listened politely but didn't seem engaged and didn't respond particularly enthusiastically when it came time to applaud.

Nevertheless, spurred on by the Nazi *Diktat* and his own convictions, Kurt Singer continued his campaign in the 1937–1938 season, mounting productions of *The Golem* by Halper Leiwik and *The Judgment* by Schulamit Bat Dori, in addition to plays by Shakespeare, Ibsen, Ferenc Molnar, and Eugene Scribe. During the High Holidays in October, a new liturgical piece by Oskar Guttmann premiered at the Oranienburgstrasse synagogue, and in February came a new setting of the Friday evening service by Leo Kopf at the temple on Prinzregentstrasse. Try as he might, however, Dr. Singer could find no examples of strictly Jewish opera, so the schedule featured works by Tchaikovsky, Verdi, Offenbach, Franz von Suppé, and Adolphe Adam.

Again the attendance figures were mixed, at best. If Kulturbund subscribers didn't actually avoid the more overtly Jewish offerings, neither did they embrace them, either emotionally or in greater numbers. And, in fact, overall attendance at Kubu events began to slump as membership declined. Where there had been twenty thousand members of the Berlin Kulturbund in 1936, there were seventeen thousand five hundred in 1937 and thirteen thousand five hundred in mid-1938. Nationally, the rate of decline was even sharper, from seventy thousand in 1936 to fifty-eight thousand in 1937 and just over twenty-eight thousand in 1938. In smaller cities, when attendance figures fell below a certain threshold, the local Kulturbund was likely to close outright. Thus the national numbers reflect both declining attendance in large urban centers and the gradual shutting down of the smaller Kulturbünde.

Several factors contributed to those figures, most notably emigration, impoverishment, incarceration, and death. Emigration played a major role, as the people who had the wherewithal, the resources, and the contacts to move abroad were invariably the very ones who had expressed the greatest interest in music and theater. As employment and other opportunites for Jews declined, many former Kubu subscribers found it impossible to afford even the meager monthly subscription fee of 2.85 marks. And every week there were more horror stories of Jews who simply disappeared, either to forced labor camps or, in the worst of circumstances, without a trace.

Just as many of the Jews of Germany felt that emigration was a last resort, so too did the artists of the Kulturbund. They had been born in Germany, had studied in Germany, spoke, thought, and felt German. But as the years went by, the lure of freedom became more attractive to actors, dancers, and musicians, as it did to bakers, bankers, and carpenters. At the beginning of 1937, the various Kulturbünde employed 1,425 artists, including 197 opera singers and chorus members, 192 actors, 174 instrumentalists, 61 dancers, 54 speakers, 49 cabaret artists, 21 graphic designers, and 396 stagehands. Slowly, however, that population began to follow its audience across the German border. And that was very bad news for Kurt Singer.

His devotion to the cause of the Kulturbund was so great that he couldn't bring himself to realize that emigration often meant survival for an artist and his family. When an artist left the country, Kurt Singer saw the action as a betrayal of the noble ideals of the organization. He felt betrayed personally as well, especially since having fewer artists available made staging a particular play or performing an elaborate opera or symphony considerably more difficult. Observers within the Kulturbund, even close friends of Dr. Singer, noticed his already somewhat arrogant and demanding personality become more pronounced.

At first he tried persuasion. When one of his actors approached him with the news that he was considering leaving for the United States, Dr. Singer asked him, "Why would you possibly want to go there? We're building the great Jewish State Theater right here." When the actor left anyway, Dr. Singer had his name stricken from the roster of that year's artists. To avoid an unpleasant scene, another actor who was planning to emigrate told Dr. Singer he was going on vacation.

Soon, however, Kurt Singer went a step beyond discouraging artists from leaving; he began using his influence to stem the flow of emigration. Kurt Sommerfeld, the first musician to be employed by the Kulturbund back in 1933, had left the ensemble in 1936 to join the Palestine Orchestra. Quite a few former members of the Kubu, including Hans Wilhelm Steinberg, the conductor of the orchestra in Frankfurt, had done the same. In September 1937, Singer wrote Sommerfeld a letter in which he pleaded for his help in keeping the door to Palestine closed.

> It is so important at this time to try to maintain stability in our orchestra. For this reason I have urgently begged your conductor, my good friend Steinberg, to no longer place ads for

musicians from here. There is no new generation of musicians for us here in Germany and I don't want to make the work of our very talented and conscientious conductor Rudolf Schwarz unneccesarily more difficult. You can see from the enclosed program that we have great things ahead.

With the whole weight of the Kulturbund on his shoulders, and now with the added burden of trying to keep his company together, Singer's temper began to fray. Always strict at rehearsals, his patience now wore thinner faster. Hannah Kroner, a dancer in the production of Tchaikovsky's opera *Eugen Onegin* that Dr. Singer directed in November of 1937, remembers an afternoon rehearsal in which the glittering polonaise in Act Three was not going well. At one point Dr. Singer stopped and shouted, "My chorus can dance better than that! If you can't execute a simple polonaise step, perhaps we should stage this opera without any dancers at all!" Kroner recalls fearing Singer, whom she always called *Herr Doktor.* "He was God," she says ruefully, "and if you wanted to stay in the theater you had to smile and do what he wanted."

But artists who had the means and didn't share Dr. Singer's messianic vision for the Kulturbund continued to flee the country for freedom abroad. Kurt Katsch, the actor who had starred in the title role of *Nathan the Wise,* the Kubu's very first offering in October 1933, made his way to Hollywood, where, ironically, he made a good living portraying Nazis in a succession of war movies. Joseph Rosenstock, who had conducted the organization's first opera production, Mozart's *Marriage of Figaro,* emigrated to Japan and, eventually, to the United States. The actress Ruth Anselm, knowing of Dr. Singer's feelings, asked him into her dressing room one night to explain to him her reasons for emigrating. He abruptly got up and left without a word. The next day he sent her a letter in which he told her she was being fired. "For someone who possesses this sense of duty, there is no room in the Kulturbund!"

Kurt Singer's anger and frustration briefly fermented into bitterness in a letter he wrote to a friend late in 1937. There were some people in the Jewish community of Berlin, he charged, who were more interested in being seen at the "right" theaters than in supporting the worthy work of the Kulturbund. "It is well known," he wrote darkly, "that a large number of Berlin's Jews keep their distance from us; these are people who consider it more important to find their way to the other theaters of Berlin, people who don't want to be 'ghettoized.'"

In another stroke of irony, the same sentiment was being uttered at almost the same time by the Kulturbund's Nazi overseer, Hans Hinkel. He, too, was troubled by declining attendance figures and what they might portend. His concerns were personal, however, driven by a fear that his pet project would fail and thwart his ambitions. Writing to a colleague, he described his disbelief that the Jews of Berlin weren't supporting each other more.

Don't these people understand? Their own Jewish artists would also profit, they would earn more and would have more opportunities to work if all Jews went to the Jewish performances. Of the more than 150,000 Jews in Berlin only about 14,000 are in the Kulturbund. That's a sign of too little Jewish racial consciousness. They possess not one iota of self-respect.

Meanwhile, racial consciousness or no, the artists of the Kulturbund continued to provide their audiences with up to two hundred performances, house concerts, and lectures per month. And despite his frustration, Kurt Singer never lost his public enthusiasm or wavered from fulfilling his role as the Kulturbund's chief cheerleader and advocate. At the end of the 1937–1938 season, Dr. Singer took note of the philosophical evolution of the organization while singing its praises and urging it forward to greater heights of achievement, always in his customary purple prose.

Today, in the year 1938, it is possible to see what ripe fruit has grown from the seeds we planted in 1933. We have, I believe in all modesty, waved the flag of Jewish art without relinquishing our traditional ties to international thoughts and experiences. With faith and the utmost trust in the Jews of Germany to support the artists among us, we have done all we could to illuminate the human spirit, and we have brought every skill we possess to this endeavor: every gesture, every breath, every musical sound, every stage setting, every feeling of pain and joy, every laugh, every tear. We have remained Jews in our play and in the passionate work of our own culture. This is who we are. We will go down in history, for all the deficiencies of our times, as having been proud, lucky, sentimental, hopeful, nostalgic and successful all in one. And let it so remain.

We have developed a platform for Jews regardless of class and world view. Next to the temple of religion we have built the temple of the stage, the temple of music. As Jews we are serving truth, beauty, art, faith, community, religion, and God. And that is our good fortune. We have within our little realm understood our times without letting ourselves be overwhelmed by them. And thus we enter, strident and happy, ambitious and modest, content and yet unsatisfied with all of our achievements, the sixth year of our existence.

10

A Protest in Paris

THE "DEFICIENCIES" of the times grew ever greater. Mocking Kurt Singer's faith in art, Adolf Hitler continued to transform Germany from one of the bastions of civilization into a land of thuggery and ignorance as he manipulated the world's leaders into accepting his vision of the map of Europe.

On March 15, 1938, Chancellor Hitler strode triumphantly through the streets of Vienna, the imperial city where he'd lived as a penniless bum nearly thirty years earlier. It was the *Anschluss*, the annexation of Austria under the threat of invasion by the German Army. Late in the day Hitler spoke from a balcony to an enormous, wildly cheering crowd that had gathered in the Heldenplatz, the Square of Heroes. "As Führer of the German nation," he thundered, "I can now report to history that my homeland has joined the German Reich!"

Over the next few weeks, an orgy of anti-Semitism spilled through the streets of Vienna. The new Nazi leaders and their henchmen forced Jewish men and women, frequently doctors or university professors, down on their hands and knees to scrub sidewalks and gutters while passersby added their taunts and jeers. And thousands of Viennese Jews, from humble tailors to Baron Louis de Rothschild himself, were commanded to surrender personal possessions as "protection money" or risk a visit from Nazi goon squads.

A musical consequence of the Anschluss was a further loss of repertory for Dr. Singer. Now that Austria was part of the Reich, Austrian-born composers were as off-limits to Kulturbund musicians as were those who had been born in Germany. A directive issued from Hans Hinkel's office in June informed the Kubu that it was now illegal for them to perform any music by Franz Schubert, Joseph Haydn, or Wolfgang Amadeus Mozart.

The authorities in the Ministry of Propaganda were concerned primarily with their pet organization, less so with individual musicians. So in threes and fours and fives, Günther, Rosemarie, and their friends continued to play chamber music by Schubert, Haydn, and Mozart in the relative safety of their homes during the summer and autumn of 1938, always taking a grim satisfaction that in doing so they were breaking the law.

But there were always more laws being issued, most of them impossible to break, and all of them designed simply to obstruct, to hinder, to hurt, to humiliate. On August 17, 1938, an edict was issued by a certain Hans Globke, a particularly nasty member of the Ministry of the Interior. As of the first day of the coming new year, declared the law, all Jews living in the Reich would be required to add an identifying name to their existing names: Sara for women, Israel for men. My mother thus became Rosemarie Sara Gumpert, my father Günther Ludwig Israel Goldschmidt.

Of all the brutal legal actions taken by the Nazis in the days preceding the Final Solution—including the ordinance of September 1941 that required Jews to wear a yellow Star of David on their clothing—I think the Globke Law was the cruelest and most inhumane. In nearly all societies, the right to name a child is clearly reserved for that child's parents. A child grows into that name; it becomes a vital part of the person's identity. To impose a name is an invasive act rooted in a lust for power and control. "Israel" and "Sara" are beautiful names, meaning "God's fighter" and "princess," but to the Nazis, people blind to beauty, they meant merely "Jew," an adjective of scorn. I think I can trace my father's unease with his Jewish identity to this law: if the Nazis forced him to assume the name of Israel, then he was damned if he would accept a Jewish self once he no longer had to. I can understand his deep-seated feelings; when I see "Günther Ludwig Israel Goldschmidt" on his passport, or read "Toni Sara Goldschmidt" on the return address of his mother's letters, my blood boils.

Meanwhile, Adolf Hitler's empire continued to expand. On the last weekend of September, at a conference in Munich attended by Chancellor Hitler, Italian Duce Mussolini, French Premier Daladier, and British Prime Minister Neville Chamberlain, Germany was allowed to take possession of eleven thousand square miles of land that had belonged to Czechoslovakia. Hitler claimed that nearly three million ethnic Germans lived in that territory, which he called the Sudetenland, or lands of "South Germany," and he threatened to seize the region by force. But in return for this massive concession, he agreed to muffle his guns. Prime Minister Chamberlain returned triumphantly to London bearing a piece of paper proclaiming that Germany and England had pledged "never to go to war with one another again." At 10 Downing Street, serenaded by repeated choruses of "For He's a Jolly Good Fellow," Chamberlain declared that his trip to Munich had produced "peace in our time."

Many people around the world breathed a sigh of relief at the end of that September weekend. Hitler's bellicose pronouncements had instilled fears that the crisis could set off a string of events that would all but certainly lead to widespread war. Günther was among those who believed that the granting of this *Lebensraum* to Hitler would assure peace and provide an opportunity for the world to gently nudge *Der Führer* toward more humane policies. But it proved—in short order—to be a vain hope.

For several months a dispute had simmered between Germany and Poland regarding the fate of more than fifty thousand Jews of Polish ancestry who were living in Germany. The Nazis favored rounding up this identifiable population of Jews and expelling them. But the Polish government wanted no part of them, declaring that Poland already had more than three million Jews within its borders and that these other Jews were rightfully Germany's responsibility and not Poland's. The two countries went back and forth through the summer and early fall. Finally, emboldened by the bloodless triumph of Munich, Germany decided to act.

During the last week of October the Gestapo, the SS, and members of the German Army began forcibly transporting about fifteen thousand Polish-born Jews to the east. But the Polish border guards, acting on orders from Warsaw, would not allow them to enter the country, instead forcing them to wander in no-man's-land for several days. The weather was foul—rainy and cold—and many of the deportees, rounded up only hours before their journey, had no food and little protection from the elements. Finally, several thousand of them were allowed to enter a displaced-persons camp just inside the Polish border. Conditions were chaotic, and the homeless were all hungry, dirty, wet, and miserable.

Among the transported Jews was a man named Zindel Grynszpan, who had moved from Poland to Hannover in 1911, the same year Alex Goldschmidt bought his store in Oldenburg. Zindel had a daughter named Berta and a son named Herschel; Herschel had left Hannover in 1936 to study in Paris. On November 3, from the border camp, Berta wrote Herschel a letter describing what had happened to the family. The letter reached her brother on November 6. That night, he purchased a pistol.

The following morning, Herschel Grynszpan wrote a note, in Hebrew, to his uncle, who was also living in Paris: "My heart bleeds when I think of our tragedy, and that of other Jews. I have to protest in a way that the whole world hears, and this I intend to do. I beg your forgiveness."

That afternoon, he made his way to the German Embassy in Paris and asked to see someone in authority. He was sent to the office of First Secretary Ernst vom Rath, who hailed from Düsseldorf. Once inside the office, Herschel Grynszpan drew his pistol and fired; vom Rath fell, fatally wounded. Rushed to the hospital, he clung to life for forty-eight hours. He died at 5:30 P.M. on November 9.

The incredible violence of the next forty-eight hours was described by the Nazi press as a spontaneous expression of public outrage over the death of Ernst vom Rath. But there are mountains of evidence that suggest that Herschel Grynszpan's act of wrath was merely a convenient excuse for a pogrom that had already been planned well in advance. For fifteen years, ever since Adolf Hitler's putsch against the Weimar government on November 9, 1923, that date had been warmly celebrated by the National Socialists. Since the Nazi accession to power in 1933, the day had become particularly unpleasant for the Jews. Another resident of Düsseldorf, Karl Heinz Adler, remembered past November 9ths this way:

It was a day for these glorious gangsters to remember their heroes. It was a day of flags, early-morning assemblies by the SA and SS, with everyone bragging in fullest uniform that he is a comrade of conviction, when youth marches through town with trumpets and drums, and the Storm Troopers sing their own beautiful songs: "Line the Jews, line the barbarians, up against the wall." You quickly learn that this is not a time for Jews to appear on the streets.

As this particular November 9 approached, there were signs that something was up. A synagogue in Munich had been torched in June, another in Nuremberg set on fire in August. The American ambassador to Germany, Hugh Wilson, cabled his concerns to Washington about increased anti-Jewish violence. On November 8, the day after vom Rath was shot but the day before he died, the official Nazi newspaper, the *Völkischer Beobachter*, published a front-page article promising a new German attitude towards the Jews. In public speeches and private diary entries on both November 8 and November 9, neither Adolf Hitler nor Joseph Goebbels mentioned the shots fired in Paris as the catalyst for the violence in the streets of Germany.

During the night of Wednesday, November 9, 1938, Nazi gangs, many in the brown and black uniforms of the SA and SS, roamed through German cities, looting Jewish homes and businesses. Synagogues and the treasures they held were set on fire. People were dragged from their homes, beaten and stomped, sometimes to death. Thousands more were arrested. The thugs smashed so many windows with clubs, chains, bricks, and stones that the shattered glass lay in heaps, reflecting the glare of spotlights and dancing flames. Seeking to downplay their action against the Jews, the Nazis gave it the name *Kristallnacht* (Night of Crystal), which is usually translated as Night of Broken Glass. The Jews themselves, however, remember that night simply as the November Pogrom.

As German skies glowed red from border to border, there were countless calls from local Nazi officials to local fire departments instructing them to save "German" possessions but to do nothing to thwart the burning of Jewish property. By the weekend, more than two hundred synagogues had been burned, seventy-five hundred Jewish shops and businesses looted or destroyed, nearly one hundred Jews murdered, and more than twenty-five thousand Jews arrested. The Nazis leveled huge fines against Jewish congregations throughout Germany. The government ruled that the Jews themselves were responsible for the "spontaneous demonstrations," since Herschel Grynszpan was a Jew; therefore, they were responsible for cleaning up the mess. Reichsmarshal Hermann Göring decreed that not only were the Jews to be fined one billion marks as "reparation" for the death of vom Rath, but that Jewish properties were to be confiscated as well.

"That will do the trick," Göring declared. "The pigs won't commit a second murder so quickly. I must say I wouldn't want to be a Jew in Germany."

11

Chocolate and Canaries

LATE ON THE AFTERNOON of Wednesday, November 9, 1938, Günther sat alone in his room on Alte Jakobstrasse, practicing his flute. In only six days he was scheduled to participate in his first rehearsal as the principal flutist of Berlin's Kulturbund Orchestra, and he wanted to make a good impression. He had stayed in the capital following the closing of the Kulturbund's production of Verdi's *Rigoletto* to study with a member of the Berlin Philharmonic. Rosemarie had gone back home to Düsseldorf to stay with her parents in the apartment on Boltensternstrasse. These past few weeks represented the longest time the two young lovers had been apart in months, and Günther had discovered that the more time he devoted to his instrument the less time he had left to miss his friend.

That afternoon Günther had spent more than an hour working on some of the fantasies for solo flute written by the prolific Baroque composer Georg Philipp Telemann; they are superb exercises and fun to play. Then he set the Telemann aside and looked at a familiar score: the *Rustic Wedding* Symphony by Karl Goldmark. The boisterous symphony by the son of a cantor had opened the previous season in Frankfurt, and now conductor Rudolf Schwarz had chosen it to open the new season at the theater on Berlin's Kommandantenstrasse. Günther spent another thirty minutes or so with the tricky runs and trills that Goldmark had left for him in the symphony's finale, going over them again and again until he felt confident he had them down cold.

Günther finally put his flute aside, feeling tired and exhilarated, sure that he would shine at that first rehearsal. Stretching, he walked over to the window and looked out at the evening sky, enjoying an almost palpable sense of accomplishment and savoring the peace and quiet of the empty house.

Then suddenly his peace shattered. The front door banged open and then slammed shut. Günther heard footsteps pounding up the stairs and then his landlord, the attorney Otto Hoffmann, stood before him, panting, his eyes wide.

"Get out!" he gasped. "Get your things and get out of here! Now!"

"What do you mean? What's going on?" was all my father could manage to say.

"A riot, that's what's going on. They're coming for us. Those Brownshirt bastards. They're breaking things, and smashing things, and burning things up, yelling, 'Get the Jews!' and . . . Look, there isn't time . . . Run . . . *Now*, dammit!"

At that moment there came a savage knocking on the door downstairs. Otto and Günther froze, then stared at each other. The attorney turned slowly to descend the stairs and Günther quickly disassembled his flute and put it back in its case, not bothering, as he normally would have, to pull a handkerchief through the wooden tubes to dry the condensation. He then dove into his closet, pulled out his old brown suitcase, and stuffed a few things, including the flute, his music, a toothbrush, and Rosemarie's favorite blue sweater, inside. By this time, cries of "Open up!" had joined the percussive pounding on the front door, and Günther's heart was pounding as well. He managed to make his way downstairs and pull on his coat and hat. Hoffmann was standing there helplessly, gnawing on a knuckle.

"How about you? Aren't you getting out?" my father whispered.

"No," he said, in a quavering voice. "My wife . . . she's not home yet. I must wait for her. But you, please, go!"

The knocking on the door resumed with such force that one of the small lintel windows cracked. Feeling as though he were abandoning a sinking ship with many people still on board, Günther turned and headed for the back door. Just as he stepped outside, he heard the front door opening and an excited high-pitched voice saying, "Otto Hoffmann, the Jew Hoffmann? You are under arrest . . . "

My father didn't linger to hear any more. Spared, for the moment, he realized that he had no idea what to do or where to go—only that he must go somewhere, and quickly. There was an alley at the back of the house and he began walking briskly along it, but he didn't dare break into a run for fear of attracting attention. At the end of the alley he turned left onto Hollmannstrasse, away from the Hoffmann residence on Alte Jakobstrasse. Günther's senses seemed unusually acute as he walked; he heard many sounds—shouts, footsteps, a child crying, a dog barking, the clang of a streetcar, the wind—and they all kept increasing in volume, becoming sharp and jarring and ugly, until it became impossible to notice individual sounds and he was only aware of an indistinct roaring in his ears. And there was more. Above the clangor whirled the simple question, "Why? Why are they doing this?" But he knew he had to remain calm and as clearheaded as possible.

Günther came to the corner of Hollmannstrasse and Lindenstrasse. Down Lindenstrasse to the left he caught sight of a small group of men, maybe five or six of them, running pell-mell and whooping, like dogs after their quarry. Günther lowered his head and turned right. A few blocks farther on, he knew, there was a small public park. He decided to go there to catch his breath and to think. Just then, as he was passing the City of Berlin Museum, a gust of wind blew his hat off. He didn't dare stop to retrieve it, but turned his head enough to see it skittering down the street into the gutter.

Those few blocks! It seemed to take an eternity to get to the park. Günther's shins were throbbing, and he had to keep switching his suitcase from one arm to the other because his shoulders ached and his hands were sweating. He found himself turning away from the few people he passed, fearing all of them. And, worst of all, he realized that he was actually feeling guilty; he was a wanted man, and despite having done nothing wrong, he found himself accepting the role of a fugitive, slipping on the suit of criminality that he knew was being fitted for him. Passersby, who might strike him or judge him, were only to be avoided. Even his physical surroundings seemed to conspire against him. Each time he came to an intersection, it was all he could do to force himself to step off the curb. It was as if he were crossing a border into enemy territory, and he felt relieved when he reached the next sidewalk safely.

Just inside the park, Günther found a bench underneath an oak tree and sat down, his legs weak and his chest heaving. He felt shaken, badly scared, utterly alone. Taking off his glasses with his right hand, he covered his eyes with his left and, trying his best not to cry, went over his options.

First he thought he might call on his teacher at the Philharmonic, Herr Strubhauser. But all Jews had been fired from the orchestra long ago, and no matter what the old man's private sympathies might be, it didn't seem likely to Günther that he would be welcomed into the flutist's home that night. He knew practically no one else in Berlin. Going back to the Hoffmanns' was out of the question. And sharing the streets with brown-shirted thugs was hardly appealing. So Günther realized he'd have to go elsewhere, and immediately thought of catching the first train for Oldenburg to be with his family. Had he acted on that thought then and there, his life would have taken a different track, one that might well have carried him, ultimately, to even graver dangers than those he faced that night. As he never speaks of it, I can only imagine that the decision he reached has come back to him again and again when sleep has abandoned him in the small hours of the morning.

Rather than attempt a reunion in Oldenburg, my father decided instead to travel to Düsseldorf to be with his sweetheart. His devotion to Rosemarie comes as no surprise to me; after all, he had abandoned the safety of Stockholm and returned to Nazi Germany to be with her. And when your life is threatened, as my father's most certainly was on that violent night, it makes perfect rational and emotional sense to seek out the person who gives your life meaning. I don't stand in judgment. But given the events of the next few years, his choice must haunt him still.

After deciding to go to Düsseldorf, Günther returned his glasses to his nose and made ready to leave, only to be stopped by a tremendous shattering crash. It was nearly dark, but there was still enough light in the west for him to see smoke rising from the synagogue on Oranienburgerstrasse. It was the grandest and most ornate temple in Berlin.

Günther had never attended services there, but he had been inside a few times to enjoy its spacious peace. Among its adornments was a beautiful painting of Queen Esther, who had saved the ancient Jews by foiling the evil plots of Haman. And the previous week, Günther had attended a concert in the temple, a recital by a young soprano who had sung some of the tender and moving songs by Gustav Mahler. Now it was on fire—the temple, the peace, the painting, the music—all on fire, set ablaze by brainless bullies. At that moment Günther felt more assaulted than if he had been set upon by a mob with clubs. Witnessing this attack on peace and beauty made him sick, and angrier than he had ever felt in his life. But there was nothing for him to do but flee, so he stood up, a little shakily, grabbed his suitcase, and headed for the station.

Not chancing a streetcar, Günther walked west down the broad avenue of Unter den Linden, eyes down. Again his senses were on edge. Each time he heard a noise—a shout, a car horn, even a kicked pebble— his head jerked in that direction as if it were on a string. His mouth was parched and his breath came in little gasps that rattled his throat. Any moment he expected to be stopped, perhaps violently.

Günther's route to the Zoological Garden railway station took him by the base of the Victory Column, built to celebrate the defeat of France in 1871. Since 1933 the tower had been adorned with Nazi banners extending nearly its full height of two hundred feet. Column and banners were ablaze this November night, not consumed by the flames that licked the synagogues, but by the white radiance of spotlights that highlighted the menacing black swastika and its blood-red background. Doing his best to keep his eyes fixed on the pavement in front of him, Günther nevertheless felt the full fury of the regime that hated him as he hurried past.

Arriving at the station without incident, he made his way to a ticket window and found a train leaving for Düsseldorf at 10:50 P.M. Inside the station it was a typically bustling Wednesday night, with no evidence that the city and country outside were in a state of convulsion. Each time the public address system crackled to life with the announcement of an arrival or departure, however, Günther flinched, hearing in the clipped tones of the railroad official an echo of a more malignant authority. He was far too nervous to eat, but he cooled his throat and fortified his resolve with a glass of beer. At 10:50 precisely, his train pulled out of the station. And there he sat, alone in a second-class compartment, a refugee in his own country.

As the train rolled westward, he was conscious of a deep weariness, but his taut nerves permitted no sleep. For many miles the tracks ran along a canal, and Günther watched the moon and the moon's reflection. But fire vied with water for his attention that night. As the train neared the town of Wolfsburg, he saw flames shooting up from a building across the canal and assumed for a moment that he was witnessing another hateful act of arson, but it turned out to be a Volkswagen plant in the full throes of production. A few miles farther on, another flame caught his eye, but this, too, turned out to be benign: a torch on a tugboat peacefully pushing a barge on the canal. But then, as they slowly approached the station in the heart of Hannover, capital city of his father's native province, Günther saw another burning synagogue. Firemen had gathered, but instead of fighting the fire they simply trained their hoses on neighboring buildings to ensure that the conflagration wouldn't spread to more precious property. As Günther looked on in horror, a man rushed out of the temple clutching something to his bosom; his clothing was on fire and he was obviously in agony, but no one stepped forward to help. Günther instinctively reached out and his hand struck the window as his train continued on its journey.

Wunstorf, Minden, Lohne, Bielefeld, Ahlen, Hamm, Dortmund, Essen. The towns he passed all had their own tales of terror to tell that crystal night, but none he would know. At 6:10 Thursday morning, he started awake from the conductor's call of "Düsseldorf, next stop!" His flight was over.

But there remained the three-mile walk to the Gumpert house on Boltensternstrasse. Again, hoping to remain as inconspicuous as possible, Günther chose to travel on foot rather than chance an encounter with hostile streetcar passengers or drivers. From the Central Station he headed north along the Königsallee, Düsseldorf's main thoroughfare, a lovely urban setting of shops, galleries, restaurants, and cinemas, its lanes of traffic separated by a canal populated by ducks, geese, and swans. But on that overcast Thursday morning, all my father saw was ruin, the results of the previous night's rampage. Heaps of broken glass. Overturned tables and chairs. The word *Jude* scrawled on a door in red paint. An upright piano lying on its side, missing most of its keys. Günther bent to strike a remaining G but received no answering sound; the instrument's felt hammers had been gouged out by an ax.

He came upon Bloomberg's Haberdashery, its windows smashed and its inventory looted. Clothing had been shredded and strewn about, some on the floor, some out on the sidewalk. Two mannequins had been left in a copulatory position; they were naked, of course, and one of them, a Star of David painted on its back, had been beheaded. A few doors up the street, Günther passed a confectionary, Wilder's Fancy Chocolates. One of the hooligans had known that chocolate and water don't mix; a hose had been turned on Herr Wilder's creations in their neat displays, and also back in the kitchen where vats of chocolate were cooking. Now everything was ruined, sweetness drowned.

As Günther continued north on the western portion of Königs-allee, he noticed a gang of people coming slowly towards him, a van in their midst. The van had a loudspeaker mounted on top; as it drew closer, my father could make out the words: "The German people are outraged by the cowardly assassination in Paris. Our people have seen to it that this will be the last detestible expression of the Jews, this soci-ety of international criminals and war-mongers . . . "

Not waiting to hear more, Günther ducked down Grünstrasse and walked rapidly westward toward the Rhine. As he passed Kasernen-strasse, he saw another crowd of people, gazing silently at the still smoking remains of the city's main synagogue. Nearly all its windows had been smashed, and shards of glass crunched under his shoes as he hurried on.

In this city of Heinrich Heine, one line of his poetry ran through Günther's memory that morning, the same line he'd recited to Rose-marie just two months before during their happy journey down the Rhine: "*Ich weiss nicht was soll es bedeuten, dass ich so traurig bin.*" That day, the first line of the poem "Die Lorelei" had contrasted so sharply with their sunny happiness, but now my father understood the reasons for his overwhelming sadness and shock all too well; the evidence was everywhere. He turned north up Bilkerstrasse, deciding to approach

Rosemarie's house via the street where Robert Schumann had lived more than eighty years ago. Perhaps the composer's spirit would spare him another ugly sight.

But more evidence of violence awaited him, and in another place that Günther held holy. Halfway up the narrow block stood a handsome house, painted green. A plaque over its second-story windows proclaimed "Here lived Robert and Clara Schumann from September 1852 until March 1854," the month, Günther knew, when Robert, in the grip of oncoming madness, had jumped into the Rhine. Since 1927, the house's first floor had been home to Alena Klein, a sculptress who fashioned whimsical birds out of plaster. The models for her creations, a matched set of canaries, lived in a cage that hung from a hook in the studio's bright yellow ceiling. Günther and Rosemarie had visited the shop during his visit in the summer of 1937 and had promised each other that they would one day buy one of Fräulein Klein's ceramic songsters.

Now, approaching the house, Günther saw that the windows, glass and frames alike, had been driven back into the studio and that the door was half off its hinges. Not wanting to, but drawn by a morbid curiosity, my father stared into what was left of the studio. Alena Klein's potter's wheel, broken in two, lay on the floor, surrounded by the ruins of the windows. The bird sculptures had all been smashed, too. And on the far wall, impaled on twin kitchen knives that had been driven into the plaster, drooped the lifeless bodies of the two canaries. Two trails of blood ran down the wall to mix with the mess on the floor. Sickened, Günther turned away and blindly stumbled on.

Through all the insults and setbacks and limitations of the past five years, he had never quite known the fear and helpless rage that surged through him that bleak morning. He had finally seen the true face of National Socialism, and the image was terrifying. Not just because it was cruel and violent, although that was certainly a major aspect of the terror. No, the main reason was that the New Germany could not seem to abide the presence of gentleness and beauty, but ruthlessly stamped it out wherever possible. As he walked the streets of Düsseldorf that day, Günther felt like an unwelcome visitor to a strange and hostile land. But it was his land, he thought bitterly, and that of his family. Enemies have taken it over, he brooded, and one day they will surely leave.

It was about half-past seven when Günther left the street and entered the Hofgarten, the beautiful park that had been expanded by Emperor Napoleon. He followed a path that wound its way northward along a pond lined with oaks and sycamores, their branches nearly denuded of leaves. As he crossed a bridge over the stream that fed the pond, he noticed four young men dressed in workers' clothes approaching from a path on his right; three of them carried beer bottles, one of them a paint can. Günther lowered his eyes and walked more briskly, hoping they wouldn't notice him. But perhaps they sensed his fear; they stopped and stared as he hurried past. And then, "Hey, Jewnose," one of them called out.

Günther thought for sure his time had come. He pictured himself beaten and bloody, left by the side of the path or perhaps flung into the pond. They would steal his suitcase, he feared, break his flute or set fire to his music and, with it, burn down a beautiful building. He was conscious both of being terrified and of hating them deeply. But all he could do was run, so run he did, as fast as he could, with his suitcase bumping his knees and almost tripping him. He followed the path where it wound up a hill and at the top took a chance and looked behind him. Instantly, warm relief replaced cold fear. What had obviously been a night of revelry had left the four lads in no condition to mount a pursuit; they were still standing near the bridge, swigging beer and laughing uproariously. From a safe distance they appeared ridiculous, small and ignorant and foolish. But they represented what Günther had been fleeing all night, what had taken over his country. He was sick to death of running, of humiliation, angry both at them and at his own cowardice. But he knew also that he really had no choice. Panting, sweating, and sorrowful, he turned his back on them and trudged on.

About forty minutes later, footsore and weary but safe, he found the apartment at 17 Boltensternstrasse. He rang the bell, and after a few moments the door swung open and there stood Julian Gumpert, his long, thick white hair neatly combed, a violin in his right hand. He smiled broadly.

"Günther, what a most pleasant surprise! Please come in."

And when the door had been safely shut, "I can't believe you came all this way. Are you hurt?"

"No, everything's fine. I mean, I'm very tired, but—"

Günther realized that he had no words to describe all he had experienced over the past fifteen hours. And he feared breaking down before this imposing man, this violinist, composer, conductor, and father of his beloved. Suddenly, there she was.

"Günther, what on earth are you doing here? I thought you were in Berlin. Is everything all right?"

She seemed about to embrace him but then, conscious of her father's presence, merely extended her right hand, which he grasped tightly. In her left she held her viola.

He was about to pour out his overflowing heart when Julian spoke first.

"I'm sure you two have much to talk about, but Rosemarie and I were having a lesson. Mornings in this house always start with music. Günther, why don't you rest or have some breakfast and we'll hear all your news. Rosemarie's mother is still asleep, but feel free to help yourself in the kitchen. Afterwards you may join us in my study."

Rosemarie squeezed Günther's hand, smiled at him a bit ruefully, and followed her father down the hall.

A few minutes later, having found nothing in the kitchen but not wanting to search too thoroughly, Günther knocked softly on the open door of the study. He had washed his hands and face and changed into the blue sweater that he had worn to his first Kulturbund rehearsal in Frankfurt, the day he'd met Rosemarie. He was still carrying his suitcase.

"Ah, Günther, yes. We were just playing through one of the Mozart duos," said Julian, waving him inside. The room was warm and dark, illuminated by a single floor lamp. Overflowing bookshelves lined all four walls, leaving just enough room for a set of pencil sketches of Beethoven, Brahms, Schumann, and Mahler. On a small table in one corner stood a metronome and a small bust of Bach.

"Do you happen to have your instrument with you?" continued Julian. "Wonderful. Here, let's the three of us try a bit of the Beethoven Serenade."

Günther could hardly believe his ears. Here he had barely survived the night, and this man was acting as if it were just another lazy morning.

"Excuse me, sir," he said. "But haven't you heard what's been going on? Have you been outside and seen the streets? Aren't you afraid?"

"Of what?" Julian replied. "Of a few drunken idiots? Of course not. Look, I made a few telephone calls last night, made a few inquiries. I know a few important people and they all told me this rowdiness will blow over very soon. In any event, in my house music comes first. So, Günther, your flute. Here's your score. Slow movement."

For a moment, all my father could do was stand and stare, dumbfounded by this display of complete self-assurance. Was Julian really aware of the situation outside, or was his head so completely in the clouds that he would never understand? Günther glanced over at Rosemarie, who was smiling at him and his sentimental choice of the blue sweater. Then he sat down in the offered chair, put the score on the stand in front of it, took out his flute. Nervous in the presence of the Conservatory director, he played a few scales to warm up, then nodded.

The slow movement of the Beethoven Serenade begins with the violin and viola playing a tender melody of the utmost sweetness, their respective lines twining around each other and yearning upward. As Günther sat listening to Julian and Rosemarie, he thought about all he had seen and heard and felt since he had last played his instrument in his peaceful room in Berlin: the knocks on the door, the painted epithets, the smoke and flames, the ruined synagogues, the chocolate and the canaries, the pain in his feet and the tightness in his stomach, "Jewnose," the glittering mountain of shattered glass that included the window of his heart. And he thought that now he was here, safe in his best friend's home, safe—for now—in the world of Beethoven. When it came time for my father to enter with his part, he couldn't see the score. His eyes were full of tears.

12

Two Newspapers

THE *NEW YORK TIMES*, Friday, November 11, 1938:

NAZIS SMASH, LOOT AND BURN
JEWISH SHOPS AND TEMPLES

By Otto D. Tolischus

BERLIN, Nov. 10—A wave of destruction, looting and incendiarism unparalleled in Germany since the Thirty Years War swept over Great Germany today as National Socialist cohorts took vengeance on Jewish shops, offices and synagogues for the murder by a young Polish Jew of Ernst vom Rath of the German Embassy in Paris.

Beginning systematically in the early morning hours in almost every town and city in the country, the wrecking, looting and burning continued all day. Huge but mostly silent crowds looked on and the police confined themselves to regulating traffic and making wholesale arrests of Jews "for their own protection."

All day the main shopping districts as well as the side streets of Berlin and innumerable other places resounded to the shattering of shop windows falling to the pavement, the dull thuds of furniture and fittings being pounded to pieces and the clamor of fire brigades rushing to burning shops and synagogues. Although shop fires were quickly extinguished, synagogue fires were merely kept from spreading to adjoining buildings.

As far as could be ascertained the violence was mainly confined to property. Although individuals were beaten, reports so far tell of the deaths of only two persons—a Jew in Pomerania and another in Bunzdorf.

By nightfall there was scarcely a Jewish shop, cafe, office or synagogue in the country that was not either wrecked, burned severely or damaged.

All Jewish organizational, cultural and publishing activity has been suspended. It is assumed that the Jews, who have now lost most of their possessions and livelihood, will either be thrown into the streets or put into ghettos or concentration camps, or impressed into labor brigades and put to work for the Third Reich, as the children of Israel were once before for the Pharaohs.

In any case, all day in Berlin, as throughout the country, thousands of Jews, mostly men, were being taken from their homes and arrested—in particular prominent Jewish leaders who, in some cases, it is understood, were told they were being held as hostages for the good behavior of Jewry outside Germany.

All pretense—maintained during previous comparatively minor anti-Jewish outbreaks—to the effect that the day's deeds had been the work of irresponsible, even Communist, elements was dropped this time and the official German News Bureau, as well as newspapers that hitherto had ignored such happenings, frankly reported them.

Berlin papers also mention many cities and towns in which anti-Jewish excesses occured, including Potsdam, Frankfurt, Leipzig, Lübeck, Cologne, Nuremberg, Düsseldorf and Eberswalde. In most of them, it is reported, synagogues were raided and burned and shops were demolished. But in general the press follows a system of reporting only local excesses so as to disguise the national extent of the outbreak, the full spread of which probably never will be known.

Generally the crowds were silent and the majority seemed gravely disturbed by the proceedings. Only members of the wrecking squads themselves shouted occasionally "Perish Jewry!" and "Kill the Jews!" and in one case a person in the crowd shouted, "Why not hang the owner in the window?"

In one case on the Kurfürstendamm actual violence was observed by an American girl who saw one Jew with his face bandaged dragged from a shop, beaten and chased by a crowd while a second Jew was dragged from the same shop by a single man who beat him as the crowd looked on.

One Jewish shopowner, arriving at his wrecked store, exclaimed, "Terrible," and was arrested on the spot.

In some cases on the other hand crowds were observed making passages for Jews to leave their stores unmolested.

To some extent—at least during the day—efforts were made to prevent looting. Crowds were warned they might destroy but must not plunder, and in individual cases looters either were beaten up on the spot by uniformed Nazis or arrested. But for the most part, looting was general, particularly during the night and in the poorer quarters. And in at least one case the wreckers themselves tossed goods out to the crowd with the shout, "Here are some cheap Christmas presents."

Children were observed with their mouths smeared with candy from wrecked candy shops or flaunting toys from wrecked toy shops until one elderly woman watching the spectacle exclaimed, "So that is how they teach our children to steal."

No photographing of the wreckage was permitted and Anton Celler, American tourist, of Hamden, Connecticut, was arrested while trying to take such pictures, although he was soon released. Members of a South American diplomatic mission likewise got into trouble on that account.

In a tour of Berlin this afternoon this correspondent saw few Jewish stores or synagogues that had escaped damage. Many buildings were destoyed.

The rioting reached a high point in the center of Berlin, where, at noon, thousands gathered in the streets to watch gangs pound to bits dozens of stores.

This correspondent saw dozens of men and women rush into a toy shop in the Arcade between Unter den Linden and Friedrichstrasse and scoop up what they could get. They went in after gangs of youths had smashed the plate glass windows. Inside, counters, partitions and everything breakable or loose were thrown to the floor and smashed.

Five other stores in the Arcade also were plundered. Few policemen were visible.

A short distance away, at the corner of Jägerstrasse and Friedrichstrasse, a second-story pawn shop came in for vengeance. Youths with lead pipes broke windows, then threw fur coats from the pawn shop's racks down onto the heads of several thousands watching in the street.

Around another corner in the center of the city a tailor shop was looted. In the doorway a tailor's dummy with a hat on its head hung with a rope around its neck.

While a large section of the German population seemed thoroughly ashamed at the exhibition of mob rule, those who participated in anti-Semitic actions had a gay time.

Before one Friedrichstrasse shop devoted to the sale of magic apparatus, children lined up with brass poles that had hooks at the ends. With these they fished magicians' boxes of tricks for themselves out of the interior of the shop through a broken store window.

Older boys unconcernedly threw tables, chairs and other furniture out of smashed windows.

Near Alexanderplatz some twenty workers from the city market helped themselves at a shoe store. When this correspondent got there they were sitting on the curb, laughing and trying on pair after pair of shoes.

Before synagogues, demonstrators stood with Jewish prayer books from which they tore leaves as souvenirs for the crowds.

The noise of breaking glass and cracking furniture accompanied loud anti-Jewish jeers. When the smashing crews had passed, it looked as if a tornado had swept the street. The pavement was covered with broken glass.

Restaurants that previously had made no distinction between Jews and non-Jews posted signs: "No Jews Wanted."

The official German News Bureau expressed indignation
that some Jewish proprietors had compelled "Aryan" employees
to clean up the debris.

The *Rheinische Landeszeitung,* Thursday evening, November 10, 1938:

GERMANY RESPONDS

DÜSSELDORF—Spontaneous demonstrations against Jews took
place overnight as a direct result of the outrage felt by our
fellow citizens at the crime committed by the Jewish murder
clique.

The citizens of Düsseldorf moved in large groups through
the streets and it is only thanks to the extraordinary discipline
of the public that the racial brothers of the cowardly murderers
were spared their lives. The crime of the Jewish clique was too
inhuman, however, to be dealt with only by choruses of talk.
The Jewish shops—a sign of the audacity of the "chosen people"—which even in the sixth year of the New Germany are
prominent in the main streets of Düsseldorf, felt the brunt of
the people's anger. There, where the Jews were trying to do
business up until now, the goods were radically removed. In
order to counteract any insinuation of wrongdoing from the
very beginning, there was in no case any plundering. Our people are much too proud to enrich themselves with the belongings of Jews. However, an essential lesson was provided to the
Jewish community, which had always tried to remain mute in
Düsseldorf.

The righteous outrage of our people understandably extended itself to the private homes and rooms of the Jews. The
Jewish clique got what it deserved with the destruction of
housing for the crime committed against fellow Germans. The
payback was considered very mild by the Jews themselves,

otherwise it would not have been possible that, as was credibly told us in one case, a Jewish apartment owner thanked his German intruders for having dealt so leniently with him and above all for sparing his life. They probably expected worse based on their guilty consciences. However, there were no bodily injuries to Jews. The Jews were offered protection by the police, who nevertheless could not entirely deflect the justified anger of the crowd.

The primary rage of the people of Düsseldorf was directed at the synagogue on Kasernenstrasse. Through all the years since the National Socialist takeover of power, the people have been provoked by the Star of David, the symbol of Jewish hate, which perched on the roof of the house of prayer.

The synagogue was stormed in the course of the evening by an ever increasing crowd of people. The interior was fully destroyed when, apparently as a result of a short circuit, it went up in flames. The fire moved quickly and took over the whole building so that the firemen were unable to stop it. The synagogue was completely burned out and the firemen had to resort to protecting the surrounding buildings. There was loud applause when the Star of David fell into the burning interior.

The people of Düsseldorf moved all night through the streets, giving expression to their disgust at the Jewish criminals. Towards morning the crowds began to disperse.

The citizens' outrage had not yet wholly subsided by Thursday morning, however. In fact, for those people who only learned of the tragic death of the diplomat vom Rath from the newspapers, their rage was at its peak in the morning hours. Thus scarcely a compatriot could remain at home or at his place of work, and crowds of people gathered downtown until finally the congestion on the Königsallee was so great that it was hard to get through.

Around noon thousands of compatriots marched to the barracks of the Old Guard where they spoke through loudspeakers and expressed their outrage that a high-ranking officer there is still married to a Jewess. The downtown demonstrations only slowly quieted down. The destruction of the synagogue and Jewish businesses that had occurred overnight repeatedly aroused the crowd's scorn and led to a few more lively demonstrations against individual Jews. In some instances the anger was such that it was vented in the further destruction of Jewish businesses and apartments.

13

The March

IN ITS EDITION of November 11, 1938, Günther's hometown newspaper gave scant coverage to the national day of violence. On its front page that Friday morning, the *Oldenburger Nachrichten* reported the death, at age fifty-eight, of Turkish President Mustafa Kemal Ataturk, as well as Chancellor Hitler's message of condolence to the people of Turkey. Also on the front page were an analysis of British rearmament and a dispatch detailing recent Communist activities in France. On the second page, underneath a weather map of Europe, a listing of the day's radio schedule, and an advisory about continuing construction on the road to Bremerhaven, there appeared a single paragraph under the heading "The People's Revenge." The story mentioned that, as revenge for the "Jewish murder" of the German diplomat vom Rath, several synagogues in the vicinity—including the temple on Peterstrasse in Oldenburg—had caught fire early Thursday morning. In addition, two Jewish businesses on Kurwickstrasse had been damaged, but police stood guard all day Thursday to prevent further incidents. Because the owners were in danger of being hurt, they were taken by police into protective custody.

The newspaper neglected to mention a few other aspects of the previous forty-eight hours.

On Wednesday night, November 9, a young man named Erich Engelbart was celebrating with a few friends at his favorite tavern, the Pape on Heiligengeiststrasse, just off the cobblestone streets of Oldenburg's city center. There were two reasons for the party. First, Engelbart had turned thirty-five on Tuesday and he always observed his birthday with a good meal and some fine wine. Second, as the highest-ranking

Nazi official in Oldenburg, Kreisleiter Engelbart was duty-bound to mark the fifteenth anniversary of the glorious Munich beer-hall putsch.

Among the guests at the Pape that night was Konrad Richter, Ortsgruppenleiter of Oldenburg and the former manager of the city's slaughterhouse.

Around eleven o'clock, Engelbart was called away from his table to take an urgent telephone call from Munich, where Chancellor Hitler and Propaganda Minister Goebbels were also celebrating the anniversary of the putsch of 1923. The voice on the other end of the line told Engelbart to listen carefully, that these instructions were to be issued once and once only and that he was not to respond, but only to see that the orders were carried out.

Jewish businesses were to be destroyed immediately. Afterward SA men, in uniform, should stand guard to see that no looting occurred. All valuables, including money, were to be "secured." All weapons should be taken away from Jews. Synagogues were to be set on fire. The local fire department should only get involved to protect Aryan homes. Jewish houses in the immediate vicinity were to be hosed down, as well, but the Jews themselves were to be driven out because German citizens would be moving into those houses soon. After the synagogues and shops had been destroyed, slogans should be painted on the walls: "Revenge for the murder of vom Rath!" "Death to the Jews!" And so forth.

Finally, the voice on the line exclaimed "Heil Hitler!" and the connection was broken.

Engelbart hurried back to his table and summoned Richter for a brief conference in the tavern's lavatory. They agreed to divide the responsibilities, with Engelbart taking charge of the destruction of the shops and Richter overseeing the synagogue operation. The Kreisleiter left the Pape on a recruitment expedition, taking care to bring along a few bottles of the wine he'd been drinking, while Richter immediately put in a call to his chauffeur, requesting a canister of gasoline on the pretext that a friend of his was experiencing car trouble.

Shortly after midnight, the chauffeur arrived with the gas and, after leaving the can with Richter, was dismissed. Driving away down Marienstrasse, he noticed that the big plate glass window of Lobel's Furs was lying in pieces on the sidewalk.

Herbert Wulf lived next door to the synagogue on Peterstrasse. That night he was having trouble sleeping, so he noticed when four vehicles pulled up outside and about twenty men, most of them wearing brown uniforms, piled out. It was nearly 12:30 A.M.

The Storm Troopers began by breaking down the door of the synagogue. They then carried newspapers, rags, a few wooden boxes and other flammable materials from a truck into the temple. Within a few minutes both the synagogue and the adjoining Jewish school were in flames. The Storm Troopers then began breaking into nearby houses, including Wulf's. They wanted to arrest him, but he had his identification papers handy and could prove he was a Lutheran. The Jews living on the block were not so fortunate; they were pulled out of bed, dragged into the street, and forced to watch the fire consume their synagogue. Wulf remembered the SA men screaming at their victims dementedly, "You should all be burned, too!"

The Oldenburg fire department recorded an alert coming into the station from a concerned citizen at 1:27 A.M., but by then Kreisleiter Engelbart had already paid a visit to the fire chief to explain to him the rules of the night. At about 1:45, by which time the school and temple were merely blazing shells, the fire truck arrived and firemen began spraying water on the roofs of nearby buildings. A little while later, a distinguished crowd of people strolled up to watch the fire. The gathering included Oldenburg's lord mayor, Dr. Gottfried Rabeling; Mayor Hans Bertram; Chief of Police Friedrich Köhnke; Max von Hedemann, the son-in-law of the last grand duke of Oldenburg; and Kreisleiter Erich Engelbart and Ortsgruppenleiter Konrad Richter, who hadn't had to travel very far to join the group. Mayor Bertram had brought his twelve-year-old daughter to join in the excitement. When the roof of the synagogue collapsed in a shower of sparks, she cheered along with the adults.

By three o'clock the fire had more or less died down. The spectators went home to bed and the fire truck rumbled off, its work completed to everyone's satisfaction. Erich Engelbart and Konrad Richter were the last to leave.

Engelbart was still keyed up from the excitement of the past three hours. In addition to his little chat with the head of Oldenburg's fire department, he had also summoned his Storm Troopers for an emergency meeting at the courthouse on Elisabethstrasse. When a few of them grumbled about the late hour, he assured them that this was a meeting and an evening they would long remember with the greatest satisfaction.

When everyone had assembled, Engelbart passed out maps and a list of Jewish-owned businesses. He divided his Storm Troopers into groups of three and gave them their orders. Each squad was assigned a certain section of the city and a list of establishments to destroy. Engelbart also imposed a time limit for their activities; he wanted them, he insisted, back at the courthouse by four o'clock. At that time he would issue new orders. When he dismissed his men, they strode off eagerly; even the few grumblers had been won over by the promise of fun and excitement ahead of them.

So as the fire raged on Peterstrasse, Storm Troopers fanned out across Oldenburg on their own mission of havoc. For the next three hours, even as the bells of Lamberti Church sweetly tolled the passing of the night, the sounds of the city were harsh and violent: the rending of wood, the groan and screech of iron and steel, and everywhere the shiver and shatter and smash of glass.

When his men returned boisterously to the courthouse at four o'clock, Kreisleiter Engelbart relayed the news of the synagogue's destruction. After the cheers had subsided, he dispatched his next orders. Keeping his teams of three Storm Troopers intact, he called for the systematic arrest of every Jewish man in the city. Whether to arrest whole families he left up to the discretion of the individual teams. But all Jewish men were expected to be in custody at the police station in the Pferdemarkt by daybreak.

Thus it was that at five minutes past five o'clock a heavy knock sounded on the door of Alex Goldschmidt's apartment at 53 Ofenerstrasse, and the sands of his allotted time began to run more quickly.

"Police!" came the cry, over and over from three throats. "Police! Open up! Police!" And the knocking shook the walls.

Alex stumbled to the door in his pajamas.

"What is it? What's the matter?"

"Are you Alex Goldschmidt? You are under arrest. Get yourself ready immediately!"

"What? But why? There must be some mistake! What have I done?"

"This is an action being taken at this very moment throughout the Reich. Germany is avenging itself for the Jewish murder in Paris. No more questions. You will come with us, immediately. And where are Günther Goldschmidt and Klaus Helmut Goldschmidt?"

"Günther is away . . . he's in Berlin. Helmut is here, but he's only seventeen, he's just a boy!"

"That makes no difference to us. Both of you, dress yourselves and come along. And be quick about it!"

"What do I tell my wife? What happens to my two daughters?"

"Tell her anything you like. The women may all stay here, for now. But you and the other one, come with us. And quickly!"

Alex walked back into his bedroom in a daze and began to dress. Toni watched from the bed, her eyes wide.

"What's going on? What do these people want with us?"

Alex sat on the side of the bed, kissed his wife, and stroked her hair gently.

"I'm sure it's some clerical error," he said, as cheerfully as he could. "They probably have the wrong house." He forced a laugh. "Or maybe I forgot to renew my driver's license. In any case, I'm sure it's nothing. I'll be back soon, just you wait and see."

In the hall, he hugged Bertha and Eva and repeated his words of reassurance. Then, at half-past five, Alex and Helmut found themselves herded down Ofenerstrasse towards the east. They had been permitted to wear coats and hats, which was fortunate because a sharp wind was blowing and the temperature was only a few degrees above freezing. Alex attempted to engage their three captors in conversation once or twice, but the only reply was the clatter of their boots on the pavement.

As they neared the Pferdemarkt around a quarter to six, Alex noticed more groups of prisoners, some of them containing women and children, entering the square from all sides, each escorted by three men in the uniform of the SA. The captives all wore blank expressions of the sheerest shock. A few of the women were doing their best not to cry as they clung to their husbands or fathers.

When they reached the broad expanse of the Pferdemarkt, they were ordered to line up, the men on one side of the square and the women on the other. It was cold, windy, and very dark, with only a few dim lights visible from the old city center to the south.

After a few minutes, Alex recognized a man standing in the line in front of him. It was Heinrich Hirschberg, a textile buyer who had come to Oldenburg about ten years earlier and had lived near the Goldschmidt family after their move to Wurzburgerstrasse.

"Herr Hirschberg! Herr Hirschberg!" Alex whispered. "Do you know what's going on? When did you——?"

"Silence, Jew!" came a shout from one of the men in uniform. "You, and all of you Jews, will speak only when spoken to! Is that understood?"

Herr Hirschberg, who had turned towards Alex at the sound of his name, spun around and faced front again. In the moment he had looked into his neighbor's face, Alex had noticed that, despite the cold, he was sweating copiously.

Alex felt for his son's hand next to him and gave it a reassuring squeeze. He then straightened his shoulders, thrust his hands into the pockets of his overcoat, and gazed out over the square. His eyes found the windows of the apartment where he had lived when he first came to Oldenburg as a young man, thirty-two years before. At that moment, the bells of the Lamberti Church chimed six times.

At about seven-thirty, as a gray dawn was breaking, a car roared into the square and squealed to a stop in front of the lines of prisoners. Out stepped Kreisleiter Erich Engelbart and Markus Gellert, Brigadeführer of the Oldenburg SA. Engelbart climbed up on the running board of the automobile and addressed the crowd.

"Attention!" he called out. "It has been decided that all women and all males under the age of eighteen may step out of line. You must leave here at once and return to your homes. Do not speak to each other and do not attempt to contact others on your way home. Failure to abide by these rules will be dealt with severely. I trust I have made myself clear. All right, then, disperse! Heil Hitler!"

Alex turned to Helmut and gave him a quick embrace.

"Do as he says, my boy," he whispered. "And wait for me . . . I'm sure I'll be home soon."

Helmut kissed his father's cheek, gazed into his eyes for a moment, smiled faintly, then turned away, joining the stream of women and children who walked rapidly and silently from the Pferdemarkt, their eyes on the ground and their hearts pounding.

When the last of them had disappeared, Kreisleiter Engelbart spoke once more.

"All right, now, the rest of you . . . count off. You, here, begin . . . one, two, three . . . "

And with that, each man in line barked out a number in turn. Alex was number 19. Herr Hirschberg was number 11. And number 28 was Leo Trepp, rabbi of the ruined Oldenburg synagogue. When the counting stopped, they'd reached number 43.

Engelbart appeared satisfied.

"Forty-three Jews. Not bad."

He then cleared his throat noisily and spat on the asphalt, just missing the shoes of a man in the front row.

"I leave you now with Brigadeführer Gellert. I'm sure you will afford him the same respect you granted me. *Auf wiedersehen.*"

And with that Erich Engelbart got into the back seat of the automobile. The uniformed chauffeur at the wheel drove smartly away down Donnerschweerstrasse.

Markus Gellert then stepped forward.

"All right, you Jewish pigs!" he bellowed. "Shut your mouths and stand up straight! Take your hands out of your pockets, or I'll hit you so hard I'll make you blind and deaf! Listen to me, you damned Jew criminals!"

The silence that had followed the departure of the automobile grew deeper. It was broken, over the next hour and a half, only by the wind and by the 8:10 train to Bremerhaven rattling over the bridge that spanned Bruderstrasse across the square.

When the Lamberti Church bells struck nine, Alex started out of a reverie. His leg muscles were sore and cramped. His shoulders ached and his hands, which he had not dared to stick back in his pockets, were numb. He had just begun to shift his weight from foot to foot and move his hands surreptitiously behind his back to rub them together when six policemen marched up to where the prisoners were standing. They wore the uniform and tunic of the SA, but one of them had a rotund figure and a walrus mustache that made him look like a character in a music-hall entertainment. Alex almost smiled when he saw him; surely this whole enterprise would now be revealed for the charade it was.

But no; the ordeal had just begun. Brigadeführer Gellert reappeared, having retreated from the morning chill, and shouted at them again.

"Come along, pigs! Off you go! Quickly, now!"

"Where? Where are you taking us?" came a small but clear voice. Alex turned to see who would dare to confront their captors and saw a small elderly gentlemen with hollow eyes and a mustache, wearing a dapper little hat and leaning on a cane. The man spoke up again.

"Why are you doing this to us?"

"Silence!" shrieked the Brigadeführer. "You are here because you are Jews, you are criminals. You will go where we tell you to go. And you will keep your mouths shut!"

And with that, the forty-three prisoners and their ten guards began a shuffling march through the streets of Oldenburg. Leaving the Pferdemarkt, they walked west for a block on Bruderstrasse before turning left down the broad avenue of Peterstrasse. A crowd, some people on their way to work and others drawn by the spectacle, gathered silently on the sidewalk to watch them pass. From time to time Markus Gellert would call out to the crowd of spectators, "These are the criminals, these are the enemies of the Reich."

A quarter of a mile down Peterstrasse, they passed the smoking remains of the synagogue, its stately cupola in pieces on the ground, its gracefully arched but doorless entranceway revealing a ruined interior surrounded by blackened brick. Brigadeführer Gellert took in the sorrowful gazes of the men as they passed their temple and sang out, "See how a righteous and angry citizenry has responded to your crimes. This act of revenge is richly deserved." A few small boys, released from school because of what had happened overnight, were poking around the rubble with sticks. On seeing the procession of downcast men and hearing them branded as criminals by the men in uniform, the boys began laughing and jeering. "Look at the dirty old Jews," they called out as Markus Gellert smiled his encouragement.

A hundred yards or so past the synagogue, the Nazi leaders herded their charges to the left, down Haarenstrasse and into the narrow, wind-

The shameful march of the Jewish men of Oldenburg through the city's winding streets, November 10, 1938. They look remarkably poised and at ease, considering the night they have just passed. A greater ordeal lies ahead for them.

ing streets of the central city. The mid-morning bustle of a normal Thursday was at its height and the streets were crowded. But all activity on the cobblestones and within the shops halted, the chatter of conversations fading into an uneasy silence as the procession passed by. A thin blond woman who was pushing a baby carriage into a bakery called out, "Cut off their heads!" She was answered by a loud guffaw uttered by a man in an undershirt who was watching from a window two floors above Haarenstrasse, but for the most part the people of Oldenburg just stared in silence. Alex wasn't sure what he saw in their eyes, whether pity and helplessness or tacit approval, but he didn't spend a great deal of time looking; he felt such shame that he largely kept his eyes on the stones at his feet.

They came to the corner where Haarenstrasse intersects with Langestrasse and Schüttingstrasse. Alex prayed that they would be herded to the right down Langestrasse and not to the left down Schüttingstrasse, because going to the left would take them, in one block, to the corner of Achternstrasse and the site of his old Haus der Mode. Walking these streets under these forced circumstances was bad enough, but being forced to march past the store that was once his under the mocking gaze of Magnus Sander would have been excruciating.

Alex's prayer was answered; his captors' route led down Langestrasse. But as he passed Schüttingstrasse he permitted himself to gaze down the street toward the corner he knew so well, toward the building he had purchased with so much hope and pride twenty-seven years before, to the place where his son Günther was born and where he had tried to do his best to contribute to the well-being of his city. He'd worked hard—his fellow prisoners had all worked hard—to make Oldenburg a better place to live. And this degrading public spectacle was their reward. Alex suddenly stopped walking as this truth hit home and he felt overwhelmingly sorry for himself, for the other forty-two marchers, for the people who silently watched their humiliation, and for his country, for the Germany he had defended with his very life.

A moment later he felt a sharp pain in his left elbow. Markus Gellert had struck him with a hard rubber truncheon and had drawn the weapon back to swing again.

"What are you staring at, Jew? Thinking of buying something? Well, the shops are closed to you and your Jewish money today, so just keep walking!"

Alex grabbed his elbow with his right hand and scurried into the mass of marchers. They continued down Langestrasse, past the Lamberti Church, past the old ducal castle, out of the old city into the heavily traveled thoroughfare called the Damm, and then right into Elisabethstrasse. They were now on the southeastern border of the Schlossgarten, and Alex could look across the pond and through the graceful trees now largely bereft of leaves to the other side of the park. There, beyond the stone walls, was the house on Gartenstrasse where he had lived in such splendor for fourteen years before receiving that nocturnal visit from the two Nazis telling him to sell his house. How foolish his confident rebuff of their threat seemed to him now.

The marchers on Elisabethstrasse, only yards from their destination: the Oldenburg Prison. The two young women in the foreground seem to find the march a reason for merriment.

The march had continued solemnly and quietly, but along the way the procession had picked up a few spectators who evidently were enjoying the sight so much they felt compelled to march along. A few boys and two young women walked cheerfully along the edges of the crowd, smiling and occasionally whispering to each other and laughing. And Markus Gellert continued his irregular cries of, "These are the criminals!"

But after they had walked two hundred yards down the curving Elisabethstrasse, Gellert and three other Storm Troopers began trotting ahead of the procession, signaling to Alex that perhaps they were nearing their destination. And to his amazement he was right. The remaining guards directed them to the left down Gerichtestrasse, where a grinning Brigadeführer Gellert was standing before the entrance to the Oldenburg Prison.

Built before the turn of the century, the prison was then, and remains today, a squat and ugly building of dirty red brick with barbed wire and razor wire surmounting the walls and heavy iron bars covering its few windows. As if in a horrible dream, Alex found himself herded through an open iron gate to the prison courtyard and then into the prison itself. His wallet, his watch, his identification papers, and his hat and coat were taken from him. Then, along with Heinrich Hirschberg, Alex was pushed into a seven-by-ten-foot cell on the prison's ground floor. The cell sported twin bunks, a bucket in a corner, and the over-poweringly foul smell of urine.

Alex's heart thumped and his legs could barely support him, so great were his shock and disbelief. As the guard slammed shut the barred door to his cell, Alex cried out hoarsely, "There must be some mistake! I fought for the kaiser—"

The guard looked back contemptuously. "Too bad, Jewboy. The kaiser's dead. Or hadn't you heard?"

And thus, after living peacefully and honorably in Oldenburg for thirty-two years, not counting the four years he had served his country during the Great War, my grandfather spent an afternoon and a night in prison for the crime of being born a Jew. Those eighteen hours were a watershed in his life; for the rest of the all-too-few years left to him, Alex lived under a sentence of death.

That night, like Falstaff, he heard the chimes at midnight. Each hour, in fact, tolled by the Lamberti Church bells made its way to his ears, which remained unstopped by sleep. Shortly after six, he and the rest of the forty-three were loaded into a bus and driven, this time, to the train station. There they met another thirty-four Jews who had been rounded up from the surrounding countryside. These men had spent much of the past twelve hours cleaning up the rubble from the burned synagogue, glass and stones that had spilled into Peterstrasse and disrupted traffic. Now these seventy-seven citizens were loaded onto a train headed east, a train with 938 Jews between the ages of fourteen and eighty-two crammed into a series of cattle cars, a train bound for the concentration camp called Sachsenhausen.

The new "protective custody" camp of Sachsenhausen had been built by Nazi engineers during the summer of 1936, just as the Nazi government was attempting to prove its legitimacy by hosting the Olympic Games in Berlin. It was located just outside Oranienburg, a town twenty-five miles northwest of Berlin's Olympic Stadium. The new camp was designed to be more modern and efficient than the older facilities that had been used to incarcerate political prisoners of the Reich. The architect had laid out Sachsenhausen in the shape of a massive triangle, with the entrance located in the base of the triangle and the prisoners' barracks ranging out towards the triangle's tip. But so many Jews were shipped to Sachsenhausen after November 9 that the architect's plans had had to be scrapped. The triangle shape was compromised when an additional sixteen barracks were added to the area just below the right-hand portion of the base. Later, the camp's facilities would be augmented by a gas chamber, but not until 1943. One aspect of the original design that the architect insisted on maintaining was the huge *Appellplatz*, or roll-call area, located just inside the main entrance and in front of the first rows of barracks. In this effort he was supported by Sachsenhausen's commandant, Hermann Baranowski, as well as by Baranowski's second in command, a young man who would soon achieve greater notoriety when he was appointed commandant of the extermination camp at Auschwitz. His name was Rudolf Höss.

The train from Oldenburg arrived in Oranienburg at about seven in the evening on Friday, November 11. The fact that the Jewish sabbath had begun probably added to the wretched state of mind of many of the prisoners, as it no doubt did to the pleasure of their captors. The Jews were ordered to make the twenty-minute journey from the train station to the entrance of the camp on foot, but this march was considerably more brutal than the walk through Oldenburg. The prisoners were lined up in rows of five, then quick-marched down the dark road through a light flurry of snow. Every so often, one of the rows of five would be ordered to halt at once. When they did, the row of men behind would stumble into them and fall to the ground, where they would be kicked and beaten with nightsticks and hard rubber truncheons.

At the entrance to Sachsenhausen, the prisoners were handed over to the SS and Commandant Baranowski. Alex Goldschmidt, Heinrich Hirschberg, Leo Trepp, and the hundreds of other Jews walked through the black iron gates that proclaimed the infamous and cynical motto of the camps, *Arbeit macht frei*, or "Work makes you free." They lined up at

The entrance gate to Sachsenhausen Concentration Camp. I took this picture in November of 1998, sixty years after my grandfather passed through the gate as a prisoner. Even empty, and preserved as a memorial, it's a pretty bleak place.

attention in the Appellplatz, standing in the cold wind with the cold harsh glare of spotlights trained on them from the nine lookout towers built into the camp's eight-foot-high walls. There they stood until morning, faced with the threat of a beating if they fell or if they had to urinate, a need that many of them yielded to as the dark hours passed. During the night more than a dozen of the older men dropped dead of exhaustion, cold, or shock.

When gray dawn broke overhead, Alex was issued the standard gray-striped prisoner's uniform, given prisoner number 9961, and assigned to Barracks Number 42, in the new Jewish section of the camp. For the next twenty-five days he arose every morning, lined up for roll call, and then marched to the work zone outside the barracks area, where he assisted in the manufacture of bricks and shoes. He was fifty-nine years old.

For more than five years, the leaders of the Third Reich had been making life increasingly miserable for the Jews of Germany. But many Jews had refused to believe the worst of their country and had continued to hope for the best. Even as law after statute after decree after regulation had been enacted, many Jews retained a naive hope that, with each successive action, the worst was now over. Some persisted in viewing the Nazi propaganda and hate-mongering as essentially harmless, as mere words designed to impress an ignorant fringe of the population. Alex himself would occasionally find solace in the saying, "No meal is eaten as hot as it's cooked," meaning that all the heated rhetoric concealed a cooler, more rational attitude towards the Jews.

But the November Pogrom changed all that, providing conclusive evidence of the ugly, violent soul of National Socialism. In his study of Nazi Germany, Saul Friedländer entertains the possibility that the pogrom was an aspect of some sort of rational policy agenda before concluding that only the basest human emotions were at play on November 9. "At that moment total, abysmal hatred appears as the be-all and end-all of the onslaught. The only immediate aim was to hurt the Jews as badly as the circumstances allowed, by all possible means: to hurt them and to humiliate them. An explosion of sadism threw a particularly lurid light on the entire action and its sequels; it burst forth at all levels, that of the highest leadership and that of the lowliest party members."

Rabbi Leo Trepp, who entered the gates of Sachsenhausen on the same night as my grandfather, was more direct. Writing in his memoirs, Rabbi Trepp declared, "On the 9th of November, 1938, if not before, Germany was morally bankrupt."

14

Vaterland und Vaterhaus

IN DÜSSELDORF, Thursday, November 17, 1938, was a day marked by flags and banners and orotund oratory. First Secretary Ernst vom Rath, a native of Düsseldorf and an utter nobody just two weeks earlier, received a state funeral on that day, a ceremony held in the Old City's Rheinhalle and attended by such luminaries as Adolf Hitler and Foreign Minister Joachim von Ribbentrop. They hailed vom Rath as a hero who had sacrificed himself in defense of the New Germany, an honored and martyred comrade in the ongoing struggle against the Jewish murderers. The *Rheinische Landeszeitung* described the scene as a "gloomy day" in which "we bore Ernst vom Rath to his grave" and "a hundred thousand German citizens lined the streets in silent greeting" as the funeral procession passed by.

On the other side of town, it was a banner day of a different sort. Günther Goldschmidt celebrated his twenty-fifth birthday. And he and Rosemarie Gumpert made a momentous decision.

Ever since he had arrived in Düsseldorf a week before, Günther had lived the life of a fugitive, spending his days inside the small apartment at 17 Boltensternstrasse and venturing outdoors only at night. He occupied himself with practicing his flute—sometimes alone, sometimes with Rosemarie and Julian. They worked on the Beethoven Serenade and another piece for flute, violin, and viola by the German composer Max Reger. But the long-awaited first rehearsal with the Berlin Kulturbund Orchestra did not take place as scheduled; in response to Julian's telephoned inquiry, Günther and Rosemarie learned that the new orchestra season had been indefinitely postponed. On the one hand, Günther felt relieved that he didn't have to take another train back to Berlin so soon after that night of violence. But both Günther and Rosemarie were frustrated that their new life in Berlin would not be starting when they had hoped it would.

Each time the doorbell rang, Günther would run upstairs to a small room underneath the roof, Rosemarie's room, where, much to the consternation of Julian and Else, he slept during his time in the Gumpert home. The apartment was simply too small for him to sleep anywhere else. While that arrangement was certainly pleasurable at night, retreating up the stairs eight or ten times a day only added to my father's feelings of being a man on the run, a criminal. Luckily, the doorbell had always proved harmless; the police had not come looking for him simply because they didn't know he was there.

On Sunday, November 13, he had called home, spoken to his mother and found out that his father had been taken away. Now he knew that his instincts on the park bench in Berlin had been right. What if he had gone home to Oldenburg and joined his family? He certainly could have done nothing to help his father; more than likely he, too, would have met his father's fate. All those rational thoughts notwithstanding, deep feelings of guilt gnawed at Günther, and not for the last time.

The modest celebration of his birthday did little to lighten his mood. Else cooked a special sauerbraten, and after dinner Julian played a movement from one of the Bach partitas for solo violin in his honor. At about nine o'clock, Günther and Rosemarie slipped outside for a walk. It was a warm, windy, cloudy night. The remaining leaves on the linden trees lining the street rustled overhead as the two young people strolled along, eyes down, hands clasped.

"I spoke with my mother again today," he said. "She's very upset, naturally. The police are maintaining their ridiculous story that my father was taken into custody for his own protection. She doesn't believe a word of it, of course, but she can't get them to tell her when he'll be released or what he's doing or even exactly where he is. She sounded terrible; I don't think she's slept a wink all week."

"Did she remember to wish you a happy birthday?" asked Rosemarie.

"She did, and then she started to cry. It was pretty horrible, really. I almost cried, too . . . Maybe I should have gone home. Maybe I should go there now."

"No," insisted Rosemarie. "You did the right thing in coming here, the safe thing. And it's so important to me that you came here. You could have gone anywhere, but you chose to be where I am. Two years ago, you could have stayed in Sweden, yet you chose to come back to Germany to be with me. And now, with your life in danger, you chose me again."

She stopped walking and looked up at him as linden leaves drifted down from above.

"All I've ever really known in my life so far has been music. And that's been wonderful—this gift I've received from my father. He's been such a good teacher, he's shown me so much: how to make a phrase lead naturally and beautifully into the next phrase, how to make music a substitute for words so that I can tell people the most marvelous stories."

She looked away, shut her eyes.

"But away from music, I hardly know my father at all. And he's not been at all kind to my mother. You know, for a time back at our house in Hösel, he had one of his students actually living upstairs! Frau Wunderwald, her name was. My mother and I did our best to convince ourselves that she really *was* just a student. But I think we always knew better."

Rosemarie bent down to pick up a fallen leaf, and twirled it by its stem.

"So I've learned a lot from my father. But I've learned so much from you, too, these past two years. About music, yes, but also about art and poetry and . . . " She smiled. " . . . about how to pack a picnic basket. And now, with everything that's happening all around us, I'm worried about losing you. Thank you for coming here last week!"

Günther's pulse quickened. A few half-remembered lines from Heinrich Heine whispered to him as he put his arms around Rosemarie and kissed her.

"Let's go inside," he said.

Half an hour later they lay snugly in her little bed in the room under the roof. They had turned out the lights and lit a small candle that stood on a bookshelf beside the bed. The single window was open a crack to let in the warm and breezy night, and shadows cast by the candle's dancing flame cavorted across the walls. They held each other and listened to each other's breathing and the wind in the trees outside.

A knock sounded softly on the door, which opened slowly a moment later. Else's gray head appeared. She whispered, "I've just come to say good night, children. I hope you had a nice day, Günther." A pause. "Sleep well, both of you." The gray head shook, there was a thin little sigh, then the head withdrew and the door swung shut.

Günther and Rosemarie looked at each other a moment, then pulled the covers over their heads and exploded in a storm of silent giggles. The bed shook violently for a full minute as they gasped and choked and struggled for air. Finally they managed to control themselves and they lifted the covers from their faces and wiped the tears from their eyes. Rosemarie coughed and grinned wickedly at Günther.

"We've shocked her no end, you know. Just think, her little daughter in bed with a man who isn't her husband!"

"Well," replied Günther, "I guess it *is* shocking from her way of thinking. And she was very nice about it. After all, I *am* just a guest."

Rosemarie flopped over on her back, staring up at the ceiling.

"At least she came in to wish us good night. My father won't even do that. He's even more shocked than she is, which is just a little hypocritical, wouldn't you say?"

They lay side by side in silence for a few minutes, watching the shadows, listening to the wind. Then Rosemarie spoke again.

"When do you think we'll be able to go back to Berlin and continue the season? I was so looking forward to getting out of here and making music again."

"I don't know. Your father said 'indefinitely postponed.' I suppose it could be a few weeks or months. I'm not sure it's even safe yet for me to walk the streets in the daytime, let alone travel back to Berlin. I don't even know if we have a place to live. God knows what happened to Herr Hoffmann."

"Oh Günther, what's going to happen to us?" A note of despair sounded in her voice.

It was then that those words from Heine, those lines that had tickled Günther's memory on the street, came to him.

Entflieh mit mir und sei mein Weib, und ruh an meinem
*   Herzen aus;*
Fern in der Fremde sei mein Herz, dein Vaterland und
*   Vaterhaus.*

He rolled over, clasped her to him, closed his eyes, and began to speak from deep inside.

"When I was living in Oldenburg, so often I felt like a stranger in my own home. Then I left home to study in Sondershausen and Karlsruhe, but even before I was asked to leave those places, part of me still felt like a stranger, an outsider. I'm not sure why. Of course the Nazis did their very best to make me even more of an outsider, so I left before they could really hurt me. Then I lived in Sweden and again I was a stranger, though I could live freely. But by then I had already met a wonderful young woman in Frankfurt, someone who immediately made me feel at home and at peace. So when she told me there was a way I could live near her and see her and work with her, I jumped at the chance, even though it meant moving back to this land where I'm not welcome, where I, we, all of us are in danger."

He swallowed, continued.

"She, you, have become my home these last two years. That's why I came here last week, because this is my home, wherever you are. But this week I've noticed that you feel like a stranger in your house as I did in mine. Maybe it's your father, maybe it's something else. I think you need a home away from this house. But I don't think you should go anywhere alone. And I don't think I can go anywhere alone. Not anymore. Certainly not now, not with all this ugliness and violence everywhere."

He took a deep breath.

"Rosemarie, *entflieh mit mir und sei mein Weib.* 'Come fly with me and be my wife, and rest yourself in my heart. Even in this strange land my heart will be your Fatherland, your father's house.' Rosemarie, marry me. We'll create a home for each other. We'll make music together. We'll protect each other. We'll make each other happy."

She looked at him in the half-darkness. And then she smiled. *"Mein Vaterland und Vaterhaus.* Yes, Günther, I'll fly with you. Yes."

My father returned her smile, laughed joyously, blew out the candle. Smoke wreathed and curled upward. Silently, awed but very pleased with what they had pledged, Günther and Rosemarie held each other tightly in the little bed in the room beneath the roof.

THEY INFORMED the municipal officials of their desire to get married and were told that the first available date in Düsseldorf's City Hall was December 13. I think it's a nice coincidence, because Heinrich Heine was born in Düsseldorf on December 13, 1797. Since he had already played an important part in their lives and then helped inspire Günther's proposal, I've always imagined him as an unseen guest at the wedding.

There were precious few corporeal guests. On December 7, Alex Goldschmidt was suddenly released from the camp in Sachsenhausen, with the understanding that he must leave the country within six months. He arrived home in Oldenburg the following day and immediately took to his bed to recover from more than three weeks of physical labor and abuse. He was still feeling weak and ill five days later, so only Günther's mother, Toni, took the train to Düsseldorf to join Julian and Else as witnesses to the marriage of their children.

Tuesday, December 13, dawned on a leaden sky and occasional snow. That afternoon the five members of the wedding party took a taxi to Düsseldorf's sixteenth-century City Hall, arriving early for their four-thirty appointment. Günther and Julian were clad in dark blue suits, the older women wore their best skirts and freshly pressed white blouses, and Rosemarie wore her favorite outfit—a white blouse and a deep blue skirt with white polka dots. She carried a bouquet of yellow and purple pansies. It was the first time the five of them had all ventured downtown since the violence of November 9, and the mood in the taxi was both giddy and apprehensive.

On the way into the Old City, Günther found himself mulling over a question that had occurred to him more than once since the night of the pogrom: why had Julian Gumpert escaped arrest? As a prominent musician and teacher, he was one of the most visible members of Düsseldorf's Jewish community. With his own father's fate weighing heavily on his mind, and vaguely aware of what had happened to other Jews around the country, Günther found it hard to believe that the Nazis had decided to leave Julian alone out of either inefficiency or compassion. Then he remembered Julian's outsize personality and his skill at making friends and wondered whether the local Party members might have more than the usual weakness for bonhomie.

The unsettling question of the source of Julian's freedom occurred to Günther again after they had all walked up the steps of City Hall and asked directions to the office of the Justice of the Peace. When they entered the official chambers, Günther saw a man in the brown uniform of the SA come striding toward them and thought at first that they had stumbled into the wrong room. But the man was smiling broadly, and he and Julian shook hands as heartily as if they had been neighbors.

"Mr. Gumpert, how nice to see you this afternoon. I hope you have been well."

"Yes, Mr. Haas, quite well, quite well. This is my wife, Else; this is Toni Goldschmidt, the mother of the young man you are about to make my son-in-law; and of course this is the happy couple, Günther Goldschmidt and my daughter, Rosemarie."

Mr. Haas gave the "happy couple" a tight-lipped smile and a proper German bow, clicking his heels together and inclining his head sharply.

"Yes, this is an important day, a very important day. Now, if you would please come this way."

He led the party through a doorway and into an adjoining room, a space dominated by an enormous portrait of Adolf Hitler. Der Führer was standing in a pristine flowery meadow near his Alpine retreat of Berchtesgaden. His soldier's cape was draped theatrically over his shoulders, his back was straight, his gaze directed solemnly toward the distant peaks. His right hand rested on the noble head of a large German Shepherd that sat proudly at his feet. Here was a man watching tenderly yet protectively over the welfare of his people. And today he would oversee my parents' wedding.

Mr. Haas directed everyone to a small table, on which they found an inkwell, a pen, a stamp, and a pile of documents. Seating himself at the table, he proceeded to fill out an official Family Book, recording the fact that on this 13th of December in the City of Düsseldorf the musician Günther Ludwig Goldschmidt, Jewish, born in Oldenburg on November 17, 1913, and Rosemarie Gumpert, Jewish, born in Düsseldorf on January 6, 1917, entered into matrimony. He then listed the parents: of Günther, Alexander Goldschmidt, salesman, Jewish, and Toni Behrens, Jewish; and of Rosemarie, Julian Gumpert, musician, Jewish, and Else Hayn, Jewish.

All this time, Günther was somewhat nervously wondering what he should say if Mr. Haas happened to ask him where his father was. "Oh, he couldn't make it. He's home in bed, trying to recover from what your friends put him through last month." But luckily Mr. Haas just kept his head down, writing busily. When he finished filling in all the lines in the Family Book, he notarized the document with a red postage stamp bearing the words "City of Düsseldorf" and then canceled it with the official seal of the Third Reich, an eagle with spread wings bearing in its talons the sign of the swastika.

Finally he stood up, straightened his uniform, and arranged Günther and Rosemarie into position directly beneath the portrait of Hitler. The three parents stood awkwardly a few feet away. Mr. Haas asked Günther if he was entering this marriage of his own free will. He said that he was. Mr. Haas then asked the same question of Rosemarie. She said that she was. Mr. Haas then repeated the question to them both and together they answered that they were. The Justice of the Peace then said, "In the name of the Reich I declare you to be henceforth and forevermore husband and wife."

There was a moment of silence. Günther had been gazing dreamily at Rosemarie but was suddenly startled into the realization that the ceremony was over. Mr. Haas walked over to Julian Gumpert and began pumping his hand enthusiastically. The two mothers embraced. As Günther turned to kiss his bride, his eyes were intercepted by those of the man on the wall above his head; when his lips met Rosemarie's he felt a chill run through his body.

The little family spent a minute embracing, clapping one another on the back, and murmuring words of congratulations, then turned and followed Mr. Haas back to the outer office. The whole thing had lasted less than twenty minutes. As everyone struggled into their coats, Julian and Mr. Haas shared a moment alone together; they laughed heartily and Günther recalled his thoughts about his father-in-law's singular fortune where the police were concerned. When they left his office, Mr. Haas called after them, "Merry Christmas!"

Snow was falling as they walked down the steps of City Hall into the old square, which was dominated by a statue of the seventeenth-century duke, Jan Wellem. Just then the bells in nearby St. Stephen's Church, a fourteenth-century edifice with a tall and twisted spire, began to chime the hour of five o'clock. It was the only music my parents heard that dark afternoon, and to Rosemarie the deep hollow sound was gloomy rather than joyous. They rode back to Boltensternstrasse in silence.

That evening Else prepared a simple meal in honor of the newlyweds. Julian tried to be cheerful, offering toast after toast, but Toni began to cry during dinner and excused herself from the table. As soon as they decently could, Günther and Rosemarie escaped to their little haven under the roof. Their first day as husband and wife had been dark and sad, slightly unreal, and utterly without festivities.

That night Günther dreamed that he and Rosemarie were on a train, happily setting off on an exciting journey. But outside, rain poured down, lightning flashed, the wind howled. And they both realized they had lost their timetable and forgotten their destination. When they sought help from the conductor, he only grinned and said nothing. All they could do was cling to each other as the train hurtled on into darkness.

15

"One Slap after
the Other"

IN THE DAYS immediately following the November Pogrom, newspapers around the world carried the shocking news to their readers. Most major American dailies carried front-page stories that attempted to describe the damage. Among the headlines on November 11 were these: in the *Dallas Morning News*, "Hysterical Nazis Wreck Thousands of Jewish Shops, Burn Synagogues in Wild Orgy of Looting and Terror"; in the *San Francisco Chronicle*, "Germany Goes Berserk in Orgy of Jew-Baiting; Hate-Crazed Mobs Mill in Streets Burning and Looting as Police Look On Indulgently"; and in the *Baltimore Sun*, "Nazi Reprisals Believed Doom of Jewish Life."

Editorial writers, too, had their say. Nearly a thousand different editorials appeared in American newspapers alone, in journals of all sizes and circulations, all of them condemning the events of the previous days in the strongest possible terms. The European press was no less vehement. A single example is the Danish *Nationaltidende* of Saturday, November 12:

There happen in the course of time many things on which one must take a stand out of regard for one's own human dignity, even if this should involve a personal or national risk. Silence in the face of crimes committed may be regarded as a form of participation therein—equally punishable whether committed by individuals or by nations. One must at least have the courage to protest, even if you feel that you do not have power to prevent a violation of justice, or even to mitigate the consequences thereof . . .

The Nazis took note, although at first they insisted that such reactions would have no effect. On that same Saturday, the first full day of Alex Goldschmidt's incarceration, Propaganda Minister Joseph Goebbels wrote an article in the Nazi newspaper *Völkischer Beobachter* titled "The Grynszpan Case." In part, it read:

The death of Ernst vom Rath was supposed to be a beacon of hope for all of world Jewry in its fight against Germany. The murder was meant as a warning. But in the end the shot backfired. The German people rather than the world were warned.

It is obvious that a nation of 80 million people cannot accept such provocations in silence. The spontaneous acts of revenge against Jews in Germany, the outbursts that erupted in the night from November 9 to 10 showed that the German people's patience had run out.

How does the German-hating, largely Jewish, foreign press respond to the spontaneous consequences of the shots fired in Paris that took place in Germany? It tries to give the impression that a civil war is going on. Endless gruesome fairy tales are invented. Above all, the Jewish press in North America rises to a fever pitch as never before. The spontaneous reactions of the German people are explained as having been the work of organized groups. These word manipulators have no idea what Germany is about. What would the reactions have looked like had they indeed been organized!

The German-hating foreign press should know this: by misrepresenting what happened by manipulation and lies, they are helping neither themselves nor the Jews in Germany. To the contrary. The German people are an anti-Semitic people. They neither wish nor desire any longer to have their rights limited by a parasitic Jewish race. What privileges the Jews of Germany are afforded in public, private or business life depend entirely on the behavior of the Jews themselves and above all on that of the Jews of the world. In any event, the German government is determined to maintain peace and order at home, and peace and order are best achieved when the wishes and needs of the German people are reflected in the solution to the problem.

The German-hating outside would be well served to allow the problem to be solved by the Germans themselves. But to the extent that others feel the need to speak on behalf of the German Jews or to take them in, rest assured that Jews in any numbers are at their disposal.

Let us all be clear about one thing: the Jew Grynszpan was a representative of world Jewry. The German vom Rath was a representative of the German people. Thus, Jewry shot at the German people in Paris. The reaction of the German government has been, and will be, legal but harsh.

The reaction, as rendered in the next wave of anti-Jewish decrees, was harsh indeed. First came a four-hour meeting at the Air Transport Ministry, the headquarters of Field Marshal Hermann Göring, on that eventful November 12. This was the session that produced the notorious fine of one billion marks against the Jews for causing all the damage during the night of November 9. The meeting was attended by Göring, Goebbels, and ten more cabinet ministers and high-ranking German officials.

A representative of the German insurance companies, Eduard Hilgard, pointed out that damage to the shattered windows of Jewish shops alone was expected to run well over five million marks, and that figure did not begin to cover the damage to other materials and to the businesses themselves; Hilgard estimated that the total bill might exceed twenty-five million marks. Many insurance companies in Germany would go bankrupt if forced to honor the thousands of claims that were starting to pour in.

"So, don't honor them," shrugged Göring.

But Hilgard pointed out that many of those same insurance companies had clients in foreign countries, and if word got out that certain firms had reneged on their policies, they could forget about doing business in London, Brussels, Amsterdam, or Paris. In short, concluded Herr

Hilgard, the German insurance industry had a serious problem on its hands and, by extension, so too did the German government.

The Field Marshal considered the dilemma for a few minutes and then announced his solution: the insurance companies would pay the Jews in full, thus honoring their contracts and preserving their reputations. Then the government would step in and confiscate all payments, returning a portion of them to the insurers. Herr Hilgard grumbled that his people would still be out a fair amount of money, but Göring replied that he should be grateful for what he got, and then abruptly showed him the door.

As the meeting continued, Field Marshal Göring introduced his "Decree to Exclude Jews from German Economic Life." As of January 1, 1939, all Jewish business activity would come to a halt with the introduction of a process of "Aryanization." Jews would be forbidden to act as managers, and Aryan surrogates, mostly appointed by the Party, would be installed. The new managers would first take over the books and eventually the whole enterprise. The same decree compelled Jews to sell, usually at rock-bottom prices, their land holdings, stocks, jewels, and works of art, thus inaugurating the infamous confiscation of private treasures that has enriched many a museum over the past half-century.

With economic matters out of the way, the meeting descended to the realm of how to exclude Jews from the pleasures of ordinary civilized living. Göring and Goebbels began to argue about how best to segregate Jews from Germans on railway trains. If, for instance, you had a separate car just for the Jews, what would happen on a crowded train if the Aryan cars were full and the Jews in their own car had plenty of room to stretch out and enjoy the ride? Wouldn't that be an intolerable situation for the Aryans who, of course, couldn't be expected to find a seat in the Jewish car but would be left with no choice but to stand in their own? Ah, said Goebbels, let's pass a law that forbids Jews to sit down until every German has found a seat. To which Göring responded, "Should the train be overcrowded, we won't need a law. We'll just kick the Jew out and he will have to sit all alone in the toilet the whole way."

Goebbels then raised the idea of separate benches for Jews in public parks, which indeed led to the installation of benches marked with signs reading "Aryans Only!" But the propaganda minister was only getting started. Regarding the matter of the hundreds of ruined synagogues that now dotted the German landscape, Goebbels suggested that Jews be made to level the remains with picks and shovels and turn the sites into parking lots for the convenience of Aryan citizens. He then insisted that Jews be excluded from nearly all aspects of daily life in Germany: from schools, movies, parks, beaches, ice-skating rinks, resorts, even forests.

"These days packs of Jews run around loose in the Grunewald; it is a constant provocation, we constantly have incidents," said Goebbels. "What they do is so annoying and so provoking that, naturally, there are brawls all the time."

The ever-practical Göring replied that they could reserve certain areas of the forests for the Jews, and stock those sections with animals that resemble the Jews, so that each species could feel acclimated. For instance, he said, "the elk has a crooked nose, just like they do."

Before the meeting broke up, a man who had remained largely silent throughout the proceedings raised his hand. It was Reinhard Heydrich, head of the SD secret police, a shadowy and particularly ruthless member of the inner circle. (Shortly after the Nazi takeover in 1933, while various factions and individuals were jostling for power and position under Hitler, someone started a rumor that Heydrich's grandmother was Jewish because her middle name was Sarah. To protect his reputation, he had her headstone dynamited and replaced with a new one that omitted the offending name.) He reminded Göring and Goebbels that the main challenge that faced them all, beyond such petty matters as trains and forests, was how to make sure that every Jew was properly identified and, ultimately, how to get the Jews out of Germany once and for all. It was then that Heydrich proposed the idea that would become reality less than three years hence: that every person defined as a Jew by the Nuremberg Laws be required to wear a special badge or emblem. They would fill in the detail, the yellow star, later.

During the meeting's final minutes, Göring declared that only the economic measures would be announced as official decrees that day. But Goebbels took one last opportunity to remind the group of the importance of his ideas, that economic issues were fine as far as they went but that they should be "underpinned by a number of propa-ganda and cultural measures so that everything should happen right away and that, this week, the Jews should have their ears slapped, one slap after the other."

The slaps came as promised, although it took longer than a week to administer all of them. The first slap came the following Tuesday, November 15, when all Jewish children in German public schools were expelled. The official announcement stated:

> After the heinous murder in Paris one cannot demand of any German teacher to continue to teach Jewish children. It is also self-evident that it is unbearable for German schoolchildren to sit in the same classrooms with Jewish children. Therefore, effec-tive immediately, attendance at German schools is no longer per-mitted to Jews. They are allowed to attend only Jewish schools. Insofar as this has not yet happened, all Jewish schoolchildren who at this time are still attending a German school must be dismissed.

One of the thousands of German Jewish schoolchildren affected by this order was seventeen-year-old Helmut Goldschmidt, Günther's brother, who was expelled from the Oldenburg Realschule two years short of his expected graduation.

Next came the edict of November 19, which excluded Jews from the general welfare system. Ten days later, Jews were forbidden to keep carrier pigeons. On December 3, driver's licenses belonging to Jews were declared invalid. And then, on December 6—the Christian feast of St. Nicholas—Propaganda Minister Goebbels's exclusionary ideas were revealed en masse: Jews were banned from all theaters, cinemas, caba-rets, concert halls, museums, fairs, exhibition halls, stadiums, sports fields, and skating rinks. From that day forward, the only entertainment venue open to Jews was the Jüdische Kulturbund.

In the month since the pogrom the Kulturbund's value to the Nazis had increased, albeit strictly for propaganda purposes. Goebbels's tough talk regarding his indifference to the foreign press notwithstanding, he and Chancellor Hitler were well aware of the international outcry. The reaction was not limited to the newspapers; on November 14, two days after the Air Transport Ministry meeting, President Franklin Roosevelt recalled the U.S. ambassador to Berlin, Hugh Wilson, for what were termed "consultations." Ambassador Wilson never returned to Germany. That same day, the German ambassador to Washington, Hans Dieckhoff, cabled Berlin that, because of the pogrom, "a hurricane is raging here." On November 18, Ambassador Dieckhoff, too, was recalled; he also never returned to his post.

In that atmosphere, the Kulturbund suddenly appeared to the Nazis to be their ace in the hole, a device to show the outraged outside world that Jewish activities in Germany were proceeding normally. Minister Goebbels, who on November 10 had curtly informed the Kubu that it was to be shut down until further notice, instructed Hans Hinkel to get in touch with the board of directors on the evening of November 12 to tell them that "soon" the Kubu would be permitted to perform again. But even the Nazis couldn't restore the Kulturbund to life immediately.

For at this most turbulent time in its history, the Kulturbund was something of a rudderless ship. In mid-October, soon after *Rigoletto*'s closing night, Heinz Condell, who had created the sets and costumes for that opera and many others in the past five years, had traveled to the United States with another Kubu official, Herbert Fischer, for what they said would be a six-week vacation. During the first week of November, just days before the pogrom, a letter arrived from America informing the Kulturbund that, despite their contracts, neither Condell nor Fischer was planning to return to Berlin.

Coincidentally, Kurt Singer was also in the United States, having sailed to New York for a fund-raising and fact-finding tour. Concerned about the Kubu's membership figures, which had continued to decline even after the success of *Rigoletto*, Dr. Singer had dreams of discovering some wealthy American investors and maybe even arranging for a few benefit performances in the New World by Kubu artists. So it was that on the afternoon of November 9, the Kulturbund's director was four thousand miles away from Kommandantenstrasse. The next day, after hearing the shocking news on the radio, Kurt Singer immediately boarded a ship bound for Amsterdam.

During Singer's absence, the leadership of the Kulturbund had fallen to Werner Levie, the onetime journalist and economist who had joined the organization in 1933 as its administrative director and, since the creation of the umbrella organization—the Reichsverband—in 1935, had served as its general secretary. It was Levie who received the message from Goebbels on November 10 that all Kulturbund activities were to be suspended. From the tone of the message and a follow-up call from one of the minister's assistants, Levie assumed that the whole operation was going to be shut down for good, and he shared that impression with his staff. He was very surprised when, two days later, he and two members of the Kulturbund's board were summoned to Hans Hinkel's office and informed that matters had changed.

Hinkel began the meeting by reminding Levie that the theater and offices on Kommandantenstrasse had escaped the destruction so common among Jewish establishments on Wednesday night. It was true. Thanks to two uniformed Storm Troopers who stood guard all night, not a pane of glass had been destroyed at Kulturbund headquarters. Why would your offices be spared, Hinkel inquired, if we didn't have a plan for your return to work? He then revealed that it was Minister Goebbels's desire that Kulturbund performances resume "soon," if at all possible. Something in his manner suggested to Levie that Hinkel was under some pressure to see to it that Goebbels's wish should come true.

Levie went back to Kommandantenstrasse and called a meeting of the whole board to inform them of the situation and to decide on the nature of their response. Some board members were of the opinion that the Kulturbund should refuse to go back to work. Thousands of Jews across Germany had been arrested, including scores of Kulturbund artists. Among them were the actor and director Fritz Wisten of their own Berlin theater and the composer Max Kowalski, Günther and Rosemarie's friend from Frankfurt, who had been sent to the Buchenwald concentration camp. Given all of that, these board members declared angrily, how could the Kulturbund, in good conscience, continue to do Minister Goebbels's bidding?

Others, however, saw an opening and perhaps even an opportunity in what Werner Levie believed was a certain urgency in Hinkel's message. If reopening the Kulturbund was important to Goebbels, they reasoned, maybe they could use his desire against him as a kind of moral leverage. Slowly the board arrived at a strategy aimed at getting as many of their colleagues released from custody as possible.

The next day Levie went back to the Ministry of Propaganda with a list of about two hundred people who had been arrested during the pogrom. He told Hinkel that, although the Kulturbund would be more than willing to mount performances in the coming days, the detention of these people made it impossible, since many of them—Fritz Wisten in particular—were essential to the organization. If something could be done about their absences, Levie coolly informed Hinkel, the season could be resumed.

Commissioner Hinkel left the room. When he returned, he announced that Wisten would be released from "protective custody" within forty-eight hours and that the others on the list would follow shortly thereafter. Hinkel then wanted to know if the Kulturbund could present a performance in three days' time. Levie asked for nine days, explaining that rehearsals were needed. His request was granted, and the two adversaries agreed that the theater would open for business on Tuesday, November 22. Hinkel promised that the Nazi press and radio would promote the evening and assure the Kulturbund's audience that they would be in no danger if they attended.

Some members of the Kulturbund's board were unhappy at the prospect of giving the Nazis more protective cover. And, indeed, the government immediately spread the word of the reopened Kubu as proof of a "return to normalcy." But the majority thought that they had accomplished something tangible in their negotiations with Hinkel. Kurt Baumann, the man who had created the original concept of the Kulturbund in 1933, wrote in his memoirs: "Apart from everything else, the fact that we succeeded in saving two hundred Jewish people from the concentration camps made the founding of a Jewish Kulturbund and its continuation in that critical time worthwhile."

The next debate to embroil the Kulturbund board was what play they should perform on November 22. What would be appropriate, which choice would make the proper statement, what could they do that would satisfy both their desire to mark the calamitous events of November 9 and their need to steer clear of further Nazi sanctions?

In the end, it was decided that the safe choice and the practical choice would also be the most satisfying choice: on November 22, the Kulturbund theater would reopen with the scheduled production of *Rain and Wind* by W. Somerset Maugham. They had already secured permission to perform the play, so that wouldn't be a problem. Rehearsals, under the direction of Fritz Wisten, had begun a few days before the pogrom. Once Wisten was released, the process could just pick up where it had been abandoned; a week's time was enough, the board reasoned, to prepare for opening night. And by quietly picking up the pieces of the season and going forward with their original plans, the Kulturbund would demonstrate that no amount of terror or brutality could subvert the organization's true purpose of bringing art and entertainment to the Jews of Berlin. A subtle statement it may have been, but it was put forth with deep conviction and all the moral strength the Kulturbund could muster.

On the evening of November 22, the actors arrived at the theater on Kommandantenstrasse fully believing that they would play to a half-empty house. In the aftermath of the pogrom, who would venture out at night to an openly Jewish establishment to see a German translation of an English drama? To everyone's surprise, however, every seat was full by curtain time. The Nazis had kept their promise to promote the event heavily in the newspapers and on radio, and doubtless that effort had an effect. But also, after two weeks of ugliness and uncertainty, the Kulturbund audience was more than ready for a little beauty.

The people not only came, they came dressed as for an important night out. And far from sitting there woodenly, as many of the actors had feared, they responded enthusiastically, laughing at the play's occasional lighthearted moments and applauding vigorously at the end of each act. The actors were amazed, and very moved. There were tears in the dressing rooms when the final curtain fell.

So the Kubu was back, but what of its future? Two days later Werner Levie, Dutch by birth, traveled to Amsterdam to meet with Kurt Singer, whose boat from New York had arrived the previous week. Levie had expected to find Singer full of plans and ideas for this next phase of Kulturbund activity. Instead, Levie was shocked to find a Kurt Singer who didn't even want to accompany him back to Berlin. For three days the two men discussed the situation from morning until late at night.

In the end, Levie returned to Germany alone and reported to Hans Hinkel that Kurt Singer saw no point in taking up the reins of the Kulturbund again as, in his opinion, it was on the verge of becoming a moribund organization.

Levie also shared Singer's conclusions with his colleagues at the Kulturbund. Nothing the Dutchman said, however, could have prepared them for the extraordinary letter that Kurt Singer sent to Kommandantenstrasse on December 4. Dramatic, sentimental, self-important, a touch overwrought, it was typical Singer. And yet its message must have been a severe jolt.

> Dear friends, if I can finish this letter without breaking my heart then I know that my nerves are of steel. I know at this moment, and have felt this way for weeks, that your strength to carry on must be incredible. And in such a difficult time, in which everything seems to be threatened, I stand apart from you even if in my spirit I am amongst you. I'm looking at you from afar, from a very lonely distance. I'm like a wild duck who cannot fly. I have been deeply wounded. The Kulturbund without me, I without the Kulturbund . . . this is the very end. What we have achieved together from our heroic beginnings— the stormy rise, the victories, the failures—what a courageous pillar it was, even as the ground shook beneath us. What a cooperative, mutual effort—a personal gain for us and even a bigger gain for all the Jewish people. It is a possession, an eternal gift, we cannot lose.

> We have overcome many crises together. But the crisis facing us now seems to me to be so fundamental that I no longer see a solution. My optimism has collapsed. In the face of this shock to our Jewish souls I am without strength, and lost. I mourn the work that must be sacrificed to this situation. I suffer with those who have to carry the wreckage on their strong shoulders. And thus I must say to you after long reflection: "Take my crown and glory away from me."

> From afar I cannot see into your souls. I hope that all of you still believe in the rest of your accomplishments and that

you fulfill your tasks with all the passion of the artist. I myself in the last weeks of doubt have become a nonbeliever, without hope. I returned from America in order to be with you in the hour of your most difficult fight, even though people tried to keep me back and even though I could have stayed. At a time of utmost need I wanted to and yet could not be a private person in a secure situation. Here in Europe I was first able to calculate the chances of the work of the Jüdische Kulturbund to succeed. The result of my calculation was abysmal.

I had to and must believe that in a short period of time no Jewish actors, musicians, or artists who are of good quality will be left in Germany. There won't be enough people who will be receptive to our concerts, plays, cabarets. There won't be enough money. I see in front of me a path that leads into provincial efforts at scenery, costumes, selection of material. I see a deadly lack of energy in all departments. The press is quiet. There's no reaction from the public. If I came back, it would be like a captain trying to get the water out of an already sunken ship using just his bare hands. I don't believe that I would be able to reconstruct that which has fallen or to lift that which has sunk. I no longer believe that I could be anything more to the people that I led than a comrade in suffering.

Maybe you'll succeed once again in raising this sunken ship. My blessings accompany such a rescue attempt in which I cannot participate. But this one guilt I do not want to burden my conscience: that I came back and, despite all my efforts and the last of my strength, I still couldn't make the enterprise work again. If the Kulturbund fails—and I can't envision anything else—then it will not be for lack of virtue and courage. But I couldn't even maintain the great talent we used to have. The time has come for us to take a step backward. The idea of the Kulturbund belongs to history. But in the great book I shall write, your names will be written as if etched in marble.

I want to assure you that I will be with you even as I am apart from you, no more at the head but one of many. As long as I am in Holland I will serve the committee in an honorary way. I will keep my eyes open. I will direct your wishes to the center of the art world. I will work, work, work for you. I will be more effective here than I ever could be in Germany. So I don't feel separate from you and I know I haven't broken the ties of loyalty. Every sign that you are thinking of me and remembering me will keep me going. And this spiritual strength should help you in some way.

In this hour of external separation accept my thanks, my recognition of your, our, joint work. Accept my praise. I will not forget a single worker, from the man who cleans the toilets to the department heads, the actors, musicians, singers. I have loved you all and I will protect this love until my last breath. If the administration remains the same, if Wisten directs the theater, Schwarz and Sander direct our music, Bab does the lectures, Sondheimer oversees the staging and costumes—then I am replaced and will continue my work quietly.

Live well, retain your strength, be united, and hold the belief, the Jewish faith, high. In unchangeable loyalty, despite everything, Kurt Singer.

What a blow this must have been to the staff of the Kulturbund! Their founder and leader no longer saw their efforts as worthwhile; the Kulturbund, in his eyes, was a ship that had already sunk and could not be salvaged. And their future promised nothing but provincial mediocrity. Nevertheless, they should carry on. It would take five people to replace him, Dr. Singer immodestly pointed out, and even then it wouldn't really be the same without him.

And what an effort it must have taken Dr. Singer to write that letter! He had put so much of himself into the Kulturbund over the past five and a half years: planning, directing, organizing, cajoling, promoting, negotiating, always trying to stay one step ahead of the next institutional or ideological objection the Nazis would be sure to raise, all the while living under the same soul-sapping tyranny that was the lot of every German Jew. Then, during his few days in New York he was a free man, able to go anywhere and do or say anything without fear of running afoul of the authorities. When he heard of the terror of the November Pogrom, his laudable instinct was to join his Kubu colleagues in their "time of utmost need." But he had several days aboard ship to think things over, to compare the freedom he'd just enjoyed with the oppression that waited for him back in Berlin. By the time he landed in Holland he must have felt a most understandable concern for his personal safety. Surely it was the prudent thing to stay in Amsterdam, far (for now) from the reach of his oppressors. But he was still the same Kurt Singer who had excoriated the artists who had had the temerity to think of their own skins before the good of the Kulturbund. So in his guilt-laden letter he needed to construct a justifiable reason to stay away, and he found one in his image of the Kulturbund as a sunken ship. But how painful it must have been for him to abandon his post on the bridge. And, despite his assertion that he had not "broken the ties of loyalty," how disloyal he must have felt. I think Singer must have borne a heavy burden of guilt after sending that letter, a burden that helps to explain his decision in 1943 to accept enthusiastically the German order that sent him to the "model" concentration camp of Theresienstadt.

Meanwhile, life went on in the offices on Kommandantenstrasse. The board of the Kulturbund named Werner Levie artistic director, Hans Zander administrative director, Fritz Wisten theater director, and Rudolf Schwarz music director. Within a few days, word came from Hans Hinkel's office that the Nazis approved of those choices and that money would continue to be made available to assist the Kubu in its efforts. Those funds would either come directly from the Reich in the form of a grant or from what were termed "Jewish means," Nazi code language for money or goods confiscated from the Jews in the aftermath of the pogrom.

On December 16—Beethoven's birthday—Werner Levie was summoned to a meeting in the offices of the Ministry of Propaganda. There he was informed of several significant changes in the organizational structure of the Kulturbund. First of all, the Reich Association of Jewish Culture Associations was to be abolished as of January 1,

1939, and no Kulturbund outside of Berlin would continue to exist. The name of the single remaining organization would be Jüdischer Kulturbund in Deutschland, e. V. (Incorporated). From now on, the leaders of the Kulturbund would be required to open their books to the Nazis every month to insure no financial improprieties or precipitous losses. Permission would have to be obtained for any special expenses or purchases. All hires, even temporary employees, would have to be approved by the Ministry of Propaganda. And Werner Levie would be expected at the ministry two or three times a week to report on Kubu activities and to receive orders.

Why were these new strictures and regulations put into effect at that time? Well, they seem a logical extension of the post-pogrom crackdown resulting from the Air Transport Ministry meeting on November 12. In other words, these were just the latest "slaps" administered by Minister Goebbels. And I can only imagine that the Nazis resented the fact that they needed the Kulturbund as a propaganda shield and were highly annoyed that Werner Levie had manipulated them into releasing those two hundred Jewish artists. If the Kubu was to remain alive, the cost would be tighter controls.

And there was to be one more turn of the screw. Also as of January 1, all existing Jewish publishing houses in Germany were to be closed down, as would all Jewish newspapers. Now the Kulturbund would take over those activities. And the Kulturbund would be allowed to show films; thanks to the Goebbels decree of ten days earlier, it would now be the only place where Jews could attend movies. The Nazis had thus succeeded in moving all Jewish cultural activities—music, theater, lectures, film, and publishing—under one roof and under a single surveillance. The Jewish cultural ghetto was now complete.

Having received their marching orders, Levie, Zander, Wisten, and Schwarz trudged doggedly forward. The next Kubu play, *Benjamin Wohin?* ("Benjamin, Where To?") by Hermann Sinsheimer, directed by Fritz Wisten, had opened on December 15. The next orchestral concert was scheduled for December 27. And two days later the Kulturbund screened its very first film, an American movie called *Chicago*. The new Jewish newspaper, the *Nachrichtenblatt*, reviewed the film in language that must have resonated with every Jew who had survived the horrors of the previous month's pogrom and now feared what might come next:

> A city goes up in flames and the firefighters stand by without taking any action. All the hoses are poised, the ladders have been prepared, but no hand moves to use them. Only when the city has burned down and is lying in cinders and ashes, an order arrives; but the firefighters are already driving away. A malicious invention? An ugly tale? No. The truth. And it was revealed in Hollywood.

As another new year began, tens of thousands of Jews had left the ashes of the Germany they had known and started new lives in new lands. For the thousands who remained, the Jüdische Kulturbund in Deutschland was the sole remaining source of information and organized entertainment.

16

Prinzenstrasse

IF THE "SPONTANEOUS DEMONSTRATIONS" of anti-Semitic hatred that had exploded across Germany during November 9–10 were designed to let the Jews know, once and for all and in no uncertain terms, that they were no longer welcome in the country of their birth, they were largely successful. In 1938, the number of Jewish emigrés from Germany numbered about thirty-five thousand. During the following year that figure nearly doubled, to sixty-eight thousand. In the days and weeks following Kristallnacht, lines were long outside foreign embassies and consulates in all major German cities, as Jews waited to obtain the necessary papers to apply for visas. While every German Jew felt the pressure to leave, some were under more immediate duress than others.

When Alex Goldschmidt was released from Sachsenhausen concentration camp on December 7, he was informed that he had six months to leave the country or face further charges. So he returned home to Oldenburg, and, after spending a week or so recovering from his ordeal and talking matters over with his family, he took the train to Bremen and visited the Cuban consulate. There he applied for permission to emigrate to Cuba in the spring, filling out one application for himself and one for his son Helmut. The plan was for them to establish residency in the Western Hemisphere and for the rest of the family to follow a few months later. It seemed like a perfectly sound strategy.

Meanwhile, on November 26, two weeks after the pogrom, Julian Gumpert paid a visit to the consulate of Ecuador in Düsseldorf. The difference was that neither Else nor Rosemarie knew of his plans and that when Julian filled out his emigration application, he did so for himself alone.

What drove the former court concertmaster to seek asylum overseas, I don't know. He had not been personally touched by the violence
of the pogrom and neither had the Gumpert Conservatory. Perhaps a
friend of his, a teacher in his school, or a musician in one of his many
ensembles had been arrested, his house badly damaged, or his instrument shattered. Or maybe Julian simply came to the realization, as so
many German Jews did, that he no longer lived in a civilized country.
So his action of visiting the Ecuadorian consulate I can understand.
That he kept his visit a secret from his family I cannot. I realize that I
am judging a man I never knew, and from a distance of six decades, but
his secret visit to the consulate seems very much in character. Julian
Gumpert usually thought of himself first, and of those around him
only afterward.

The other, more jovial and generous, side of his character was on
display on December 15—ten days before Christmas and two days
after his daughter's wedding—when he and Else saw Rosemarie and
Günther off on their journey to Berlin. The four of them arrived a few
minutes early at Düsseldorf's Central Station. As the time of their
departure approached, Else gave the newlyweds a small basket containing some cold chicken and a bottle of wine. Julian presented his daughter and son-in-law with a wooden carving of a man playing the violin.
He also bestowed upon them a little speech about how to get along in
the big city, but Rosemarie and Günther giggled through so much of it
that he finally gave up in good-natured disgust.

"Just remember one thing," he said at last. "You are both fine musicians with the souls of artists. You have much to give, both to the people who will come to hear you and to the other musicians with whom
you will play. Remember your talents, and be proud."

At those words, the two young people stopped their foolishness and
smiled shyly at Julian. They then embraced the older man. Rosemarie
whispered, "Thank you."

As the train pulled out and the receding figures of Julian and Else
grew smaller and smaller, Günther suddenly and fearfully recalled his
wedding-night dream. But it was a bright, cold day, he and Rosemarie
knew just where they were going, and they arrived in Berlin right on
schedule.

Almost immediately they found an apartment, the first address they shared as a married couple. Their room was at 93 Prinzenstrasse in the eastern section of Berlin, about a seven-minute walk from the theater on Kommandantenstrasse. Despite the name of the street, their apartment offered less than princely lodging. To get to their room, Günther and Rosemarie had to walk through a courtyard surrounded by little repair shops for bicycles and sewing machines, past a print shop with end-lessly clattering presses, and up two dark flights of stairs illuminated at night by only a single weak bulb with neither a globe nor a shade. Their room contained a bed; a tiny kitchen area with a sink, a collapsible table, and an icebox; two music stands; a wooden bookcase painted brown; and a studio sofa covered with a fabric of yellow and rust, my father's favorite colors. On the walls they hung Julian's little fiddler and reproductions by Van Gogh, Matisse, and Albrecht Dürer. Rosemarie sewed curtains for the apartment's three little windows. It wasn't long before they felt right at home, and their happiness in their new life was nearly complete.

Their landlord was a thin wisp of a man named Adolf Cohen, whom my father remembers for his kindness and for his habit of stor-ing charcoal briquettes in the apartment bathroom, thus making the already small room even smaller. Since Berlin was experiencing a paper shortage, Herr Cohen devised another memorable bathroom adorn-ment: on a wire hook he hung a stack of neatly cut five-by-five-inch squares of newspaper for his tenants' most private use. Their landlord also kept, by the door in his own room, a small suitcase. Günther once asked him what was in it.

"Just the few things," he replied, "that I want to take along when the Gestapo comes for me."

"What are you talking about?" asked my father.

"Haven't you heard?" came the answer. "Don't you know we all will be burned?"

"Come on," protested Günther. "Those are rumors, fairy tales."

Their landlord looked at him solemnly. And all he would say was, "You will remember Adolf Cohen."

Not surprisingly, music played a major part in my parents' lives during their first weeks in Berlin. They spent most of their free time practicing their instruments. They'd work in shifts: after a breakfast that usually consisted of a soft-boiled egg and a cup of coffee or tea, Rosemarie would play for an hour or so while Günther read; then he would play his flute while she left for a walk or to buy a few things at the market. After lunch, they would sometimes take a nap or go out for a walk together, often finding their footsteps leading them toward the zoo. Then, back in their room, Günther would practice for another hour, followed by Rosemarie. At night, if they didn't leave Prinzenstrasse to visit friends, they might each spend another hour on their instruments. They were both acutely aware of how important it was for them to be well prepared for each rehearsal. They also wanted to do their best to live up to Julian's praise and confidence. Work, they knew, was the truest road to artistry.

I think that, at least subconsciously, their steadfast schedule of making music was a form of self-protection; as long as they concentrated on their instruments, they had less time to reflect on the danger and uncertainty of their situation. They had jobs, to be sure, but still very much at the pleasure of the Nazi authorities. It was much easier on their spirits to work out a difficult passage in Mendelssohn or Mahler than to think too far into the future and ponder the fate their landlord had predicted.

Once orchestral rehearsals began, Günther and Rosemarie spent less time playing on their own. But these sessions with their Kulturbund colleagues were equally stimulating, if not more so. They again worked with Rudolf Schwarz, who had conducted *Rigoletto* in October. They learned that he had worked in cities with ties to both of them; he had made his debut with the Düsseldorf Opera in 1924 and, until he lost his job in 1933, had conducted the Karlsruhe Opera. They also found him to be an exceptional musician who knew what he wanted and how to share his ideas with his orchestra so that everyone was working toward a single musical goal.

The first concert of the long-delayed season was scheduled for December 27. Before the November Pogrom, Schwarz had intended to conclude the initial concert with the *Rustic Wedding* Symphony by Karl Goldmark. Now, wanting to make the kind of splash that would attract an audience still leery of venturing forth at night, he decided to begin the concert with the noble tone poem *The Moldau* by Czech composer

Bedřich Smetana, play only the scherzo movement from the *Rustic Wedding,* and conclude with the youthful and heaven-storming Symphony No. 1 by Gustav Mahler.

Although Rosemarie had played the Mahler One in Frankfurt, it was brand-new to Günther. Mahler's music made a deep impression on them both. (To the end of her days, however, my mother would complain that Mahler was among the most difficult composers to play.) What sonic splendor he created, what emotions he plumbed, with what huge issues of life, love, and death he wrestled in his massive symphonies! He referred to himself as thrice an outsider: a Bohemian-born citizen of Austria, an Austrian among Germans, and a Jew on top of that. Mahler later exacerbated his feelings of not belonging when he converted to Catholicism and found that, in the end, he remained an unbeliever. His sense of being alone in the universe, even after his marriage to Alma Schindler, kept him in a permanent state of agitation and unhappiness, but, like many a great artist, he distilled his pain into beauty for those who would listen.

Mahler published his First Symphony in 1898, just forty years before Günther and Rosemarie encountered it in Berlin. Most of the themes he would explore in his later symphonies he introduced in his First: romantic yearnings, restless rootlessness, questions of faith, the struggle to defeat death. Throughout the symphony's first movement he quotes a cycle of songs he had written earlier, the *Songs of a Wayfarer,* beautiful and wistful meditations on lost love. He includes a mysterious slow movement based on the folk melody "Frère Jacques," inspired, he said, by a picture in a book of fairy tales that depicts a funeral procession for a dead hunter borne to his grave by an array of woodland animals. And Mahler concludes his symphony with an epic battle in which life triumphs over death to the accompaniment of some utterly exuberant music. On more than one occasion during rehearsals, Rudolf Schwarz drew parallels between Mahler's struggles and those of the musicians of the Kulturbund and their audience. Günther and Rosemarie found themselves mesmerized by the music and looked forward eagerly to the first concert on December 27.

But unbeknownst to them, as they rehearsed Mahler on Kommandantenstrasse and honed their craft at home, an event took place far from Berlin that would profoundly affect their lives. A letter arrived for Julian Gumpert at his conservatory in Düsseldorf. It was from a former student, who wrote to tell Julian that he was now living in New York and teaching young children himself. He went on to say that he had been profoundly disturbed by the reports he had read of the violence and brutality of November 9. Matters were obviously difficult and probably dangerous, he wrote, and he wondered if there was anything he could do to help Mr. Gumpert or his family.

With his own secret emigration plans already under way, Julian wrote back to his former student saying, yes, there was something. Would it be possible to arrange visas for his daughter, Rosemarie, and her new husband, Günther, so that they, too, could live in America?

Julian made no mention of Else, his wife.

My father learned of this exchange of letters only much later, and not from the man who started the correspondence. To this day, I have no idea of the man's identity. I only know that this stranger wrote a letter to my grandfather, himself a stranger to me, and began the process that would save my parents' lives and make mine possible. We truly live in a random, mysterious universe. But I would so much like to find this man, or his children, and say thank you.

On Christmas Eve, knowing nothing of the machinery that had been set in motion to save them, Günther and Rosemarie felt only a little loneliness as they gazed out their window to the south and saw the thin spire of the Church of St. Simeon outlined against the stars. They rejoiced in their togetherness, but, still new in Berlin, they missed their friends and families on this night that had always brought them a special sort of excitement and eager anticipation.

"Let's walk over to the church," said Rosemarie. "Maybe they have some nice music."

So the two young people descended the stairs and, hand in hand, strolled through their courtyard and out into the street. After a couple of blocks they came to the brightly lit facade of St. Simeon's. There was a sign proclaiming *Alles Willkommen* (All Are Welcome), but Günther and Rosemarie knew enough to realize that, even in church, "All" no longer meant "All" in Germany. Not wanting to risk the embarrassment of having to identify themselves and then being asked to leave, they were content to stand in the dark alley behind the church, where they could hear the organ and the voices of the congregation as they sang carols of peace and goodwill. The service closed with "Stille Nacht, Heilige Nacht," and, eyes closed and holding each other tightly, Günther and Rosemarie sang along with the people on the other side of the church's thick brick walls. Then they smiled at each other and walked silently home, a newly kindled warmth in their hearts.

The next day they placed telephone calls to Oldenburg and Düsseldorf to wish their families well and then invited Adolf Cohen to their apartment to share in a Christmas dinner of roast goose, potatoes, and red cabbage. It was Rosemarie's first opportunity to cook for a guest in her new role as a wife. As she would for the rest of her life, she agonized for hours over each detail, making herself more nervous than she ever felt for a recital. But, also foreshadowing her later efforts as a dinner hostess, everything turned out splendidly. When Herr Cohen finally left around eleven o'clock, he stood in the door a moment to wish his tenants well.

"Thank you, thank you," he gushed, having had an extra glass or two of the Rhein wine he had brought to the feast. "It is good to have you two living here. I look forward to the time when we can enjoy a truly Happy Christmas together!"

Two days later, Günther and Rosemarie played their first concert with the Kulturbund Orchestra in the company's headquarters on Kommandantenstrasse. The seats were full, as usual, and as the triumphant last notes of the Mahler symphony were still ringing in the electrified air of the theater, the musicians were rewarded with cheers and shouts of approval. On New Year's Eve, the orchestra gave its Smetana-Goldmark-Mahler concert a second time.

As Günther and Rosemarie took the by now familiar seven-minute walk from their home on Prinzenstrasse to the theater, they talked over the momentous events of the year now ending—from their first lovemaking exactly one year ago to their last concert in Frankfurt to the horrors of November 9 to their wedding just eighteen days earlier to their new lives in Berlin. So much had happened to them personally, much of it good, amid all the bad that had befallen them and their Jewish countrymen. A similar mood of ambivalent nostalgia prevailed at the theater. The *Moldau* and the Goldmark Scherzo went well, but there was an undertone of sadness, of resignation, that weighed everything down and prevented the proceedings from gaining the necessary emotional altitude. At intermission, before the musicians played the Mahler First, conductor Rudolf Schwarz gathered them all together backstage.

"Ladies and gentlemen," he said, "you do not need me to tell you that these are abominable conditions under which to make music. I know that many of you have lost members of your family in these last few weeks. I also know that some of you will leave this ensemble in the weeks and months ahead. That is entirely understandable, as are certain emotions and feelings I have discerned among you tonight as we bid farewell to a year of unusual cruelty, a year none of us will miss.

"So," Schwarz continued, "I want to offer you tonight my sincerest thanks for your heroic efforts these last twelve months and remind you that they are deeply appreciated, both by me and by the other leaders of the Kulturbund who have had to soldier on in the absence of our leader, Dr. Singer. You are also appreciated, most especially, by the members of our audience, who continue to fill our theater by night even as our days become emptier of those things that make life truly worthwhile. What we do here is obviously of great importance to a great many people. And, may I say, to ourselves."

Schwarz took off his glasses and cleaned them thoroughly with a handkerchief. When he resumed speaking, his voice was huskier.

"Permit me, please, to urge all of you wonderful artists to work as hard as you can on what remains of this New Year's Eve to reveal Herr Mahler's music in all its strength and color and nobility and beauty. Let us play as if our lives depended on it."

With that, Rudolf Schwarz turned and hurried back to his dressing room. The members of the orchestra slowly filed out on stage and began to warm up. As he blew a few scales and looked over his part, Günther felt enormously proud to be a member of the Kulturbund.

"This is why I practice," he thought. "This is why I perform. This is what I'm meant to do. And for as long as I can, I must continue to make beautiful music. In an ugly time, the best protest is beauty."

Conductor Rudolf Schwarz.

A moment later, Herr Schwarz strode out on stage to the applause of the audience. He swept his eyes over the stage, then raised his baton. Günther, sitting with the flutes at center stage, exchanged a smile and a wink with Rosemarie in her position with the second stand of violas on stage left. The Symphony No. 1 by Gustav Mahler begins mysteriously, with the full orchestra sounding softly the notes that, over the course of fifty minutes, will shape a universe of human pain and triumph. Rudolf Schwarz gave the downbeat and, as if their lives depended on it, my parents began to play.

17

Sempre Libera

ON JANUARY 30, 1939, the sixth anniversary of his appointment as chancellor, Adolf Hitler gave a speech at the Reichstag. He began at 8:15 P.M. and spoke for more than two and a half hours. First he sketched a colorful history of National Socialism and repeated for his eager followers the legend of their rise to power, a story that for them had assumed the proportions of myth. He then sharply criticized Winston Churchill, Anthony Eden, and the other English leaders who had spoken out against his regime, referring to the "Jewish and non-Jewish instigators" of this utterly unfair attack. Next he turned on his American enemies, both for entering the Great War against Germany in 1917 and for their "unfounded" printed attacks following the recent unpleasantness of November 9. American editorialists, Hitler shouted, had criticized him for what his people had done to the Jews and for encouraging them to leave Germany. Well, then, he continued sarcastically, if the Jews are such wonderful, cultured people, shouldn't world leaders be grateful that the chancellor was sharing them? Where, anywhere in the world, he asked, was there a movement to take in these "magnificent people"?

Hitler paused to let his point sink in. Then he continued by stating publicly a threat that, up to that point, had usually been confined to Nazi back rooms.

In my life I have often been a prophet and people have often laughed at me. At the time of my struggle for power, it was mostly the Jews who laughed loudest at the prophecy that one day I would be the leader of the German state and that then, among other things, I would discover the solution to the Jewish problem. I think it safe to say that the uproarious laughter of those days has stuck in the throats of Germany's Jews. Today I am going to make another prophecy: If the Jewish international financiers succeed in precipitating another world war, the result will not be world Bolshevism and therefore a victory for the Jews, but rather the annihilation of the Jewish race in Europe.

On that same Monday night, the Kulturbund theater company was rehearsing William Shakespeare's *The Winter's Tale,* a production directed by Fritz Wisten that was due to open the following week. The Kubu had undergone a very trying four weeks. On New Year's Day the organization was nearly two hundred sixty thousand Reichsmarks in the red. The financial situation was so bad that actors and musicians were sometimes paid in single marks, and in mid-January many artists still hadn't been paid for services rendered back in November. A few artists had been let go, the number of full-time singers in the opera company's chorus had declined from twenty-one to twelve, and the future of the Kulturbund cabaret was in serious doubt. The threat of the November Pogrom had speeded emigration, and as a result membership in the Kulturbund had declined from 13,186 Berlin subscribers on November 1 to 12,055 on January 1 and 11,403 on February 1. Since subscriptions were the main source of the organization's income, something would have to be done, and soon.

On one of his thrice-weekly visits to the Ministry of Propaganda, Werner Levie was informed by Hans Hinkel that he would have to seek out some of the Kulturbund's Jewish debtors and ask that those debts be forgiven. Otherwise, said Hinkel coldly, the entire enterprise would be declared bankrupt and the complete roster of artists, technicians, and support staff would be out on the street. That prospect was, of course, very unpleasant to Dr. Levie and his colleagues, from both an artistic and a practical perspective.

I wonder if Hinkel was prepared to follow through on his threat to shut down the Kulturbund. It was still a useful propaganda tool, and so long as it was, the Nazis had every reason to insure its survival. Hinkel could have been thinking in purely financial terms: if the debts must be paid, better that the money should come from Jewish businessmen than from the Nazi propaganda budget. Perhaps he was using his power to force Levie to scramble for money, and enjoying the side benefit of turning the screws on Jewish businessmen. Maybe this latest threat was tied to the Nazis' annoyance at having been forced to release the two hundred Jewish artists as the price for having the Kulturbund reopen as soon after the November Pogrom as possible. Or maybe Goebbels and Hinkel were truly prepared to cut off support to the Kulturbund if they were not able to retire their debt.

In any event, Dr. Levie went back to his board of directors with this latest financial information, and two members of the board—Arthur Lilienthal and Heinrich Stahl—volunteered to assist Dr. Levie in what they termed the "cleansing" of the Kubu's books. The three men spent several weeks in earnest consultations with the Jewish heads of companies with which the Kulturbund had done business and was in debt to—building supply stores, carpenters, painters, wig makers, luthiers, piano tuners, delicatessens—and convinced them that losing a little money now was preferable to losing the Kulturbund's business permanently. By early March, Levie, Lilienthal, and Stahl had succeeded in retiring all but fifty-three thousand Reichsmarks of the organization's debt, a figure they all agreed would soon be paid up, thanks to two recent Kubu success stories.

The first big success was the Kulturbund's new film bureau. With the showing of *Chicago* on December 29, 1938, the Kubu had become the one and only place in all of Berlin where Jews were allowed to attend the movies. A man named Manfred Epstein was hired to run the new film bureau. He immediately set to work renovating a room in the Kommandantenstrasse theater to accommodate about fifty patrons, taking care not to violate the city's fire code. Epstein had to clear his choice of films with the Reich Film Chamber so that nothing provocative or insulting to the regime would be screened. He was also in charge of the film bureau's books and saw to it that a complicated fee structure was set up and satisfied. Of each night's box office revenues, 9.4 percent was sent to the Ministry of Propaganda as an entertainment tax and 35 percent of the remainder went to the film's distributor. The Kubu kept the rest, and right from the start there was a lot to keep.

Epstein instituted a ticket policy for the film bureau that was markedly different from the standard Kulturbund practice. First of all, patrons could request a particular seat when they called to reserve a ticket. And second, it was possible to purchase a ticket for a particular film without buying a subscription for the whole series. The roster of films shown by the Kulturbund wasn't especially stellar—the titles for the first six months included *Lord Jeff, Mississippi Melody, The Blue Fox, Tarantella, Tanz auf dem Vulkan,* and *Hoheit tanzt inkognito*—not exactly Academy Award material in a year that would see the release of *Gone With the Wind, The Wizard of Oz,* and *Stagecoach*—but the cinema-starved Jewish population of Berlin ate up the offerings as if they were buttered popcorn. All shows on Saturday and Sunday nights were sold out and there was respectable mid-week attendance as well. In the first six months of 1939, the Kulturbund presented three hundred fourteen screenings and pulled in a profit of 129,000 Reichsmarks.

The other successful new venture was the Kulturbund's publishing activity. The most visible aspect of that venture was the newspaper, the *Jüdische Nachrichtenblatt,* which came about as the result of another Nazi act of aggression. Joseph Goebbels's decree of December 6, 1938, had banned the Jewish press from operating in the Reich. However, the propaganda minister saw an advantage to having a single Jewish paper publishing just what he wanted it to, and so the *Nachrichtenblatt* was born. One day in late December, Erich Liepmann, who had spent years at the helm of another newspaper, was summoned to appear before Goebbels at the ministry. As Liepmann recalled the encounter, Goebbels greeted him by shouting, "Is the Jew here?" from his office. Then, when Liepmann entered the office, the minister "was sitting at his desk. I had to stand some eight meters away. He yelled: 'An informational paper must be published within two days. Each issue must be submitted to me. Woe to you if even one article is published without my having seen it. That's all!'"

The first issue of the *Nachrichtenblatt,* with Erich Liepmann as publisher and a man named Leo Kreindler serving as editor in chief, appeared on New Year's Day, 1939, and thereafter on Tuesdays and Fridays. Werner Levie attended one of the paper's editorial meetings each week and served as liaison to the Propaganda Ministry. In that capacity he ran everything by Goebbels's watchful eyes and also obtained information concerning the latest Nazi restrictions and emigration policies, all of which found its way into the pages of the *Nachrichtenblatt.*

The paper ran many stories on the intricacies of emigration, including how and where to obtain visas and the latest shipping news, as well as articles of general interest to its Jewish readers. Its editorial stance, with a careful nod to the Nazis, was bipartisan on the emerging Middle East question, friendly toward the concept of a Jewish Palestine but in no sense Zionistic. Much of its space, which ranged between eight and sixteen pages per issue, was given over to advertisements and announcements of births, deaths, marriages, and bar mitzvahs.

Almost immediately, the *Nachrichtenblatt* took off like a rocket. It was, after all, the only Jewish newspaper left, and Germany's declining yet still substantial Jewish population snapped it up eagerly. Following the Kulturbund practice of encouraging subscriptions over individual performance tickets, Erich Liepmann established a policy that made single issues hard to come by. Within six months, circulation hit sixty-two thousand, with editions in eleven cities that left room for local ads in each town. Community announcements and Kulturbund notices were given free ad space; even so, nearly 170,000 marks in advertising revenue poured in during the first six months of 1939. Income from subscriptions amounted to 286,000 marks during the same period.

The Kulturbund's publishing activities also extended to the printing of books and magazines. In the aftermath of the December decrees and regulations, Hans Hinkel announced that all existing Jewish publishing houses were to be closed. Henceforth there would be no independent Jewish publishing concerns or independent Jewish bookstores other than the Kulturbund. Bookstore owners were required to send a list of their inventories to the Propaganda Ministry as of December 31, and all of their titles were then to be handled by the Kulturbund.

Werner Levie traveled to Vienna in mid-January to meet with representatives of Jewish publishing houses. He had only a few weeks to become acquainted with the intricacies of the book business. Fortunately, it didn't take him long to grasp the essentials, and by the spring of 1939 he was making regular trips to London and Amsterdam to oversee his organization's book enterprises. In a report he filed with the

Kulturbund's board in early summer, Dr. Levie estimated that he was spending approximately half his time overseeing the publishing concerns and the other half with the Kulturbund's original activities, the theater and music performances.

In retrospect, naturally, it's impossible to avoid wondering why Werner Levie didn't simply stay in London during one of his visits and save his own life. As with so many other members of the Kulturbund, the answer seems to lie in a combination of naïveté and a deep dedication to the Kubu's ideals. And of course Levie, no less than Kurt Singer and Günther Goldschmidt, was powerless to predict the future.

In the early months of 1939, however, the present was full of activity for the Jüdische Kulturbund in Deutschland, e. V. The Kubu had indeed become the sole source of culture, entertainment, and information for the Jews of Germany. It was the cultural ghetto that the Nazis had longed for, a bell jar clamped securely around the bright Jewish butterfly. But for the leaders of the Kulturbund, who had just confronted the real possibility of bankruptcy, the spring of 1939 was a time to breathe a sigh of relief.

With healthy revenues from the film and publishing ventures flowing in, the Kulturbund showed a profit of over 25,000 Reichsmarks for the month of January. That figure increased to 49,000 marks in February, 103,000 marks in April, and 125,000 marks in May. With the approval of the board (and, of course, the Ministry of Propaganda) the Kulturbund donated more than 30,000 marks to the Reich Federation of Jews in Germany to assist in emigration efforts. And nearly 50 percent of their income went to pay taxes to the Reich. Nevertheless, matters had stabilized to such a degree that more than fifty employees, most of them in the film and publishing departments, were added to the Kubu's staff in the first six months of 1939.

In this time of surplus, the thoughts of the Kommandantenstrasse staff turned towards those citizens who no longer had access to organized entertainment—the Jews beyond the boundaries of Berlin, whose Kulturbünde had been shut down at the end of 1938. So, in acts of cultural solidarity, members of the Berlin troupe, in groups of two and three and four, began to go out on the road in late February. They paid visits to Hamburg and Frankfurt, Breslau and Hannover, Leipzig and

Cologne, staging piano and lieder recitals, offering lectures and reciting scenes from plays, presenting puppet shows for children, and occasionally borrowing a spare projector to show films. With the national organization in ruins, there was no one in those cities to handle publicity or tickets, or to arrange for a place to perform. But with the help of the *Nachrichtenblatt* and heavy reliance on word of mouth, these heroic artists staged 214 events for more than 44,000 of their fellow Jews in those six cities between February and June.

Meanwhile, the main focus of Kulturbund activity remained the performances in Berlin. In a series of concerts in February and April, Rudolf Schwarz conducted the orchestra in music by Slavic composers (Smetana, Tchaikovsky, Stravinsky, Borodin, and Jiri Weinberger) and a repeat of the Symphony No. 1 by Mahler. But the musical highlight of the spring was a series of performances of the opera *La Traviata* by Giuseppe Verdi. As the fortunes of the company began to rise after the horrors and disappointments of the autumn and winter, everyone involved was determined to demonstrate—to friends and foes alike—that the Kulturbund could still mount a handsome and musically thrilling production.

Rudolf Schwarz conducted, Kurt Baumann directed, and the cast was headed by Fritzi Merley and Dolly Salkind, who shared the role of the courtesan Violetta Valéry on alternate nights; Igo Guttmann and Richard Dresdner, who shared the role of Alfredo Germont; and Günther's and Rosemarie's old friend Wilhelm Guttmann, who sang the part of Giorgio Germont, Alfredo's father, the character who convinces Violetta to break off her affair with his son. At the time, Werner Levie proclaimed the production one of the strongest in the entire history of the Kulturbund.

To this day my father names *La Traviata* as his very favorite opera, and he traces his love for it to the nearly twenty performances he spent down in the pit in the theater on Kommandantenstrasse in March of 1939. The story of the selfless Violetta, the headstrong Alfredo, and their hopeless love is marvelously romantic and therefore perfect for my father's poetic sensibilities. Verdi spins out some of his most tragically beautiful music in this opera, particularly in the magnificent duet the two reconciled lovers share in the third act.

But the moment Günther looked forward to most at every performance was Violetta's brilliantly spirited aria in the opera's opening act, when she proclaims her independence and her devotion to pleasure. "*Sempre libera*," she sings. "Always free am I, flying from joy to joy. As each day dawns, as each day dies, I turn always to new delights that make my spirit soar!" Tragically, Violetta, only twenty-three years old, suffers from consumption and is doomed to an early death even as she utters her defiant credo in the carefree maelstrom of Paris society. Her determination to live and love fully amid difficult circumstances appealed deeply to Günther as he attempted to do the same. He would often play the lighter-than-air melody of "Sempre libera" as he warmed up before a performance and frequently found himself whistling the tune as he and Rosemarie walked home from the theater.

"'Always free,'" he thought to himself on those walks. "What must it be like to live a life in which one can so confidently sing 'Always free'?"

In late April, after *La Traviata* closed, Günther and Rosemarie attended a Kulturbund performance of *People at Sea*, a drama by the Englishman J. B. Priestley in a German translation by Leo Hirsch. Fritz Wisten directed. The play concerns the plight of twelve people on a ship in the Caribbean. The ship has been disabled by fire and is in danger of sinking. Günther was particularly drawn to the subject because his father, Alex, and brother, Helmut, had just obtained tickets for an ocean voyage that would take them to freedom in the Caribbean. They were bound for Cuba on a sturdy vessel of the renowned Hamburg-America Line.

In *People at Sea*, the characters are all rescued. My grandfather and uncle would not be so lucky. They had booked passage on a ship called the *St. Louis*.

18

New World—
and Old

"THE *ST. LOUIS* is a ship on which one travels securely and lives in comfort. There is everything one can wish for that makes life on board a pleasure!"

Those friendly words greeted Alex Goldschmidt from a gleaming brochure that he acquired from the Hamburg-America Line in late April of 1939. The *St. Louis* was due to set sail from Hamburg to Havana on May 13, and both Alex and his younger son, Helmut, were in the market for tickets. They had obtained visas from Cuba and were on the verge of securing their passports from Germany. Alex's waking nightmare, which had begun in January 1933 and had horribly intensified in November 1938, seemed finally to be nearing its end.

As matters turned out, however, it was only the end of the beginning.

After his release from Sachsenhausen on December 7, 1938, and his application for a Cuban visa, Alex realized that he and his family would have to conserve all of their resources if they hoped to carry out their plan to emigrate to the New World. Alex's work as a buyer had paid less and less in the months leading up to Kristallnacht. And now, he knew, there would be many fees, both legal and extralegal, associated with the emigration process. So on December 28 he moved his family from the apartment on Ofenerstrasse to a smaller, less expensive apartment on Nordstrasse, just a few blocks from the railroad station.

Alex, Toni, Bertha, Eva, and Helmut spent the next few months nervously waiting for news to arrive from the Cuban consulate in Bremen. Bertha was approaching her thirtieth birthday and searching for a career in what were now very inhospitable circumstances. In late February, she announced to the family that, through a school friend, she had secured a position for herself as a domestic and family gardener in the northern English city of Leeds. This required another train trip to Bremen to stand in line at the British consulate, but it was a welcome relief from the tension of doing virtually nothing every day except wait, all the while restricted to the confines of a small apartment.

Finally, in early March, the family learned that Cuba had granted visas for Alex and Helmut. But then the next day a letter arrived from a certain Manuel Benitez Gonzalez, the director-general of Cuba's Office of Immigration, informing them that Alex and Helmut would each have to purchase a special landing certificate if they intended to disembark in Havana. The price for each certificate was 450 Reichsmarks, a small fortune for the Goldschmidts.

Alex realized that the family would have to tighten its belt one more time before the journey west. So on March 21, the first day of spring, they moved a final time, to an even smaller apartment at 17 Staulinie. They were now only a block from the train station, and the chug and chuff of engines became a constant accompaniment to daily life.

A month later the so-called Benitez Certificates arrived. Alex placed the precious documents with the visas into a cardboard folder, which he stored under his mattress. He checked their safety every night and every morning and several times during the day; other than his wedding ring, he owned nothing of greater value than those four pieces of paper.

The time had now come to secure passage to Cuba. It was then, in late April, that Alex learned of the *St. Louis*. She was one of the Hamburg-America Line's luxury liners. Although at first glance she was not the sort of craft one might expect to take on the responsibilities of a refugee ship, an interesting series of events had led to her selection.

On January 24, 1939, Field Marshal Hermann Göring had appointed Reinhard Heydrich, one of the men who had been with him at the fateful meeting at the Air Transport Ministry on November 12, to lead the Central Office for Jewish Emigration. The Final Solution to the Jewish Problem still lay several years in the future; for now, the goal was simply to get as many Jews out of Germany as possible. Heydrich knew Claus-Gottfried Holthusen, the director of the Hamburg-America Line and one of the most powerful men in German shipping. He also knew two vital bits of intelligence regarding Herr Holthusen: the director had Nazi sympathies, and in recent years his company had suffered some financial setbacks. Just recently the *St. Louis* had sailed from New York to Hamburg with only about one third of her berths occupied.

Heydrich immediately recognized a mutually profitable situation for the Reich and the shipping line. He informed Göring and Propaganda Minister Joseph Goebbels about the situation, and by the middle of April they had arranged that the *St. Louis* would sail from Hamburg to Havana on May 13 bearing nearly a thousand Jewish refugees. Everyone involved was satisfied. Göring relished the opportunity to demonstrate to his Führer that he was ridding the Reich of Jews. Goebbels immediately saw the propaganda possibilities: Germans could be informed of the happy news that more Jews were leaving, while the international audience would have clear evidence that Germany was graciously allowing its Jews to leave unharmed and unimpeded—and on a luxury liner, no less. The Hamburg-America Line would enjoy a profitable voyage; while the *St. Louis* passengers would be refugees, to be sure, they would be charged the standard fares of 800 Reichsmarks for first class and 600 Reichsmarks for tourist class. And last, and certainly least, the Jews themselves would surely appreciate this highly civilized manner of being booted out of their country.

And so now Alex, in Bremen in late April to book passage to Cuba, held in his hands the glossy advertising brochure for the *St. Louis*. He purchased two tickets, one for himself and one for Helmut, at the tourist class fare of 600 Reichsmarks each. He was obliged to pay an additional 460 Reichsmarks for what the Hamburg-America Line termed a "customary contingency fee." This additional money covered a return voyage to Germany should what the line called "circumstances beyond our control" arise. The line insisted that the "contingency fee" was fully refundable should the voyage proceed as planned.

Alex returned to Oldenburg in triumph, bearing his precious purchases. They had been extremely expensive, but now he had everything he needed—visas, landing certificates, tickets—to apply for a passport.

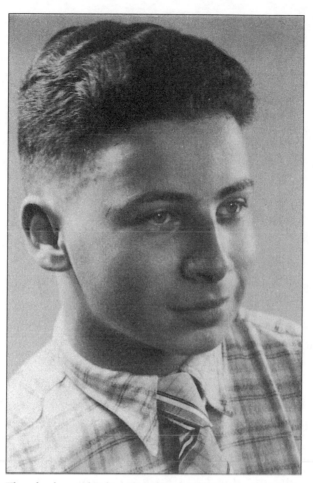

The only photograph I have of my Uncle Helmut, from his application to travel to Cuba in May of 1939. At seventeen, he seems to be a very nice young man.

On Monday, May 1, he, Helmut, and Bertha visited the Oldenburg offices of the Emigration Advisory Board to fill out individual applications for the "issuance of a single-family passport for domestic and foreign use."

The three filled out their forms in much the same manner. On the line marked "profession," Alex wrote "salesman," Helmut "student," and Bertha "gardener." On the line marked "destination," Alex and Helmut wrote "Cuba," while Bertha filled in "England." All three practiced the same small deception: under their address, which each of them listed as 17 Staulinie, there was a line requesting any previous addresses within the last year. Although the family had indeed moved from Ofenerstrasse to Nordstrasse and then to Staulinie in the past twelve months, all three declared that they had lived on Staulinie "for years." Perhaps they were simply impatient with all the paperwork. Perhaps Alex thought that a history of frequent moves might indicate to the authorities a troublesome lack of stability. Whatever the reason, their white lie seemed to pass unnoticed.

Under their signatures—and each of them signed using the repulsive additions of "Israel" or "Sara"—there appeared the official assurance that "the applicant is not listed in the register of banned permits" and two questions posed by the Gestapo: "Is it assumed that the applicant wants to use the permit to avoid prosecution or execution?" and "Is it assumed that the permit to travel would endanger the internal or external security or other demands of the Reich?" To each question, on each application, the answer was written: *"Nein!"*

For me, the most interesting, and poignant, aspect of the applications is the fact that each bears a photograph of the applicant, and that Alex's includes the only other image, aside from the 1914 family photograph, that I have of him. There he is, staring at me just to the left of the big, red, block letter *J* at the top of the form. He is wearing a prim little bow tie and his ears are still quite prominent. His mustache is gone. The hair on the top of his head is gone. And gone, too, is the confident, self-assured expression of a quarter-century before. The face on my grandfather's passport application, filled out under duress after six years of adversity and six months of hell, has a hunted, haunted look of uncertainty and fear.

But how he must have breathed a sigh of relief a week later, when his application, and those of his children, were returned to him fully filled out and signed. The passports had all been issued and were valid from May 9, 1939, to May 9, 1940. Each of them had cost 3 Reichsmarks. With Bertha's travel plans now set and with the *St. Louis* scheduled to depart the following week, the Goldschmidt family's flight to safety had finally begun.

The hunted, haunted photograph of my grandfather from his passport application.

On Saturday, May 13, the journey commenced. Preparations for the ocean voyage took very little time, as Alex and Helmut were each allowed only one suitcase and no more than ten Reichsmarks in their wallets. The family arose early and enjoyed a large breakfast; Toni was determined that her husband and son should remember their last meal in Oldenburg with pleasure. After breakfast, Alex excused himself from the apartment and took a farewell walk through the cobbled streets of Oldenburg, bidding farewell to the city he had called home for thirty-three years, a city he had served well, a city that had then betrayed him.

The family walked to the train station a little after noon; the train that would carry Alex and Helmut to Bremen, where they would catch another train to Hamburg, was scheduled to leave at 12:57 P.M. Everyone tried their best to be jovial. After all, the two men were on their way to a new and better life in the New World, a life that would soon embrace them all. And yet the uncertainty of the whole enterprise and the forced circumstances of the emigration cast a pall on their leave-taking.

At 12:55, when the stationmaster blew his first whistle, Alex and Helmut exchanged hugs with Toni, Bertha, and Eva. Husband and wife held each other the longest.

"We shall see each other again before you know it," Alex whispered to Toni. "In the meantime, remember that I love you with all my heart."

Toni, her eyes full of tears, merely nodded and tried her best to smile.

Alex and Helmut found seats in a second-class car. As the train pulled away at precisely 12:57, they both leaned from the open windows and waved their handkerchiefs to wife and children, mother and sisters. They continued to wave as the train rolled down a hill and then curved eastward on its journey to Bremen.

At 1:45 they pulled into Bremen, changed trains, and continued their journey to Hamburg. They arrived shortly before four o'clock and were greeted by Günther, who had left Berlin on a westbound train that morning. The three men then made their way on foot from the train station about a mile southwest to the banks of the River Elbe, where the *St. Louis* was anchored.

Hamburg's docks have long been notorious for their rough-and-ready characters and tinderbox atmosphere, from the days Johannes Brahms earned money as a child by playing the piano in waterfront whorehouses to the long nights a leather-clad foursome called the Beatles entertained sailors at the Kaiserkeller and the Star Club along the red-light Reeperbahn. In May of 1939, Hamburg was in the midst of a jubilant observance of its 750th birthday, and brightly colored bunting and ornate Japanese-style lanterns hanging from streetlights gave the city a festive appearance. But the celebration had not made its way down to the Elbe, where on that Saturday afternoon a sharp wind blew and occasional cold rain fell from leaden skies. Gulls wheeled and shrieked overhead and the metal pilings groaned loudly as they shifted with the tide. Longshoremen glared at the travelers, ignoring them when they asked for directions. All seemed gloomy and unpropitious until Alex and Helmut finally spotted the magnificent craft that would carry them to freedom.

The *St. Louis* was immense: 575 feet long and 16,732 tons. An impressive, imposing streamlined vessel, it had a raked bow and tapering stern. The hull was black, the superstructure white, with eight fully stocked decks. Towering above the topmost deck were two smokestacks painted black, red, and white—the colors of the Nazi flag. And, indeed, from the stern flew a swastika.

But if Alex and Helmut were at all disconcerted by the flag, their mood must have been considerably lightened when they boarded the *St. Louis* and discovered all that had been done to make the voyage, as the brochure had promised, "a pleasure." Under the orders of Captain Gustav Schroeder, who for the past six years had resisted repeated pressures to join the National Socialists, the crew of 231 had stocked the ship with all the luxuries of first-class ocean travel: caviar; salmon, both smoked and fresh; the finest cuts of meat; hundreds of cases of robust German beer and mellow Rhine wine; even the highest-quality toilet paper. There was a swimming pool and sports area, complete with shuffleboard, on A Deck; a nightclub on B Deck; a dining hall that featured crisp white linens, leaded crystal glassware, and sterling silverware on C Deck. And the first-class social hall was to be converted into a synagogue for the duration of the voyage.

But probably the most pleasant surprise was the degree of politeness that welcomed the refugees on board the *St. Louis*. Again acting under the directive of Captain Schroeder, the crew saw to it that the passengers were assisted with their luggage, ushered graciously to their cabins, and made to feel at home for the two-week cruise to Havana. For Alex, Helmut, and the rest of the passengers, this was the first instance of courtesy they had experienced from German officialdom in years.

As agreeable as the external circumstances were, however, and even though Alex and Helmut expected to see Günther again fairly soon, this was still a sad leave-taking. Shortly after seven o'clock, Günther walked solemnly down the gangway to join the other well-wishers on the pier. The members of a small band organized by the Hamburg-America Line to serenade the ship at its departure huddled under a makeshift tent to stay out of the rain, which had begun to fall more steadily. At precisely seven-thirty, the ship's horn uttered three mighty blasts, the gangways were hauled up, and the hawsers slipped from the pilings. Slowly, ever so slowly, the *St. Louis* edged away from the pier, into the River Elbe, toward the North Sea.

Günther stood on the dock, first waving and then merely watching as the ship grew smaller, as his father and brother sailed away into the fog.

"I felt somehow," he remembers today, "that I would never see them again. Even now, more than sixty years later, there are moments when I hear the eerie, moaning sound of the ship's horn, when I see the disappearing boat before my eyes, getting more and more enshrouded by clouds and rain, engulfed by an uncharted future."

After about ten minutes, Günther began to shiver, the wind knifing through his thin overcoat, and he trudged back to the train station. The band was still playing resolutely against the elements, and he couldn't help but notice that the flutist was a bit out of tune.

On the bridge of the *St. Louis*, Captain Schroeder made an entry in his diary:

> There is a somewhat nervous disposition among the passengers. Everyone seems convinced they will never see Germany again. Touching departure scenes have taken place. Many seem light of heart, having left their homes. Others take it heavily. But pure sea air, good food and attentive service will soon provide the usual worry-free atmosphere of a long sea voyage. Painful impressions on land disappear quickly at sea and soon seem merely like dreams.

Thirty-eight hours later, at nine-thirty on Monday morning, May 15, the *St. Louis* arrived in Cherbourg, France, to pick up a few more passengers and to bring aboard several crates of fresh fruits and vegetables for the ship's dining room. Early that afternoon the *St. Louis* once again weighed anchor, and glided out into the English Channel to begin the transatlantic portion of the voyage. With the newly added passengers, there were now 937 refugees on board. Almost all of them were, like Alex and Helmut, Jews fleeing the Third Reich under great duress. Most were citizens of Germany, some were from Eastern Europe, a few were Spaniards seeking sanctuary from the Civil War. None of them was traveling for pleasure.

As the ship left the European continent behind, the sun broke through a bank of clouds that lay upon the western horizon. Captain Schroeder ordered the engine room to achieve the maximum speed of sixteen knots. At that moment, only the most pessimistic of the passengers must have felt anything other than hope and relief as the *St. Louis* assumed a steady southwest course.

But they were sailing in blissful ignorance. Members of the Cuban government in Havana, Nazi leaders in Berlin, the United States State Department in Washington, and Jewish relief and refugee organizations on two continents were already aware that something was amiss, and that the passengers on board the *St. Louis* might encounter difficulties when the vessel entered Cuban waters.

A confluence of corruption, greed, and internal power plays within the Cuban government was beginning to take effect. Manuel Benitez Gonzalez, the immigration officer who had sold his landing certificates to Alex, Helmut, and hundreds of other passengers, was a protégé of Army Chief of Staff Fulgencio Batista, who in a few years would become president of Cuba. But well-connected though he was, Benitez was on the outs with the current Cuban president, Federico Laredo Bru. And Benitez had made further enemies within the Cuban government through his shameless profiteering; by selling his landing certificates without so much as checking with other officials, he had managed to amass a personal fortune of nearly a million dollars. Unfortunately for the passengers on the *St. Louis*, President Bru chose this moment to demonstrate to his countrymen just who was in charge of Cuban immigration.

On May 5, eight days before the *St. Louis* steamed out of Hamburg, President Bru issued an order—coincidentally, given the number of passengers on board the ill-fated ship, known as Decree 937—that invalidated all of the Benitez landing certificates. The decree stipulated that only with written authorization from both the Cuban secretary of state and secretary of labor, plus the posting of a $500 bond, could an immigrant gain legal entry into Havana. This announcement was for internal consumption only; unfortunately for the passengers, word of Decree 937 never reached Germany.

Other issues were at play within Cuba as well. The country was still trying to dig itself out from under the effects of the worldwide Depression, and unemployment was high. Many Cubans thought that there were already far too many immigrants competing with native-born citizens for scarce jobs. And the island's twenty-five hundred Jews were an obvious target for the usual charges of financial manipulations and shady wire-pulling. An active Cuban Nazi Party encouraged the growth of anti-Semitism, as did three Havana newspapers that were owned by the influential Rivero family, outspoken supporters of the Spanish Fascist leader Francisco Franco.

Three days after the issuance of Decree 937, forty thousand people attended a boisterous rally in downtown Havana. The organizers pointed to the imminent departure of the *St. Louis* as yet another example of the worldwide Jewish threat. A speaker at the rally called upon his countrymen to "fight the Jews until the last one is driven out."

Those words were music to the ears of Joseph Goebbels. Still smarting from the editorial pounding the Nazis had taken over the events of the previous November, the propaganda minister was eager to show the world that it was not just Germany that had no use for the Jews. Recently, he and his colleagues in the German Foreign Office had made their position clear. "In all parts of the world," read a statement from the Foreign Office, "the influx of Jews arouses the resistance of the native population and thus provides the best propaganda for Germany's Jewish policy. In North America, South America, France, Holland, Scandinavia, and Greece—wherever the Jewish migratory current flows—a marked growth of anti-Semitism is already noticeable. It must be the task of German foreign policy to encourage this anti-Semitic wave."

Now, as the *St. Louis* steamed steadily onward, mounting internal and external pressures on the Cuban government threatened to prevent the

ship from disembarking her passengers in an orderly fashion. Such organizations as the London-based International Committee on Political
Refugees, the American Jewish Joint Distribution Committee of New
York, and the Jewish Relief Committee in Havana—all of whom were
following the progress of the journey—slowly came to the realization
that trouble lay ahead.

The passengers on board the *St. Louis*, however, knew nothing of
those matters and felt only a giddy pleasure as they neared the warm
waters of the Caribbean. On Thursday, May 25, they enjoyed a costume ball in the ship's nightclub, a party that traditionally signaled the
end of a voyage two nights before landing. Early on the morning of
Saturday, May 27, the *St. Louis* pulled into Havana Harbor, her horn
blasting most of the passengers awake at four o'clock. The breakfast
gong sounded at four-thirty, and despite the early hour the dining rooms
were soon full of sleepy, eager people, excited that their two weeks at
sea were nearly over.

But as day broke, the passengers gradually became aware that something was wrong. The ship was still out in the harbor and hadn't tied
up at the dock. In fact, late on Friday afternoon, Captain Schroeder had
received a cable from Luis Clasing, the Hamburg-America Line's representative in Havana, instructing him to "not, repeat not, make any
attempt to come alongside." Cuban President Bru was standing firm
behind Decree 937 and had let the Hamburg authorities know about it
in the most unambiguous manner possible.

Over the next few days, confusion reigned, as meetings and negotiations involving President Bru, Immigration Director-General Benitez,
Captain Schroeder, Luis Clasing, and Milton Goldsmith of the Jewish
Relief Committee all failed to come to a satisfactory resolution. At one
point, Cuban Secretary of State Juan Remos met with President Bru to
argue the moral aspects of the situation and to remind the president
that his stance might cost him the disfavor of the United States. But
Bru, after realizing that Army Chief of Staff Batista was not going
to intervene on one side or the other, stood his ground, refusing to let
the *St. Louis* passengers disembark. An exception was made for twenty-
eight lucky passengers who somehow had managed to secure valid entry
documents.

At first, the 909 people left on board the harbor-bound ship passed the time as best they could in the hundred-degree heat and heavy humidity. They took snapshots of the Havana skyline and purchased bananas, coconuts, and other tropical fruits from enterprising vendors who drew their little boats up alongside the luxury liner. But eventually the tension of waiting, on top of the fear of what might be transpiring, began to wear on everyone. On Tuesday, May 30, after four days of fretting that the delay was the prelude to a Nazi plot to send the *St. Louis* back to Germany and its occupants to concentration camps, a passenger named Max Loewe slashed his wrists with a razor and leaped overboard.

From that moment on, the stakes soared. Reporters from several international newspapers, who had come to Havana to cover the ship's arrival, sent dispatches home describing the plight of the refugees. A committee of *St. Louis* passengers was formed, and they sent telegrams to Mrs. Bru and to several public figures in the United States, pleading for assistance. In response to the newspaper stories, telegrams began to flood the American consulate in Havana insisting that something be done. And in the streets of New York, Washington, Chicago, and Atlantic City, demonstrators marched in protest.

Negotiations continued. Only yards from the *St. Louis*, a seaplane landed in Havana Harbor bearing Lawrence Berenson, a lawyer representing the American Jewish Joint Distribution Committee. Berenson, the former president of the Cuban-American Chamber of Commerce and a man with extensive business experience in Cuba, exuded confidence in his abilty to work out a deal.

But President Bru would not be budged—not by telegrams, not by a personal request from American ambassador Butler Wright, and most especially not by Lawrence Berenson. Bru actively disliked Berenson, thinking him an arrogant Yankee wheeler-dealer. At a chilly face-to-face meeting on Thursday, June 1, President Bru informed Berenson that he had ordered the *St. Louis* to depart Cuban waters the following day and that no further negotiations would take place until after the ship had sailed.

On Friday morning, June 2, Milton Goldsmith of Havana's Jewish Relief Committee came on board the *St. Louis* to tell her frightened passengers that everything possible was being done to insure their ultimate safety. Captain Schroeder, well aware of his passengers' worst fears, declared, "I give you my word that I will do everything possible to avoid going back to Germany. I know only too well what they would do to you." But shortly after eleven o'clock, Goldsmith returned to his office, the captain gave the order "dead slow ahead," and the ship began its journey northward. As Havana slowly faded astern, many passengers stood on deck and wept openly.

For the next four days, the *St. Louis* treaded water between Cuba and Florida, twice sailing so close to the American mainland that passengers could see the lights of downtown Miami. On June 3, President Bru offered to allow the ship to land if the Joint Distribution Committee would post a bond of $500 per passenger, or a total payment of more than $453,500. On June 4, Lawrence Berenson, thinking that Bru had merely begun negotiating, made a counteroffer. On June 5, Captain Schroeder heard a Miami radio station announce that President Bru had decided to let the ship land at Cuba's Isle of Pines. But on the morning of June 6, the Cuban government declared that negotiations over the matter of the *St. Louis* had been "terminated." The last hope for the 908 passengers was the United States of America.

But before too many more hours had passed, that "golden door" was shut as well. There were many reasons. The Immigration Act of 1924 set rigid quotas that limited the number of people who could enter the United States each year. For 1939, the quota from Germany and Austria was 27,370. Adding nearly a thousand more, all at once, would mean that an equal number of German Jews who had already applied for visas would have to be turned away.

Then there was the matter of American public opinion. Newspapers from coast to coast had documented the increasing savagery of the Nazis' treatment of the Jews, and by and large the American people were sympathetic. But despite their compassion, most Americans did not want the United States to become a haven for European Jews. According to a poll taken in the spring of 1939 by *Fortune* magazine, 83 percent of the American people opposed relaxing restrictions on immigration.

Few politicians, including the nation's First Politician, were willing to discount such a majority. An attempt to admit twenty thousand Jewish children from Germany, the Wagner-Rogers Bill of 1939, had died in committee. President Franklin Roosevelt had spoken not a word on behalf of Wagner-Rogers. And in response to two cables from the passengers' committee on board the *St. Louis*, Roosevelt remained silent.

During those first days of June, editorials published in several American newspapers attempted to rouse public sympathy for the plight of the *St. Louis* passengers. One of the most striking was a cartoon by Fred Packer that appeared in the New York *Daily Mirror* on June 6. Under the headline "Ashamed!," the Statue of Liberty stands with eyes averted as a boat labeled "Jewish Refugee Ship" steams past. Hanging from her upraised right arm, the arm bearing the torch, is a sign that reads, "Keep Out."

That same week a telegram arrived at the White House addressed to President Roosevelt from a number of Hollywood actors, including Edward G. Robinson and Miriam Hopkins. It read, "In name of humanity urge you bring all possible influence on Cuban authorities to radio return of German liner St. Louis, now at sea returning over nine hundred refugees to imprisonment and death in Nazi Germany. Urge Cuba give at least temporary shelter until another refuge can be found in democratic country."

But the White House and the State Department maintained that they had no authority to intervene in what they viewed as strictly a Cuban matter. Some voices within Roosevelt's cabinet even suggested that Nazi secret agents were on board the *St. Louis;* thus, allowing the ship to land in Miami would be tantamount to inviting those spies to infiltrate American society. In the end the Coast Guard was issued orders denying the ship entry into any American harbor.

At 11:30 P.M. on Tuesday, June 6, Captain Gustav Schroeder received a terse cable from Claus-Gottfried Holthusen, the director of the Hamburg-America Line. It read simply, "Return Hamburg Immediately." At 11:40, Captain Schroeder ordered his helmsman Heinz Kritsch to bring the ship onto a heading of east by northeast. The *St. Louis* was headed back to Germany.

Joseph Goebbels immediately seized on the news as further proof that the world shared the Nazis' low opinion of Jews. "Since no one will accept the shabby Jews on the *St. Louis*," the Propaganda Ministry declared, "we will have to take them back and support them."

It took little imagination to conclude that Nazi "support" more than likely meant being sent to the camps, and fear on board the ship grew to crisis proportions. A band of passengers attempted mutiny, overpowering the crew and seizing control of the engine room. The uprising was quickly contained, but Captain Schroeder himself began devising a desperate plan to save his terrified passengers should all other means of rescue prove impossible. He cleared his plan with three of his most trusted officers and a member of the passengers' committee. As a last resort, said the captain, he was prepared to run the *St. Louis* aground off the Sussex coast of England, set her on fire, and evacuate the passengers to shore.

For many on board the ship, Alex and Helmut among them, that plan, ill-conceived as it probably was, might ultimately have worked out for the best. But no such dramatics proved necessary, thanks to the efforts of another member of the American Jewish Joint Distribution Committee: its European director, Morris Troper. Working feverishly as the *St. Louis* steamed on, Troper convinced first Belgium and then France, Holland, and Great Britain each to take a percentage of the ship's refugees. England's acceptance of the arrangement was brokered in part by American ambassador Joseph P. Kennedy, father of the future president, who carried a letter outlining the terms to the proper authorities.

On the night of Tuesday, June 13, a week after the *St. Louis* had headed back to Europe and exactly a month since her departure from Hamburg, Morris Troper cabled the ship from Paris of his successful negotiations: "Final arrangements for disembarkation all passengers complete. Governments of Belgium, Holland, France and England cooperated magnificently with American Joint Distribution Committee to effect this possibility." The passengers' committee cabled back, "Our gratitude is as immense as the ocean on which we have been traveling."

The next morning, in the presence of Captain Schroeder, the committee read Troper's telegram to the assembled passengers. The announcement was met with unrestrained cheering and sobs of joy, and everyone embraced. They were Wandering Jews no more.

On Saturday morning, June 17, the *St. Louis* sailed into the estuary that leads to the city of Antwerp, Belgium. At a little after nine o'clock, Morris Troper and representatives of the four concerned countries were

ZWERFTOCHT NADERT ZIJN EINDE.

„St. Louis" op de reede van Vlissingen.

Diep ontroerende begroeting.

Velen weenen van blijdschap.

Na een zwerftocht van bijna 2½ maand komt het vluchtelingenschip „St. Louis" vanmiddag in de haven van Antwerpen aan, waar de bijna duizend beklagenswaardige passagiers voet aan wal kunnen zetten.

The headlines of a Dutch newspaper heralding the arrival of the St. Louis in Antwerp on June 17, 1939. The translation: "Wandering Nears Its End. 'St. Louis' on the way to Vlissingen. Deeply emotional greeting. Many weep for joy."

taken by tugboat to the steamer. A reception line of children was wait-ing to greet Troper. A little girl named Liesl Joseph, who was celebrat-ing her eleventh birthday that very day, said to him, "We thank you with all our hearts. I am sorry that flowers do not grow on ships; oth-erwise we would have given you the largest and most beautiful bouquet ever." With that, the whole crowd of passengers surged forward to shake the man's hand. In the next few hours, as the *St. Louis* made its way to the Antwerp pier, every passenger signed a note of gratitude to Troper.

Around two in the afternoon, just as the ship was pulling into its first berth in over a month, an ugly little confrontation broke out between Belgian police and a Nazi-inspired group called the National Youth Organization. The group was protesting the arrival of the ship, distributing handbills on which was printed the cheery message: "We, too, want to help the Jews. If they call at our offices each one will receive free of charge a length of rope and a long nail." After a few minutes of pushing and shoving, the police confiscated the handbills and dispersed the crowd.

Meanwhile, Troper and his colleagues had retired to the ship's social hall to sort out which passengers would go to which country. It had already been decided that England would take 287 refugees, France 224, Belgium 214, and Holland 184. But determining how the refugees would be distributed took the better part of that sunny Saturday.

Troper announced that he would do his best to see to it that no families were broken up. He also said that he would try to accomodate people with definite preferences. At that, Alex decided to request that he and Helmut be part of the English contingent, since Bertha had secured a passage to Leeds. But he found that there was no easy way to make his feelings known; within minutes of the start of the meeting, the entryway to the social hall was packed with passengers seeking to influence the deliberations. So Alex elected to leave their selection to chance. What difference did it really make, he reasoned, so long as they were out of Germany?

So fate intervened again. And fate determined that Alex and Hel-mut would be two of the 224 *St. Louis* passengers accepted by France.

That evening a French consular official handed them special cards on which were stamped the words "Refugees from the St. Louis." The next afternoon they gathered their few belongings together and, for the first time in thirty-seven days, set foot on dry land. Their six-thousand-mile odyssey was over.

But again it was only a beginning. Alex and Helmut walked a few hundred feet along the Antwerp docks and boarded another ship, a freighter called the *Rhakotis*, which had been hastily outfitted by the Hamburg-America Line to make the quick trip to France. Two days later they arrived in Boulogne. The morning after that, Tuesday, June 20, they were taken to a displaced persons camp in Le Mans while the French government decided exactly what to do with them.

If they were frustrated that their Cuban plans had come to naught, they were happy at least that their travels were over. And they were particularly happy to have been spared being returned to Germany. Here in France, they reasoned, the Nazis could no longer harm them. It was only a matter of time before they would make their way safely to the New World, this time for good.

But the Old World and its old hatreds would not let them go so easily. Ten weeks later, as the French government continued its lazy deliberations over its refugees, Germany invaded Poland and the world was once again at war. Overnight, Alex and Helmut Goldschmidt metamorphosed, in the eyes of their hosts, from displaced persons to enemy aliens. Eventually they were transported from the overall friendly atmosphere of Le Mans to the hostile confines of a camp called Rivesaltes in the Pyrenees. There, behind barbed-wire fences, Alex and Helmut began a life in which they subsisted on ever-shrinking rations of food and hope.

A final word about the ship that carried them so far from their homeland and so close to freedom. The *St. Louis* was bombed by the Royal Air Force in 1944 as it lay at anchor in Hamburg. After the war it was partly renovated and for a time served as a floating hotel. In 1950, with their profits plummeting, the new owners sold the ship for scrap, and it was broken up.

Captain Schroeder survived the war and died in 1959. For his efforts to find a safe haven for his passengers during his voyage of May and June 1939, Captain Gustav Schroeder was honored posthumously by Yad Vashem in Israel as one of the "Righteous Among the Nations."

19

Appointment
in Quito

LESS THAN A MONTH after Alex and Helmut Goldschmidt concluded their unsuccessful voyage to the New World only a few hundred miles from where they had started, Julian Gumpert also attempted to flee Germany for the West. He was both luckier and unluckier than they had been.

By the late spring of 1939, Julian had received his visa to Ecuador. As Alex and Helmut were steaming westward on the *St. Louis,* Julian had made arrangements to emigrate. But not with his wife. And not alone.

It was only after the chaos and carnage of the November Pogrom that Julian's eyes were opened to the dangers that threatened him in his homeland. Until then he had been completely caught up in the effort of teaching and making music under increasingly difficult circumstances. But rather than concentrate on the source of the difficulties and begin preparations to leave the country, Julian had chosen to work on circumventing them. He had seen the increased number of restrictions as a series of challenges and worked hard to meet them.

For one, maintaining the health and well-being of the Gumpert Conservatory had kept him occupied. In the years following 1933, as more Jews were asked to leave German music schools for "racial reasons," Julian's conservatory increasingly was seen as a haven where all students would receive the finest instruction. As the years went by, the building at 10 Ehrenstrasse in Düsseldorf welcomed more and more students who had begun their studies in the prestigious programs of Cologne and Frankfurt, Bonn and Leipzig. The Gumpert Conservatory became one of the musical landmarks of Düsseldorf, both as a center of learning and as a presenter of public concerts.

Eventually, however, the increasing marginalization of Jews slowly began to cripple the conservatory. Since it was no longer possible for a Jew to find employment with the mainstream German orchestras, and since the Jüdische Kulturbund had only a limited number of available positions, by the middle of the decade it had become apparent that a career in music for a German Jew was destined to be extremely limited. As more and more Jews chose emigration, fewer and fewer students applied to the Gumpert Conservatory. So Julian began to consider more carefully the offers of a merger with the Buths-Neitzel Conservatory, Düsseldorf's other music school. A similar alliance had been proposed in 1918, but had been discouraged by the city. Late in 1935, the process of a merger began in earnest, an effort that eventually led to the formation of what is today one of Germany's foremost academies, the Robert Schumann Hochschule für Musik.

But Julian remained at the center of musical life in Düsseldorf. He continued to give concerts, both recitals in private homes and as the conductor of his Jewish Chamber Orchestra, which remained active until the post-Kristallnacht crackdown outlawed all ensembles save the Kulturbund. The JCO faced the same repertory restrictions as the Kubu did, with non-Jewish German-born composers forbidden. One of the ways Julian attempted to keep the interest of his audience was by writing more and more of the music himself. He had composed a few chamber works in his youth and more chamber music (such as pieces for solo piano and violin and piano) earlier in the 1930s, but now he began writing for larger forces as well, including some songs for mezzo-soprano and orchestra; a concert overture; and an oratorio for tenor, male chorus, piano, and orchestra called *Salomo*.

Julian drew most of the members of the Jewish Chamber Orchestra from his roster of faculty, students, and former students of the Gumpert Conservatory. One of the violinists in the orchestra was a young man named Siegfried Solms, who had begun his studies at the conservatory when he was about twelve years old. In the course of lessons, rehearsals, and concerts with the boy, Julian met his mother, a red-haired widow named Nellie Solms. Julian and Nellie became friends,

Jüdische Winterhilfe Düsseldorf

Sonntag, 13. März 1938, 20 Uhr, Ibach-Saal

Konzert

des

Jüdischen Kammerorchesters Düsseldorf

Leitung: Julian Gumpert

unter freundlicher Mitwirkung von *Ruth Kisch-Arndt* (Alt)

Christoph Willibald Gluck: Ouvertüre zu „Iphigenie in Aulis" (Schluß von Mozart)

Christoph Willibald Gluck: Arie des Orpheus aus der Oper „Orpheus":
„Ach, ich habe sie verloren"
Ruth Kisch-Arndt

Anton Dvořak: 2 Sätze aus dem Terzetto op. 74 für 2 Violinen und Viola
Introduzione (Allegro ma non troppo) ~ Larghetto
Paul Carsch, Charlotte Fleischhacker, Julian Gumpert

Anton Dvořak: 3 Zigeunerlieder op. 55
a) „Mein Lied ertönt" b) „Als die alte Mutter" c) „Darf des Falken Schwinge"
Ruth Kisch-Arndt — am Klavier: *Hilde Jonas-Klestadt*

Peter Tschaikowsky: Andante cantabile aus dem Streichquartett op. 11

Julian Gumpert: 2 Lieder mit Orchester (zum 1. Male)
a) „Soviel Sonne kann ja niemals scheinen"
b) „Soll ich danken"
Ruth Kisch-Arndt

Niels W. Gade: Violinkonzert d moll op. 56, 1. Satz ~ Allegro con fuoco
Wolfgang Diederich — am Klavier: *Klaus Glücksmann*

Felix Mendelssohn-Bartholdy: Hochzeitsmarsch aus „Ein Sommernachtstraum"

Texte umseitig.

A program for a concert by Julian Gumpert's Jewish Chamber Orchestra.

and then more than friends. When the time came to flee the country, Julian asked Nellie and Siegfried to go with him.

Between late November of 1938, when he first contacted the Ecuadorian authorities, and early July of 1939, Julian told no one of his plans to emigrate. Once Günther had asked Rosemarie to marry him, Julian must have felt assured that his daughter would be provided for. But he made no provisions for the well-being of his wife.

I can only imagine her shock and fear when, on the morning of July 11, 1939, Julian Gumpert came downstairs fully dressed, carrying a packed suitcase in one hand and his Stradivarius violin in the other, and curtly informed Else Hayn that he was going away. He simply walked out on her, leaving her to fend for herself, a Jewish woman alone in Nazi Germany. He had demonstrated insensitive, cruel, and caddish behavior many times before. But given the circumstances, I have difficulty not likening this abandonment to an act of manslaughter, or what a lawyer might term negligent homicide.

Günther had wondered just what it was about Julian Gumpert that had enabled him to escape personal injury or loss during the November Pogrom. Günther had also noticed the peculiar jocularity that had accompanied Julian's interaction with the Nazi Justice of the Peace during his wedding on December 13. And now I wonder at the singular aspects of Grandfather Julian's departure from Germany in July of 1939.

He did not name Nellie or Siegfried Solms in any of his emigration documents and yet the three did manage to leave the country together. Most Jewish emigrés of the time were not permitted to take more than ten Reichsmarks with them, yet the authorities allowed Julian to cross the German border with a priceless violin under his arm. And then there was the manner in which Julian and his party made that border crossing. After taking a train from Düsseldorf to Bremen on July 11, the three flew on a Dutch airplane from Bremen to Amsterdam on July 16.

Given the state of enforced poverty in which most Jews found themselves by this time, it's a curious fact indeed that Julian Gumpert was able to emigrate by air. Obviously, he was one of the privileged few. I wonder why. Was it simply that he was a hearty man with an unusual ability to charm people? Or were there other reasons, perhaps a relationship to the authorities that I would rather not know about?

Julian did not leave the country with all he had hoped to, however. The Gestapo had been tracking his movements since New Year's Eve, 1938, the day they opened a file on him. They recorded his departure from Düsseldorf on July 11 and from Bremen on July 16. From Amsterdam, Julian, Nellie, and Siegfried traveled to Quito, presumably by boat. But Julian's Gestapo file takes note of the fact that on April 16, 1941, the Bremen branch of the secret police requested that his German citizenship be revoked and that a collection of articles he had brought with him to Bremen be removed from storage and auctioned off. The weight of those possessions amounted to 1,789 kilograms, or about 3,600 pounds.

It seems that Julian and Nellie had been confident enough of their ability to circumvent the rule allowing only minimum baggage to take a large number of belongings with them when they left home. But it also seems that whatever deal they had been able to strike in Düsseldorf cut no ice with the authorities in Bremen. How Julian must have raged when he was forced to leave so much behind with a storage company and fly off to Amsterdam. And yet the fiddle, easily his most valuable possession, flew along with him. He must have thought that once he arrived in South America he could begin the process of reclaiming his other goods.

No doubt he also envisioned a new life in Ecuador. It would encompass many aspects of his old life, with music at its heart. He would teach, he would perform, he would compose. Perhaps he had plans to open another conservatory, one that could and would welcome any and all citizens of his new home. And in a land free of persecution, perhaps Julian could devote himself more fully to his new family; he and Nellie would grow old together, and Siegfried, like Rosemarie before him, would benefit from Julian's inspired teaching.

In the end, however, his plans were as forfeited as his possessions had been. He was luckier than my other grandfather in that he actually reached his destination in the New World. But within ten days of his arrival in Quito, Julian Gumpert was dead—felled by a heart attack brought on by the high altitude and thin air. He was sixty-three years old.

Word of his death reached Germany several weeks later. My father remembers that my mother, still reeling from his sudden disappearance, seemed numbed by the news. Only after many years, when they were safe and she had had time to think and feel deeply, did Rosemarie reflect on what her father had meant to her life and to her career. I'm not sure that she entirely forgave him for abandoning her mother, but she deeply mourned the man who had given her music.

To this day, I have no idea what happened to my grandfather's Stradivarius. About twenty-five years after his death, my parents retained a lawyer to try to track it down. But the lawyer's inquiries came to nothing and the violin was never found.

Ever since I learned of it, the story of Julian fleeing persecution and death in Nazi Germany only to die suddenly in a foreign land thousands of miles from his home has struck me as rich in an almost literary irony. Only recently did I come across this passage in *Sheppey*, a play by W. Somerset Maugham:

> There was a merchant in Bagdad who sent his servant to market to buy provisions. In a little while the servant came back, white and trembling, and said, Master, just now when I was in the market-place I was jostled by a woman in the crowd and when I turned I saw it was Death that jostled me. She looked at me and made a threatening gesture. Lend me your horse and I will ride away from this city and avoid my fate. I will go to Samarra and there Death will not find me. The merchant lent him his horse and the servant mounted it and dug his spurs in its flanks, and as fast as the horse could gallop he went. Then the merchant went down to the market-place and saw Death standing in the crowd and he said to her, Why did you make a threatening gesture to my servant when you saw him? That was not a threatening gesture, said Death, it was only a start of surprise. I was astonished to see him in Bagdad this morning, for I have an appointment with him tonight in Samarra.

After a life in music, one which touched many and inspired many others, including my mother, and through her, me, Grandfather Julian apparently had—and kept—an appointment in Quito.

20

Eine Kleine
Curfew Music

I sit in one of the dives
On Fifty-Second Street
Uncertain and afraid
As the clever hopes expire
Of a low dishonest decade . . .
The unmentionable odour of death
Offends the September night.

With those words W. H. Auden began his poem "September 1, 1939,"
taking sorrowful note of the start of the Second World War. On that
date, German troops began their lightning ground and air assault
against Poland.

That morning, as the musicians of the Jüdische Kulturbund gathered for a rehearsal, they were anything but uncertain and afraid. My
father remembers a tremendous excitement, a sense almost of glee, puls-
ing through the corridors of the theater on Kommandantenstrasse. Everyone was convinced that Adolf Hitler had overreached at last and that
the beginning of the war meant the eventual undoing of the Nazis.
They were right, of course, but nobody could foresee how much misery, suffering, destruction, and death the world would endure before
Hitler's defeat was assured.

The Kulturbund had already suffered a casualty before the Wehr-
macht moved on Poland. In the last days of August, Werner Levie quietly
informed his colleagues that he had managed to secure passage back

to Holland, the country of his birth. Though they were devastated to lose him and his abilities, the other directors of the Kubu solidly encouraged his emigration. The leadership of the Kulturbund now passed to a triumvirate of Martin Brasch, Moritz Henschel, and Dr. Arthur Lilienthal. When the war began, the theater on Kommandantenstrasse suffered some collateral damage. Late in the evening of September 1, Martin Brasch received a call from the office of Hans Hinkel informing him that the Kulturbund was to be shut down until further notice.

That was only the first of three directives to be issued against the Jews of Germany during the first month of wartime. On the tenth, SS Reichsführer Heinrich Himmler announced that Jews would henceforth be subjected to a daily curfew: they had to be off the streets by eight o'clock in winter and nine during the summer. And then on September 23 came the order that Jews must surrender their radios. Many Jews had already markedly decreased the number of hours they listened to the radio because of the constant polluted stream of propaganda directed at them, yet it was possible to pull in a few foreign broadcasts, and those would be missed. This decree was yet another in a seemingly never-ending series of humiliations and harassments simply, and effectively, designed to break their spirit.

German Jews had to get along without the Kulturbund's efforts to revive their spirits through most of the month of September, but on September 24 the film bureau once again opened for business, and on October 1 the order came down to resume rehearsals for plays and concerts. Despite the war—or perhaps especially because of it—the Kulturbund was still of use to the Reich.

The members of the Kubu agreed once more to shake off the debilitating effects of the latest edicts and begin another exhausting yet exhilirating season of planning, preparation, and performance. No matter what obstacles the Nazis placed in their path, the artists always seemed to find a way to continue.

But now they had to reorganize yet again to adapt to wartime and the emigration of their audience. The board of directors, led by Martin Brasch, decided to implement three new policies designed to increase attendance and reduce costs. First, he did away with one of the original

Kubu mandates. From now on, subscriptions would no longer be required, and the Kulturbund began selling individual tickets to all plays and concerts. With the loosening of the subscription policy, about thirty thousand people made their way to Kommandantenstrasse that season, a figure that represented more than a third of all Jews then living in Berlin.

The board of directors also decided to shrink the newspaper. The *Nachrichtenblatt* was reduced from eight pages to four on Tuesdays and from sixteen pages to six on Fridays. This was a far less popular decision; subscriptions to the paper fell by seven thousand in the first two months.

The final effort to lower the budget was the most drastic. All of the Kulturbund's performing artists—musicians, actors, and singers—agreed to forgo their seasonal contracts and instead be paid on a per-service basis: so much for a rehearsal, so much for a performance. The employees of the two most successful branches of the organization, the film bureau and the publishing house, were exempt from that decision and were still paid a salary, as were a few office workers deemed to be indispensable.

The artists' fees were small. For instance, during the 1939–1940 season, music director Rudolf Schwarz averaged 150 Reichsmarks per month. (At the same time, conductors Herbert von Karajan and Wilhelm Furtwängler were commanding fees of four thousand Reichsmarks *per concert* for their performances with the Berlin Philharmonic.) These belt-tightening measures proved successful, however. After an initial slump caused by its enforced inactivity during September 1939, the Kulturbund rebounded to show profits every month thereafter.

The artists always worked under the shadow of uncertainty and terror. Along with the resumption of normal activities came a requirement that the Kulturbund's employees—those men under forty-five years of age and women under thirty, that is—join the rest of the Jewish population and register with a governmental body known as the Arbeitsamt for periodic forced labor.

Rumors of labor camps had been floating around the Kulturbund for months, although no one knew quite what to believe. The rumors had led to at least one significant casting decision, however. Back in July the Kubu had mounted a production of an operetta by Emerich Kalman called *Countess Maritza*. As the run was drawing to a close, there were whispers backstage that the company's dancers were in trouble. Someone had heard that since the next production didn't call for any dancers, they would all be sent off to camps immediately after the final curtain fell. Just in case the rumors turned out to be true, conductor Rudolf Schwarz and director Kurt Baumann devised a plan to mount what they called a "ballet pantomime" based on music by the late eighteenth-century Belgian-born composer André Ernest Grétry. Schwarz and Baumann asked Kubu dancer Hannah Kroner, then nineteen, to choreograph the ballet and cast the production. She was quietly instructed to hold auditions but to make sure to reserve a role for every dancer who had been a part of the *Maritza* production. In that way it was possible for Werner Levie to protect the freedom of a few more of his charges, at least for another month.

As it happened, however, the members of the Kulturbund had a higher-placed protector than their embattled artistic director. Internal politics and savage turf wars had always played a major part in the Nazi hierarchy, and now a fight broke out between the ministries of Labor and Propaganda that actually worked to the Kubu's advantage.

Shortly after October 1, Kurt Michaelis, an oboeist in the Kulturbund Orchestra, received a letter summoning him to the Labor Department a few days hence. Michaelis had no doubt that when he got there he would be dispatched immediately to a camp and would find himself breaking up rocks. But on the day before his appointment another letter arrived, this one from the Ministry of Public Enlightenment and Propaganda. Hans Hinkel had somehow gotten wind of the fact that one of "his" artists was in harm's way and had moved quickly to parry the thrust. This second official letter informed the bearer that under no circumstances was Kurt Michaelis to be employed for any purpose other than to play his instrument.

As Michaelis remembers the incident today, "I had that letter in my pocket when I went down to that office and there was one of those nasty people, gloating that he'd gotten another victim. So I took out the letter from Hinkel and he was very angry because the victim had slipped away, had escaped him."

During the next two years there would be many such incidents. Shortly before his death in 1960, Hans Hinkel argued that his letters are evidence that he sincerely wanted to protect Jewish artists. Other observers have taken a far less charitable view of Hinkel's actions, insisting that he was acting out of a ruthless self-interest, more concerned with preserving his domain than with protecting individuals.

As official Germany continued to celebrate the fall of Poland and the inability or unwillingness of France and England to do more than declare war, the Kulturbund resumed its activities in November. Fritz Wisten directed a production of *Anatol's Wedding Morning*, a play by Arthur Schnitzler; and Julius Prüwer, who had conducted the Frankfurt Kulturbund Orchestra for several years, came to Berlin to lead a program of Slavonic Dances by Antonín Dvořák and the Symphony No. 5 by Tchaikovsky. The world might be at war, but the Kubu played on.

They could play, but they couldn't talk. That, at least, was the result of the next decree to be handed down from above. On December 1, the Kulturbund's lecture series, a staple of the organization since its beginnings in 1933, was abruptly forbidden. There was no obvious reason for the ban; nothing inflammatory or provocative had been delivered from the Kubu's modest lectern. But someone in the Propaganda Ministry, his ear attuned to the potential power of words, had decided that while music, films, and scripted dialogue were benign, a free-flowing forum where opinions could be exchanged might prove threatening, a breeding ground for infectious ideas. So, just like that, the lectures stopped.

Another Christmas season came and went and a new decade began. Günther was now twenty-six and in January Rosemarie turned twenty-three. The ugly, turbulent tempest of war raged around them, but they and their circle of friends did their best to maintain a quiet, peaceful haven of music and relaxation at its center. They went eagerly to their many rehearsals. While today a major orchestra in Europe or America usually allots three or four rehearsals per concert, the concerts at the Kulturbund were the culmination of twenty to twenty-five rehearsals. Not only did that ensure a very high level of performance once the audience was allowed into the theater, but it also enabled Günther and Rosemarie to revel in what was, to them, new literature and new encounters.

In December the orchestra performed the music that French composer Georges Bizet had written for a play called *L'Arlésienne*. A potboiler melodrama about a young man who kills himself because he doesn't get the girl, the play itself is almost never performed today. But Bizet's music is a marvel, conjuring up the heat and passion, the beauty and sensual lassitude of the south of France. My parents were entranced, Rosemarie in particular. I think I can trace the love she felt for Provence in her later years to this first encounter with its soul and spirit as she played Bizet's bright music during that dark and dreary December in Berlin.

Günther treasured his musical discoveries as well, but on a different and slightly unusual level. Most musicians who play in an orchestra tend to look after their own part. They hone it and polish it and make it shine to the best of their abilities, but rarely do they concern themselves with what musicians in other sections are doing. Second violinists, in other words, don't usually worry, or care, much about what the bassoons are doing (at least so long as they play in tune). But Günther was very interested in what was going on outside the flute section. He would often take whole scores of pieces the orchestra was playing home with him and study them so that he would more fully understand where the music was going and what the composer was trying to communicate. On the one hand, I think he was trying to be a better musician. On the other, he was simply satisfying his natural curiosity.

Günther and Rosemarie loved their cozy little apartment on Prinzenstrasse, but they would often forsake the city when they could and, as they had always done, take a train or streetcar to the distant suburbs and tramp over the hills and through the woods and fields. On those walks they would occasionally visit the charming region of Fürstenwalde to the southeast, the former royal city of Potsdam to the southwest, or the twin villages of Wernitz and Wustermark to the west. But they wouldn't travel north. Northbound trains stopped in the city of Oranienburg, which housed, just outside of town, the concentration camp called Sachsenhausen. One Goldschmidt visit to Sachsenhausen, Günther reasoned, was enough.

Their favorite recreational activity, however, involved their first love, music. Several times a month they met with friends and made music

Rudolf Schwarz conducts the Berlin Kulturbund Orchestra. Rosemarie is in the upper left center of the photograph.

in the relaxed, informal atmosphere of someone's home. On Saturday or Sunday afternoons, fifteen or twenty musicians would gather in a house or apartment to read through music of every possible description, written for every possible combination of instruments. A typical session might include performances of a sonata for cello and piano; a trio for flute, violin, and viola; a string quartet; a wind quintet; or a nonet for strings and winds. The repertory was limited only by the musicians' imagination and the available space. The hosts for these afternoons rotated among the participants, as did the honor of playing first violin, for instance, in a string quartet performance. A musician who owned a piano, however, would host these gatherings more frequently.

While one group of musicians played, the others sat in chairs or sprawled on the floor, listening intently, ready to offer opinions on questions of tempo and balance. Between performances, everyone munched

The wind section of the Berlin Kulturbund Orchestra. Günther is seated second from left in the second row. To his left is oboist Kurt Michaelis.

on fruit or crackers and discussed poetry or literature or painting. They shared suggestions for hikes or bicycle rides. But the conversation almost never turned to what euphemistically was called "the situation." The danger that forever lurked outside the walls of the chamber stayed outside. Inside was music and its stimulation and its peace.

The people who participated in these afternoons were mostly members of the Kulturbund, who enjoyed getting together away from the more regimented atmosphere of Kommandantenstrasse. But a few other musicians came as well. A young double bass player named Henry Bloch, a surgeon-violinist named Walter Kappell, and a divorce lawyer named Max Lehrmann who also played the violin joined in the performances, while a young woman named Gerti Totschek contributed to the lively conversations and also frequently brought sandwiches to share with her friends. The afternoons usually broke up shortly after seven o'clock, with the participants reluctantly heading off to be home before curfew.

Talking about those sessions today, Henry and Gerti remember Rosemarie as fairly serious and always well prepared, while Günther was more outgoing and friendly. Their long-standing memories conform to my more recent ones; music-making was always a serious business for my mother, her marvelous sense of humor notwithstanding. Her early lessons with Julian, the former court concertmaster, obviously left their mark.

Those weekend get-togethers, enjoyable as they were, were not enough to satisfy Rosemarie and Günther's hunger for chamber music and camaraderie. Once or twice during the week they would get together with a much smaller group of musicians—maybe three or four others—and play and talk some more. These sessions nearly always broke up long after curfew and would necessitate the flagrant breaking of the law as the young people sneaked home to their beds.

Although my parents spoke very little to me when I was younger of their time in Germany, they must have mentioned their illegal nocturnal journeys home from making music, because it's an image of them I have had—and held dear—for years. It may, in fact, have formed the most significant impression I possess of my parents. That image, that vision, may also have done more to shape my own relationship to life and music than anything else I can think of.

I picture two young people in their twenties, holding instrument cases in one hand and their life partner by the other as they walk quickly down a dark and dangerous street. (To risk riding a streetcar or subway would be foolhardy.) At any moment they may be stopped by a uniformed policeman or a plain-clothed partisan of the secret police. Failure to produce Aryan identification will mean immediate incarceration, and once their identity as Jews becomes known they will be sent to Sachsenhausen or Buchenwald or Dachau. They know the penalty. And they take the risk anyway.

My heart goes out to them as fools, fools for love, fools for the love of music—music that could cost them their lives, but music they cannot live without. As moviegoers cry out uselessly to the screen to warn the celluloid hero and heroine of imminent danger, I beg my mother and father to be careful, please be careful, as they navigate their way through this sixty-year-old vision. And I am so proud of them and so grateful to them for showing me what is truly important, for showing me that you must love the people and things that are important to you and that you must sometimes risk everything for that love. There is no finer lesson for parents to teach their children.

I've also learned that the things you love take care of you, sometimes in mysterious ways. Günther and Rosemarie's love of chamber music led them to someone who would prove instrumental in saving their lives.

The lawyer Lehrmann, who joined and sometimes hosted those afternoon gatherings, had somehow been invited to play chamber music at the American embassy. He, in turn, invited Günther and Rosemarie to join in. And so it happened that in late January of 1940 my parents found themselves walking into the graceful granite building located just off the avenue called Unter den Linden, a block or so east of the Brandenburg Gate, taking their first steps on what was officially American soil.

They returned several times over the next few months. They enjoyed playing, they liked the free and easy atmosphere, and Günther was particularly enthusiastic about the refreshments that were served after the performances. He was especially fond of the flavorful Swiss cheese that, he learned, was manufactured in a state he'd never heard of before: Wisconsin.

After one of these concerts, Günther and Rosemarie met an employee of the embassy, a woman my father remembers only as Mrs. Schneider. She took a liking to the two young people. They spoke often after that, sometimes in German, as a challenge to Mrs. Schneider, and sometimes in English, so that Günther and Rosemarie could practice a language they had each studied only briefly in school. They talked mostly about music, but Mrs. Schneider also spoke lovingly of her homeland and suggested to her new young friends that they consider emigrating there. She was undoubtedly aware of the conditions under which they were living, but she diplomatically never spoke of them, preferring instead to paint a beautiful picture of her United States.

Günther and Rosemarie were certainly intrigued by the thought of moving to America, but had no idea how to begin the process. But just then lightning struck, in the form of a letter from Rosemarie's mother,

Else, still living alone in Düsseldorf. Julian's former student—the one who earlier had written to Julian offering his help—had written back with the electrifying news that, unbeknownst to any of them, he had been looking for and had just found an American sponsor for Günther and Rosemarie.

If one wanted to emigrate to America, the first hurdle was also one of the biggest. It was necessary to find someone who would act as a sponsor, a person who would sign an affidavit swearing that the new arrivals could support themselves and would never become dependent on public welfare. Julian's former student had secured the promise of a well-to-do American music lover, known to my parents only as Mr. Shapiro. He would remain only a name to them. Generous as he was, Mr. Shapiro chose never to meet Günther and Rosemarie in later years. He wanted no thanks for saving their lives.

But with his promise to sponsor them in hand, they could now actively begin the process of applying for a visa. Mrs. Schneider enthusiastically helped them fill out the necessary papers. She also told them to be prepared for a long wait. This was an election year, she said, and an unusual one at that; President Roosevelt had decided, with the onset of war, to run for an unprecedented third term. Immigration issues might arise during the campaign and to postpone any heated debates on the topic the administration would probably drag its feet on processing new applications. But, she concluded cheerfully, if they were patient they would surely be successful.

So with their applications forwarded to Washington by their new friend, Günther and Rosemarie waited through the spring and summer of 1940. Those months witnessed the high noon of the Third Reich, as the Nazi sun blazed down upon the newly conquered countries of Denmark and Norway, Holland and Belgium and France. Berlin seemed more and more the capital of what was destined to become a worldwide empire, and for the first time the Kulturbund musicians who had expressed hope at the outset of the war began openly to fear that Chancellor Hitler would never be stopped.

But even as German tanks rolled virtually unopposed through the Low Countries, and as swastikas flapped from the Eiffel Tower, the artists of the Kulturbund continued to entertain their audiences. Fritz

Wisten directed productions of Shakespeare's *The Taming of the Shrew* and Molière's *The Imaginary Invalid*. The orchestra played concertos by Corelli and Chopin, symphonies by Mendelssohn and Tchaikovsky, a set of scenes from *The Damnation of Faust* by Hector Berlioz, and gave a concert performance of the opera *Cavalleria Rusticana* by Pietro Mascagni. The Kubu's film bureau screened such movies as *It Happened One Night*, *Shanghai Express*, *Anna Karenina*, the Jeannette MacDonald musical *Rosemarie*, and MGM's *Broadway Melody of 1936*.

Now more than ever, the Jews of Berlin needed the escape of theater, music, and the flickering silver screen. Rationing had come to Berlin at the beginning of the year, and everyone had been issued ration cards that delineated how much of each product the card's bearer could purchase at any given time. The cards distributed to Jews bore a bright red letter J and contained fewer items than those given to "Aryans." Then, in early July, came the next decree: from this point on, Jews were allowed to shop for groceries only between the hours of four and five in the afternoon. Most shops opened for business at eight or nine in the morning and offered fresh produce. By the time Jews were allowed inside a store, most of its shelves had been picked clean of quality items. All that remained were the leftovers: too-soft tomatoes, too-hard bread, cheese that was beginning to go bad. And often the shelves were bare.

Luckily, Günther and Rosemarie weren't terribly choosy when it came to food. They would often leave the theater about four o'clock and visit the few stores on Ritterstrasse on the way back to their apartment. Rosemarie would pick up enough items for a stew, trusting that an hour of bubbling on their tiny stove would do wonders for the frequently questionable quality of the ingredients. When they were able to find still-fresh fruits for dessert, they simply thought of those evenings as special occasions.

In September of 1940, their little family grew when both of their mothers moved to Berlin to be near them. Toni and Else had each lost a husband—one through mischance and one through betrayal—in the summer of 1939. Over the next year they wrote frequently, commiserating with each other and finding themselves drawn together by their fate and by their children. Finally they decided to pool their resources. Else sold her apartment on Boltensternstrasse and Toni didn't renew her lease on Staulinie, and the two women and Günther's younger sister, Eva, moved into a pleasant little house at 160 Manfred von Richthofenstrasse in the Tempelhof section of Berlin, just about two miles south of Prinzenstrasse.

Their two-story house was fronted by a little white fence and a tiny yard. There was more green space at the side and in the back, with a few tall, graceful trees on the property and across the street. The women maintained a few flowers in the garden and in the window boxes that hung from the second-story windows. The inside of the house was a little cluttered with two sets of furniture; neither Toni nor Else was eager to give up certain special chairs or tables, all of which contained years of memories in the grain of their wood. So everyone just accepted a little less floor space and watched their step carefully, especially when Günther and Rosemarie came over for dinner, which they did several times a month.

Within days of their arrival in Berlin, Toni and Eva proudly accompanied Günther and Rosemarie to Kommandantenstrasse to watch them perform. Else stayed home; her years with Julian had engendered a certain discomfort with music, and even the opportunity to hear her daughter and son-in-law play couldn't entice her from what she claimed was the more important job of unpacking.

That afternoon Rudolf Schwarz conducted the Kulturbund Orchestra in the beautifully sad *Songs of a Wayfarer* by Gustav Mahler, and the poetic and powerful Symphony No. 2 by Finnish composer Jean Sibelius. The soloist in the Mahler was Günther and Rosemarie's old acquaintaince Wilhelm Guttmann, the baritone who had sung the role of Rigoletto. It was one of those nights when everything comes together, when music and musicians reveal a thrilling glimpse of the human spirit. After the concert Günther bent the rules of the theater by allowing his mother and sister to join the musicians backstage. Toni and Eva were so excited they both began speaking at once, gushing with praise for the music, the performances, the conductor, and the soloist.

"And here is Herr Guttmann now," said Günther, grasping the baritone by the sleeve as he was about to stride out the stage door. The older man was stylishly dressed, wearing black trousers, a white silk shirt, a black leather jacket, a white silk scarf and a black Tyrolean hat. "Wilhelm Guttmann, my mother, Toni, and my sister, Eva."

The two women stammered their thanks and praise, while Guttmann quickly shook Toni's hand and then, turning to Eva, bowed, clicked his heels in the traditional German manner, lifted her right hand to his lips and kissed it while gazing purposefully over their clasped hands into her eyes.

"Such a charming young woman," purred Guttmann, "makes this dreary theater almost charming itself. So, Günther," he continued, returning Eva's hand reluctantly, "you never told me you had such a sister as this. So lovely, and so young . . . you must still be in school, is that right, my dear?"

"Oh, no," said Günther, before Eva could recover. "She's no longer a schoolgirl. She celebrated her twentieth birthday in June."

Eva turned on her brother, blushing furiously, but said nothing. Guttmann laughed.

"Well, you're all old enough to share a drink with me then. Come on . . . you're all invited back to my place for some vodka."

"Thank you, thank you very much, but no," said Toni. "We must be getting back home. It'll be time for curfew before we know it."

"Well, then," replied Guttmann, eyeing Eva, "perhaps in that case, the young lady. I'd be most happy to see to it that she's off the streets at the appointed time."

Eva, her eyes wide, could say nothing. Günther stepped forward, shook Guttmann's hand, and said loudly, "We're all a bit worn out, Wilhelm. But thanks again for your . . . offer of hospitality. Another time, perhaps?"

The baritone bowed again, grinned wolfishly, and swept out the door into the courtyard that surrounded the theater. He lifted his hat in ironic greeting to the Gestapo man standing guard and walked away down Kommandantenstrasse, whistling the jaunty melody to the first of the Mahler songs he'd sung that night.

"My goodness," breathed Toni. "Are all your friends so unrestrained as that?"

Günther and Rosemarie both laughed. "Oh, no," said Rosemarie. "I can assure you. There is no one here quite like Willy."

"I'm sorry, Mother . . . Eva," chuckled Günther. "I should have warned you. But he's perfectly harmless and a wonderful character. I'm sure you'll see more of him."

And they did, a few weeks later, when Guttmann sang the role of Tonio in a Kulturbund production of the opera *I Pagliacci* by Ruggiero Leoncavallo. After singing the opera's famous prologue, in which he steps in front of the curtain to warn the audience that they are about to see an example of real human behavior, the lustful Tonio plays on the jealousies of the tragic clown Canio until Canio eventually stabs his wife to death. The murder occurs in full view of an audience of townspeople who have come to see a troupe of roving players. The opera created a sensation at its premiere in 1892; less than fifty years later, it still packed an emotional punch for the Kulturbund audience, and everyone agreed that Wilhelm Guttmann's slyly insinuating Tonio was a highlight of the production.

Afterwards, Günther, Rosemarie, Toni, and Eva, all properly prepared for the experience, accepted Guttmann's offer to accompany him to his small apartment for a celebratory drink. The baritone downed several shots of vodka, Günther drank a glass of beer, and Rosemarie and Toni each had a small glass of wine. Eva brewed herself a cup of tea as Guttmann looked on in bright-eyed amusement.

After they'd settled themselves and talked for a bit, Eva shyly asked Guttmann if he would mind singing a bit more for them.

"I never sing unless my listeners pay for the privilege," he declared boisterously. "But if you, my dear, will accept two conditions I will sing the entire prologue to the opera you have just witnessed."

"And what are they?"

"A drink and a kiss. And I mean a *real* drink and a *real* kiss. From me."

The room erupted in loud applause. Even Toni joined in. Eva went deeply red, but laughed and nodded.

So Wilhelm Guttmann jumped up, walked over to the little Knabe upright piano that sat along one wall of his apartment and, accompanying himself at the keyboard, gave a riotously over-the-top performance of the prologue to *Pagliacci*, complete with exaggerated hand and facial gestures that left his audience of four nearly paralyzed with laughter.

When it was over, to thunderous applause from his guests, Guttmann grabbed a glass, poured in three fingers of vodka, draped a napkin over his forearm, bowed, and elaborately offered the glass to Eva.

"For services rendered," he said mockingly.

Eva looked around the room at her family, smiled, shrugged, and downed the contents of the glass in a single gulp. And then, while she was still absorbing the effects of her drink, Guttmann embraced her and kissed her full on the lips. He released her with a gleeful shout.

"That's more than I've been paid by those Kubu crooks for years!" he bellowed.

When the four visitors took their leave an hour later, they were all more than a little unsteady on their feet, but feeling very warm against the autumn chill.

But such evenings could not block out the reality of a world war for long. It was at about this time that England's Royal Air Force began to penetrate Germany's air defenses to inflict regular bombing attacks upon Berlin. Many nights Günther and Rosemarie would be jolted awake by the shriek of air-raid sirens. Throwing on whatever clothes were handy, they would feel their way down the stairs to the courtyard of their apartment building and then run a block north up Prinzenstrasse, their arms around each other, to the subway stop at Moritzplatz that served as a bomb shelter. At the top of the stairs leading down to the shelter was a large sign on which were printed the words *Juden Verboten*—"Jews Forbidden." During the first air raid they paused briefly when they saw the sign, only to be driven underground by the continuing wail of the siren. Günther reasoned that if challenged, they could always claim to have left their papers back at the apartment. Thereafter they ventured down the steps without thinking of any danger other than the RAF bombs dropping all around them.

Each time they sat huddled together in the shelter, the thump of exploding bombs clearly audible above, emotions raged within them. On the one hand, they feared for their own safety and that of their friends and colleagues. What would they do if they emerged one night to find their building in flames, their few possessions destroyed? On the other, they hoped that a skilled RAF marksman would score a direct hit upon Adolf Hitler's chancellory, which was just a few blocks to the west at Potsdamer Platz. Each air raid brought equal measures of terror and hope.

And yet when the all-clear siren sounded and Günther and Rosemarie climbed up the stairs with their fellow citizens to face whatever damage the bombers had inflicted upon their city, the ruin around them always deflated their spirits. On one occasion they learned of the destruction of Berlin's Staatsoper. On another they saw that the concussion of a bomb exploding several streets away had shattered the stained-glass windows of the Church of St. Simeon, where they had gone on their first Christmas Eve in Berlin.

At the sight of the broken colored glass, Rosemarie sat down on the sidewalk and began to cry.

"Oh, Günther," she sobbed. "What's going to happen to us?"

He sat down beside her, kissed her, stroked her hair.

"Our visas should be here soon. We will leave this place. We will go to America and be safe. Soon. Very soon."

Rosemarie stared at him bleakly.

"No we won't. We will never leave here. We will never get out of Berlin."

Günther helped his wife up, embraced her, and led her home to bed. He deeply hoped he was right.

The Kulturbund had lost many of its artists in the preceding months as more of them had been successful in their attempts to emigrate. But in December of 1940 the Kubu actually gained a member, a seventeen-year-old violinist from Dresden named Henry Meyer. Through a chance meeting with a Kubu musician, Meyer got himself an audition with conductor Rudolf Schwarz. During the audition, Meyer played some solo Bach and, accompanied by Schwarz at the piano, a movement from a Mozart concerto. Schwarz was so impressed that he invited the young man to that afternoon's Kulturbund rehearsal.

The orchestra was rehearsing the colorful tone poem "Sheherezade" by Nicolai Rimsky-Korsakov, a brilliant showpiece based on the *Arabian Nights*. Rimsky gives the voice of Sheherezade—the wily wife of the Caliph of Bagdad, who saves her own life by spinning fantastic tales over a thousand and one nights—to a solo violin. It's the job of the solo fiddle player to make the mythic beauty come alive, her voice sometimes soaring, sometimes whispering, always mesmerizing her husband and those of us who listen. During that day's rehearsal, Rudolf Schwarz asked several of the orchestra's violinists to play parts of the difficult solo passages, and he asked Henry Meyer to play some of them, too. At the end of the rehearsal, the orchestra broke out into enthusiastic applause for young Henry, and Schwarz immediately invited him to join the ensemble. He did, becoming, in his words, "the Benjamin of the orchestra"—in other words, the youngest.

Within a few days Günther and Rosemarie introduced themselves to Henry. The orchestra was made up largely of older people by this time, since most of the younger musicians had left. Still in their middle twenties, Günther and Rosemarie were not much older than Henry, so they felt an immediate connection with him. Then, when the three of them discovered that they shared an enthusiasm for painting, literature, and the all-important topic of chamber music, they became friends and began to spend a lot of their free time together.

On New Year's Eve, 1940, Günther and Rosemarie, along with Henry and another Kubu violinist, were invited to the home of one of their acquaintances from the American embassy chamber music series. Heinz Loewe, a very fine amateur cellist, wanted to ring in the New Year with a meal and a night of reading through some scores. He and his wife knew they were asking their guests to break the curfew, but everyone decided that the police would probably look the other way during this night of revelry.

At four that afternoon, Rosemarie paid a visit to the local grocer to pick up something she could contribute. Since the "Aryan" population of the neighborhood had been shopping steadily since morning, all she could find were a few small cherries that had been picked over and left in the corner of a bin on the floor. When she and Günther knocked on the door of the Loewe apartment shortly before eight o'clock, they had only their instruments and a bag of cherries to contribute to the festivities.

The night began with Günther, Rosemarie, and Henry playing through the Serenade for Flute, Violin, and Viola by Beethoven, the very

Berlin, 1940: Rosemarie, Günther, and Henry Meyer (left to right) playing the Serenade for Flute, Violin, and Viola by Beethoven.

piece Rosemarie and Julian had been working on when Günther had fled to Düsseldorf more than two years earlier. After a break for dinner, the four string players sat down to play the intense, dark-hued Quartet Movement by Franz Schubert. It lasts only about nine minutes and nobody knows exactly when or for what larger work Schubert composed this music, but its combination of soaring melody and underlying sense of tragedy make it one of the greatest brief string quartets there is.

But before they could play a note, the clangorous screech of the air-raid sirens sent everyone downstairs to the basement. After about twenty minutes, the all-clear sounded and the party trooped back upstairs. They had played only a few measures of the Schubert, however, when the air-raid siren, like a nasty critic, interposed itself again. The pattern continued for the rest of the night, as the RAF apparently had decided to contribute their own noisemakers to the German New Year's Eve. Downstairs, upstairs, downstairs, upstairs—all night long the determined friends made music amid the falling bombs as the calendar turned. It wasn't until dawn was breaking that the bombers flew back to their bases and Franz Schubert's Quartetsatz was allowed to play itself out in the snug little apartment. When the four musicians played their last three dramatic chords, bringing the music to an explosive conclusion, everyone leaped to their feet clapping, laughing, and crying. A final toast, a round of kisses, and the night was over.

Günther and Rosemarie walked slowly home through the gray streets. It was 1941. Their time was nearly at hand.

21

The *Resurrection* Symphony

And now there arise the great questions: Why did you live? Why did you suffer? We must answer these questions some way if we are to continue living—yes, even if we are only to continue dying.—Gustav Mahler

AS 1941 BEGAN, the Kulturbund was in trouble. For once, its difficulties didn't stem from cruel and unnecessary Nazi ordinances or dire financial straits. With Hitler planning his massive invasion of Russia, and with virtually all other aspects of the war going smoothly for Germany, there was no reason for the authorities to bother themselves unduly with their Jewish artists. And thanks to the continuing success of the film series and the artists' willingness to accept minimal pay for their efforts, the organization continued to show monthly surpluses.

No, the organization's troubles were more intangible than that. The strain of making art under stressful conditions was finally beginning to wear people down. Fritz Wisten had been the most energetic of men, directing and acting in play after play during the Kulturbund's early years. Now, as the Kulturbund's artistic director, he was unable to mount more than a single play every three or four months. Actors began to emigrate in greater numbers, further draining the organization of talent and inspiration. And while the orchestra continued to perform—with a Vivaldi, Glazunov, Liszt program in late January—more and more musicians in their thirties and forties were finding ways to flee the country, leaving, with a few exceptions, only the very young and the very old to make up an increasingly ragtag ensemble. The musicians still put forth the same effort; the desire to make music was still strong, and they continued to play for large and enthusiastic audiences. But the best artists had the easiest time landing jobs abroad, and the ones who remained found it increasingly difficult to maintain the highest standards.

Talk backstage tended to focus on musical matters—string players compared bowings, small groups planned chamber music gatherings. Occasionally, events from the outside world would intervene, as when one musician would ask another whether the previous night's bombing had caused any damage at his house. For the most part, however, as had been the case since the very beginning of the Kulturbund, within the theater on Kommandantenstrasse all conversation revolved around the work.

There were practical reasons for this, especially at a time when so many of them were attempting to emigrate. Musicians such as Günther and Rosemarie, who were waiting impatiently for their visas, didn't like to talk about their situation. Perhaps they were afraid that mentioning the possibility of leaving would jinx the whole enterprise. Also, discussing one's plans for emigration could cause ill feelings among fellow musicians who might feel envious or, quite possibly, betrayed. And people were loath to discuss their plans because it was impossible to know who might overhear a sensitive conversation and interfere.

The result of this unspoken closed-mouth policy was that from time to time a musician might simply not appear at a scheduled rehearsal or performance and his colleagues wouldn't know exactly why. Had he managed to get all the necessary papers with their required signatures and was he even now on his way to safety in another country? Or had he been visited during the night by an agent of the Gestapo and was he now on his way to a work camp? No one knew for sure whether a missing person signified good news or bad news, except that in all cases a missing musician meant bad news for the continuing health of the orchestra.

Under these circumstances it's easy to understand that morale was ebbing. For years now, the Kulturbund had represented an island of serenity in the angry Nazi ocean, a safe haven where music and drama and inspiring ideas mattered and were nourished. But now the harsh waves of the ocean were beginning to penetrate and threaten the island, and what was once a sanctuary seemed more and more to reflect the fear and uncertainty of the rest of the country.

There were occasions, however, when the Kulturbund managed to turn the stress of the times into a source of lightheartedness. As Allied bombing runs became more common, the Kubu leadership decided that it should have two members of the organization present in the theater night and day in case a bomb should fall nearby and the building catch fire. As Henry Meyer remembers the situation, "It was sometimes difficult to decide which male would get to stay overnight in the theater with which female, but we made the most of it."

Finding the lighter side of air raids was obviously an exercise in black humor. It was clear that in time a more substantial way of lifting everyone's spirits would have to be found if the Kulturbund was to maintain the energy it needed to survive. Naturally, when such a plan emerged, it was an exercise in art. In early February of 1941, music director Rudolf Schwarz announced an audacious idea: at the end of the month the Kulturbund Orchestra and Chorus would offer a performance of one of the largest, most complex scores ever composed, the Symphony No. 2, the *Resurrection* Symphony, by Gustav Mahler.

It was a proposal both inspired and foolhardy. The Kulturbund was tired, overworked, underpaid, understaffed, besieged and surrounded by official hostility. The Mahler Second is a huge undertaking, demanding an immense orchestra, a large and well-trained chorus, two vocal soloists, and bottomless energy. Fortunately, it also requires time, spirit, and dedication, and these qualities the Kubu still had in abundance. Schwarz set February 27 as the date for the performance, intending as much as anything to prove that the Kulturbund could rise above its resources and deliver a powerful message of inspiration to its followers.

Before he could begin rehearsing the *Resurrection*, Schwarz had a much smaller concert to attend to; on February 8 he was scheduled to accompany baritone Wilhelm Guttmann in a recital of songs by Mahler, Modest Mussorgsky, Gerhard Goldschlag, and Max Kowalski. Kowalski, the composer Günther and Rosemarie had known in Frankfurt, had been sent to Buchenwald in the aftermath of the November Pogrom but had managed to emigrate to London, where he was living safely in

Baritone Wilhelm Guttmann in a Kulturbund recital.

1941. Both Guttmann and Schwarz were proud to keep his music alive for his Kulturbund audience.

The two musicians met for a final rehearsal at the theater late in the afternoon of February 7. Just as they were finishing up, one of the stage managers knocked on the door of their room and slowly walked in. His face was pale.

"Mr. Guttmann, sir, I'm sorry to bother you. But we've just received a call from the police. You've been ordered to appear at their offices tomorrow morning at ten."

Guttmann glanced at Schwarz.

"Police. You mean the Gestapo, don't you?"

"Yes, sir."

"Did he say anything else? What they want?"

"No, sir."

The stage manager stood quietly for another moment and then withdrew. Guttmann sat down heavily on the piano bench next to Schwarz. The conductor put his arm around the singer's shoulders.

"What do you think it means, Willy? Do you know anything at all about this?"

"No. I have no idea. But listen, Rudy," Guttmann exclaimed, brightening suddenly. "I'm sure it's nothing at all. In any case, I won't let it interfere with the show tomorrow afternoon. We're on for three o'clock, right? See you around two-fifteen."

With that the baritone jumped to his feet, pulled on his leather jacket, swept his little pile of scores under his arm, waved farewell to Schwarz and dashed off.

The next afternoon, a crowd gathered early for the recital, which was called *Wort, Lied, Ton,* or "Word, Song, Sound." Rudolf Schwarz arrived at two o'clock and was fully dressed in his concert clothes by two-thirty. But Wilhelm Guttmann did not arrive at two-fifteen, and by two forty-five there was still no sign of him. Finally, at three minutes before three o'clock, he came rushing into the theater, gasping for breath, sweating profusely, his face a peculiar shade of gray. Hearing of his arrival, Schwarz burst into Guttmann's dressing room to find the baritone struggling with his white tie.

"What's wrong, Willy? What happened to you this morning? Are you going to be able to sing? Shall we cancel the concert? Or at least delay it by a half hour?"

"No, no. I'm here now. I'll be fine. I'll tell you what those bastards did to me later. But now, just please help me with this damned tie!"

Five minutes later, to loud and affectionate applause from yet another full house, Guttmann and Schwarz walked out on stage to begin their recital with a set of songs by Russian composer Modest Mussorgsky. After the first one, a sweet and simple song titled, simply, "Prayer," Guttmann motioned offstage for someone to bring him a glass of water. He drank it in one long swallow, set down the glass, wiped his face with a handkerchief, and nodded to Schwarz to continue. Sitting at the piano, Schwarz noticed that the baritone's face was still covered with sweat and that his eyes were darting around the theater, almost as if he were looking for someone.

They began the next Mussorgsky song, "My Tears Give Birth to Flowers." After Guttmann finished his first phrase, he suddenly uttered a peculiar high-pitched whimper, clutched the left side of his chest with his right hand, and pitched forward onto the stage.

Shrieks and gasps flew forward from the hall. Schwarz leaped from his bench and cradled Guttmann in his arms, tearing off his tie and ripping off the top button of his starched white shirt. Stage managers and other Kubu personnel crowded around. A doctor pushed his way up onto the stage from his seat in the ninth row. But nothing could be done. Wilhelm Guttmann was dead, struck down by a massive heart attack. He was fifty-five years old.

No one ever found out what had happened inside Gestapo head-quarters that morning. And no one doubted that Guttmann's summons to that building and his dramatic death were inextricably linked.

There was a brief memorial service a week later, conducted on the same stage where Guttmann had died. There were songs, the slow move-ment of a string quartet by Beethoven (allowed by the Nazis because it was not strictly a public performance), a few words. A standing-room-only crowd filled the theater, a gathering that included Günther and Rosemarie and the entire Kulturbund staff, artists and workers and everybody. But it soon became common knowledge that the real memo-rial to Wilhelm Guttmann was to be the performance of the Mahler symphony on February 27.

There was at least one rehearsal, sometimes two or three, every day for the next dozen days. The Kulturbund orchestra was augmented by a number of musicians from Berlin's Jewish community, players plucked from schools and synagogues from one end of town to the other. Blend-ing the sound of these newcomers with his established musicians was a daunting task for Rudolf Schwarz, and his rehearsals were long and intense. He swore, he pleaded, he whispered, he screamed, challenging his musicians to play as sublimely as Mahler demanded. And slowly the great composer's monumental vision of death redeemed began to take shape within the walls of the little theater on Kommandantenstrasse.

So much of Mahler's conscious and subconscious view of the world was colored by the specter of death. He came from a large fam-ily, and five of his brothers and sisters died at an early age from child-hood maladies. A sixth sibling, his brother Ernst, then died at age twelve. Gustav was particularly affected by Ernst's death; he was a year younger than Gustav, who sat by his bed for months, telling him stories and doing everything possible to cheer him up before the inevitable occurred. Later in life, Mahler confessed to friends that in dreams he often saw Ernst holding his hands out to his older brother in a gesture of supplication. In adulthood, too, Mahler confronted death; his first child, Maria, whom he called Putzi, died of scarlet fever when she was only four. He himself died of heart trouble at fifty-one.

Mahler tried to work out his feelings about death in his music. Nearly all of his symphonies contain funeral marches or dirges, and one of his finest cycles of songs he called *Kindertotenlieder*, or "Songs on the Death of Children." But nowhere did he ponder the meaning of death, and thus of life, so directly as in his Symphony No. 2.

The symphony's gigantic opening movement is a funeral service, in which Mahler wrestles with the unanswerable questions of why we suffer and die. He asks the questions tenderly and lyrically at times, but more frequently they are accompanied by anger, sarcasm, and despair— all very human responses. In the symphony's second movement, Mahler employs a traditional Austrian country dance to pose a melancholy reflection on lost youth and innocence, perhaps the cruelest casualties of death. The third movement echoes some of the opening movement's despair, evoking the absurdity and pointlessness that we all encounter in life from time to time.

Thus, in its first three movements, Mahler's Second Symphony poses the questions that the artists and audiences of the Kulturbund had been forced to ponder on an almost daily basis since the organization's beginnings in 1933. In the last two movements, Mahler does his best to answer them, as reassuringly and thrillingly as he can.

The fourth movement is a brief hymnlike song in which the composer reflects on humanity's desire to know God. And then, in the symphony's finale, with breathtaking music, Mahler first destroys the world and then shares with us his consoling, inspirational vision of ultimate redemption. In the composer's own words:

A huge tremor shakes the earth and the last trumpet sounds. The graves burst open, all the creatures struggle out of the ground, moaning and trembling. Now they march in a mighty procession: rich and poor, peasants and kings, the whole church with bishops and popes. All have the same fear, all cry and tremble alike because, in the eyes of God, there are no just men. As though from another world, the last trumpet sounds again. Then, when the earth lies silent and deserted, there comes only the long-drawn note of the bird of death. Finally, he too is silent. What happens now is far from expected: no divine judgment, no blessed and no damned, no good and no evil, and no judge. Everything has ceased to exist. Soft and simple, the words gently swell up: "You will rise again, yes again, my dust, after a short rest."

Those words come from a poem by an eighteenth-century German poet named Friedrich Gottlieb Klopstock, a poem called "Resurrection." Mahler was terrifically excited to discover the poem, which he thought provided the perfect ending for his symphony. But Klopstock's vision of redemption was not quite personal or liberating enough for Mahler, so he wrote an additional fifteen lines of verse for the chorus to sing:

Believe, my heart, you have lost nothing.
Everything you longed for is yours; yes, yours!
Everything you loved and struggled for is yours.
Believe, you were not born in vain.
You have not lived and suffered in vain.
What has been must go and
What has gone will come again.
Stop trembling.
Prepare to live.
O Pain, all penetrating one, I have escaped you.
O Death, all conquering one, now you are conquered.
With wings I have won for myself I shall soar in fervent love
    to the Light unseen.
I shall die to live.
You will rise again, my heart, in a moment,
And be borne up, through struggle, to God!

The ecstasy and exhiliration that Mahler expresses in the music he wrote for his words are among the most sublime heights of experience that human beings can achieve in this lifetime.

As they worked with Rudolf Schwarz and the rest of the expanded orchestra to bring Mahler's *Resurrection* Symphony to life, Günther and Rosemarie were astounded by the beauty and power of the music. They also found themselves buoyed up by its message, finding in the symphony's finale the encouragement to hope for a better life. Several times in the past few months Rosemarie had found herself repeating the doleful words she had first uttered on the sidewalk after the air raid, "We will never get out of Berlin." But during the days she worked on the *Resurrection*, she found herself brimming with a newfound optimism. In particular she, and Günther as well, were inspired by Mahler's words, "Stop trembling. Prepare to live."

As the performance of the symphony approached, she and Günther couldn't help but feel that something marvelous was ahead and that they should prepare for it. On February 25, 1941, two days before the Mahler, there was no orchestral rehearsal scheduled until late in the afternoon; Herr Schwarz had set aside the morning and early afternoon to work with the chorus and soloists. So that day Günther and Rosemarie rose early and got into line at the passport office. And a few minutes past four o'clock that afternoon they emerged, whooping and shouting, each with an officially stamped *Reisepass*, or passport, that would enable them to emigrate once the all-important visas came through from the American consulate. That evening, during the rehearsal, when the chorus sang their special phrase, "*Bereite dich zu leben!*" ("Prepare to live"), they found each other's eyes across the crowded stage and smiled happily. They had prepared.

What took place two days later approached, in the minds of everyone who was there, the dimensions of a miracle. The concert was scheduled for three in the afternoon; a crowd began to gather a few minutes before two, and an hour later every conceivable place a human body could inhabit within the confines of the hall's main floor, the balcony, the aisles, even along the walls, was occupied. People clutched their programs, which cost ten pfennigs each and came equipped that afternoon with a special enclosure that warned patrons not to leave

My father's passport, dated February 25, 1941.

their places should an air-raid siren sound, but rather to follow the instructions of Kubu personnel. The crowd included Toni, Eva, and Else, who had been persuaded by her housemates and daughter that the afternoon would be special and well worth her attendance.

By five minutes past three o'clock, the massive orchestra and chorus were in place. Then the two soloists, soprano Henriette Huth and alto Adelheid Müller, walked out on stage, followed closely by Rudolf Schwarz. He asked all his artists to stand, then turned to face the members of the audience, who rose and applauded a full minute before settling back into whatever resting place they had managed to squeeze into. Schwarz then turned back to face his musicians, swept his eyes across the stage, smiled grimly, and gave the downbeat to begin.

For the next hour and twenty-five minutes, Gustav Mahler's *Resurrection* Symphony took possession of the theater, of the musicians, of the audience. No one, either on stage or in the hall, was conscious of time passing, just of an immense sound and an equally immense spirit moving among them. Rosemarie, whose practical mind did not usually acknowledge such phenomena, was dimly aware of someone or something in addition to Rudolf Schwarz directing the proceedings. There were virtually no sounds—coughs or sneezes or rustling with coats or hats—coming from the crowd. More than a thousand people, men and women who had come to know danger and pain and hurt and humiliation on an almost daily basis for more than eight years, heard from a valiant ensemble of artists who had struggled along with them a vibrant musical account of their difficulties and then the infinitely hopeful message that they had not lived and suffered in vain and that from their depths they would rise again.

The final few measures of Mahler's magnificent vision of being borne upward through struggle are a wonderous clangor of open chords sounded by the strings, winds, and brass of the orchestra, undergirded by the rumbling strength of the organ and augmented by crashing percussion and pealing bells. In those last lingering moments Günther and Rosemarie both experienced an awe they had previously known only in the presence of an incandescent sunset, a tumultuous thunderstorm, or some similarly splendid composition of nature.

And then Rudolf Schwarz, his face radiant and dripping with sweat, his arms aloft urging the ultimate effort from his artists, gave the final beat and the symphony was over, the resurrection complete. For a moment there was a charged silence. Many members of the audience could only sit stunned and openmouthed at what they had just experienced. And then, almost as one, the people rose and began to applaud and cheer and stamp their feet. Many of them wept. On stage, the chorus clapped their hands, the string players rapped their stands with their bows, and Rudolf Schwarz responded to the cheers of the crowd by holding the score of Mahler's symphony high above his head where it, too, could receive its share of adulation. Pandemonium reigned inside

GUSTAV MAHLER

Zweite Sinfonie (c-moll)

für Soli, Chor und Orchester

1. Satz: Allegro maestoso (Mit durchaus ernstem und feierlichem Ausdruck)
2. Satz: Andante moderato
3. Satz: Scherzo (In ruhig fließender Bewegung)
4. Satz: „Urlicht"
5. Satz: Finale

Mitwirkende:

Das Orchester des Jüdischen Kulturbundes und der Künstlerhilfe der Jüdischen Gemeinde zu Berlin

Henriette Sara Huth (Sopran)
Adelheid Sara Müller (Alt)

und der erweiterte Kammerchor

Dirigent:

RUDOLF ISRAEL SCHWARZ

The program from what may have been the Kulturbund's greatest achievement: Gustav Mahler's Resurrection *Symphony, February 27, 1941.*

the theater for a full fifteen minutes. Of all the emotional and spiritual peaks achieved by the Kulturbund since 1933, this one afternoon, given the external circumstances, the available resources, and the magnitude of the endeavor, may well have been its loftiest.

When Günther and Rosemarie met their family afterwards, none of them could speak. Eva offered to carry her brother's flute, so Günther seized Rosemarie's viola case and the five pulled on their coats and walked slowly and thoughtfully homeward. The keen air was dim with evening and yet fragrant with the coming spring. A few crocuses pressed their way upward through the dirty patches of snow that still lined the streets. Günther could not remember the last time everything had seemed so peaceful.

When the family reached the apartment on Prinzenstrasse, Günther and Rosemarie offered to walk the others to the subway stop where they could catch a train for their house.

"Just let me drop off the instruments upstairs and I'll be right back," said Günther, and trotted off, leaving the others in the courtyard.

Toni and Eva had just begun to describe their reactions to the *Resurrection* to Rosemarie when a cry came from the landing above their heads. It was Günther.

"Wusche, everybody, come quickly! Run, run!"

The four women exchanged glances and then hurried up the darkened stairwell. Günther was standing in the doorway of their little home. He had turned on a lamp inside and its glow lit up the left side of his face, leaving the other side in shadow. But there was more than enough light for Rosemarie to see the joy and wonder in his expression as he threw open his arms and enveloped her in an enormous hug. He was holding a torn-open envelope in one hand.

"Look, Wusche! Look, everybody! They've come! They're here!"

Günther dragged his wife into the apartment and knelt on the floor with her. The others crowded in after them and stood over my parents in wonder as Günther slid out of the envelope two small but immense pieces of paper. They were Quota Immigration Visas Numbers 20182 and 20183, issued to Günther and Rosemarie Goldschmidt this 27th day of February, 1941, by the U.S. Vice Consul, Berlin, Germany. There was, incidentally, no charge.

My father's precious visa. Note the absence of the hated middle name on this U.S. document.

For a moment, no one could speak. Then Günther let out a shout and began to dance around the room with Rosemarie. Toni, Else, and Eva all shrieked and jumped up and down. Günther kissed his wife, then his mother, his sister, and his mother-in-law. The women all hugged and kissed each other. Everyone grabbed for the precious documents, reading the strange English words out loud. And then there was silence, and then tears, as the deep pent-up emotions of loss and hope from that afternoon and the realization of the overwhelming importance of this longed-for but unexpected delivery were unloosed in each of them.

A door had swung open for Günther and Rosemarie. Everything they had longed for was theirs; yes, theirs.

22

The
Inextinguishable
Symphony

NOW ALL THEY NEEDED was a ship.

With their visas hidden carefully under the mattress in their bedroom, Günther and Rosemarie began the toilsome task of booking passage to America. When they consulted the *Nachrichtenblatt* for advice on emigration, two things immediately became clear: they would have to make arrangements through a neutral country, and they would have to pay for their passage in American dollars. With only limited savings in Reichsmarks, and no prospects for earning American currency, this second item struck them as an insurmountable hurdle.

They consulted their friend Mrs. Schneider at the American embassy. She suggested getting in touch with Mr. Shapiro, the man who'd agreed to sponsor them. But even before Günther could compose a letter, Mr. Shapiro had acted on their behalf. He mentioned the plight of his young German couple to one of the teachers at the New York City public school where he was the principal. The teacher, Mrs. Lotte Breger, instantly offered to help. She rounded up every teacher she knew and sponsored a big benefit dinner in New York's Chinatown. More than a hundred public school teachers attended and they raised nearly six hundred dollars. The next morning Mrs. Breger delivered the money to Mr. Shapiro, who promptly sent it winging its way to Berlin. Günther and Rosemarie's run of good luck had continued. Now they set about searching for a vessel to transport them to the United States.

Günther began frequenting the American Express office, arriving every morning around seven o'clock. He had heard that a Mr. Wufka was the man to see, that he could secure berths on boats to the New World—for a price. But after waiting in line every day for more than a week, Günther learned that the price was not to be reckoned in dollars after all, but rather in objects such as Persian rugs, paintings, and jewelry. If you arrived with such items, your chances of booking passage were good; otherwise, there just didn't seem to be anything available that day or any day. In other words, Mr. Wufka was seeking bribes, the good name of American Express notwithstanding. As he possessed no belongings of value, Günther realized that he would have to look elsewhere.

Back he went to the *Nachrichtenblatt*, whose pages regularly included advertisements for organizations dedicated to assisting the emigration of German Jews, and among them Günther selected one. On March 21—my father remembers the date, because it was the first day of spring and the birthday of Johann Sebastian Bach—he went to a tiny office on the third floor of a building on Grosse Hamburgerstrasse, near the grand synagogue on Oranienburgerstrasse whose partial destruction he had witnessed from afar on Kristallnacht. In the office he filled out a long application form, listing his name and Rosemarie's, the name of their U.S. sponsor, the numbers of their visas, and many more facts and figures. The man on the other side of the desk promised to do all he could, and Günther walked down the stairs and out into the street, thinking to himself that now all *he* could do was wait.

And yet there was always one other thing he could do—play his flute. The next Kubu concert was scheduled for early April and there were rehearsals to attend. Günther had recently begun supplementing the family income by taking on a few students, and they required his attention. There were still the occasional chamber music gatherings at night and on weekends. So, as luck weighed their lives, my parents made music, easing their unquiet minds and tempering their enormous hopes with Schubert and Mozart and Brahms. They spoke little about their application, but Günther awoke many mornings before dawn and stared into the darkness, thinking that their future was as difficult to discern as the dim form of Julian's little wooden fiddler, which hung on the wall across the room.

Günther fills parts of his last days in Berlin as a teacher. His young pupil does not seem to be enjoying himself.

Every day he and Rosemarie awaited the arrival of the mailman with intense suspense. When they had to be away and missed the daily delivery, they would always rush home in acute anticipation, telling themselves excitedly that today would be the day they would receive news about their passage to America. But days, weeks passed, and there was no word.

No word of rescue, that is. What did arrive occasionally were brief letters from Alex and Helmut from their captivity in Rivesaltes in which they described, in guarded words, their sufferings from exposure to rain and wind and an ever-present gnawing hunger that sapped their eroding reserves of strength and hope. Günther felt powerless to shape even his own fate, yet he was tormented by the conviction that he should somehow be able to assist his father and brother. When he had wrestled with his troubled conscience for some time, usually at three or four in the morning, and concluded that there was really nothing he could do, he would resign himself to his helplessness with reassuring thoughts that at least Alex and Helmut were safe in France and far away from the dangers of living in Germany. What, after all, was the worst that could happen to them? With any luck at all they would simply ride out the war across the border, and after Hitler's inevitable defeat they would return home to the welcoming arms of their family.

In the face of such strains, it was a great relief for Günther and Rosemarie to be able to concentrate on music. On April 3, the Kulturbund Orchestra gave a concert that included the overture to the comic opera *The Bartered Bride* by Czech composer Bedřich Smetana and the *Serenade for Strings* by his compatriot Antonín Dvořák, as well as the Symphony in D Minor by the Belgian-born César Franck. The Dvořák and Franck pieces were new additions to my parents' repertory. Even though Günther's flute was not needed in the Dvořák, he characteristically studied the score and even attended a few rehearsals to heighten his understanding of the sometimes melancholy but largely cheerful *Serenade.*

This was the first concert mounted by the Kulturbund since the triumph of the *Resurrection* Symphony five weeks before. Kubu patrons had not seen a play since a production of a light comedy called *30-Second Love,* directed by Fritz Wisten, had opened on March 8. Diminished resources and dwindling energy combined to make each new endeavor an extreme test of the artists' wills. The more the Kulturbund cut back on its offerings, however, the more audiences seemed to appreciate them, and the concert on April 3 was another success, with a packed house and sustained ovations.

That evening, as the people ambled out of the theater into the early spring chill, they were confronted by an eerie and disquieting sight. A troop of Hitler Youth, both boys and girls, had assembled on the sidewalk, apparently for the express purpose of intimidation. Standing silently in neat rows and in full regalia, they stared fixedly at the older crowd of concertgoers, who averted their eyes and hurried off to arrive at their homes before curfew. The young people waited until all the patrons had left the building, then marched away, the last rays of the evening sun turning their blond heads golden.

The message was unmistakable: We have you surrounded and we may hurt you at any time. Even our children are your implacable enemies.

Three days later, on April 6, Palm Sunday, the German army continued its seemingly unstoppable advance, rolling into Greece and Yugoslavia. Excited announcers broadcast the news on German radio; one overwrought commentator likened the entry of German tanks into Athens to the humble entry of Jesus, astride a donkey, into Jerusalem two millennia ago.

The news of this latest victory inspired both organized and impromptu celebrations throughout the country. That night a phalanx of Brownshirts, augmented by a scattering of ordinary citizens, marched down Prinzenstrasse carrying flags and torches, singing Party songs and chanting paeans to their noble chancellor. Günther and Rosemarie gazed down onto the revelers from their window and then turned slowly to look at each other. They both sensed that time was running out for them; if they didn't secure passage on a ship soon, it would surely be too late.

And then, without warning, the longed-for, eagerly anticipated lightning bolt struck. On Thursday afternoon, April 10, in an unexceptional envelope, arrived two tickets for the Portuguese liner *Mouzhino*, scheduled to depart Lisbon for New York in precisely two months, on June 10.

My parents' wonder and disbelief and feelings of gratitude knew no bounds. Were they really going to escape the dangers that threatened them daily? They had secured a sponsor, passports, passage to the United States. But they celebrated quietly, secretly, not even telling their mothers the news for several days. They did not dare to believe wholeheartedly in their good fortune until they found themselves on U.S. soil. The knowledge of what had happened to Alex and Helmut weighed heavily on their minds as the next weeks slipped past.

They were busy weeks, filled with music and preparations for their journey. On May 3 Günther joined other first-chair members of the Kulturbund Orchestra's woodwind section and pianist Martin Keil for a chamber concert that included a wind quintet by Franz Danzi, a flute sonata by Giovanni Platti, and the Sextet for Piano and Winds by a Jewish German composer named Ludwig Thuille. Twelve days later Rudolf Schwarz conducted the last orchestral concert of the season, a program of Felix Mendelssohn's *A Midsummer Night's Dream* music, a tone poem by Jean Sibelius, a suite by James Rothstein, and the Polka and Fugue from *Schwanda the Bagpiper* by Jaromir Weinberger. The *Schwanda* music is particularly jolly and beguiling, and as the audience members spilled from the theater humming its tunes they had no way of knowing

Jüdischer Kulturbund in Deutschland e.V.

KÜNSTLERISCHE LEITUNG: FRITZ ISRAEL WISTEN

Zweigstelle Berlin

Sonnabend, 3. Mai 1941, 18 Uhr

Die musikantische Stunde

Programmfolge:

1. Quintett für Flöte, Oboe, Klarinette, Fagott und Horn . Franz Danzi
   Allegretto — Andante — Menuetto (Allegro) — Allegro (1763—1826)

   Günther Israel Goldschmidt, Kurt Israel Michaelis, Helmuth Israel Stiebel
   Fritz Israel Rheinhold, Alfred Israel Lehmann

2. Linkshändige Klavierstücke . . . . Karl Israel Wiener
   a) Präludium
   b) Ballade
   Der Komponist

3. Sonate G-dur für Flöte und Klavier . . . . . . Giovanni Platti
   Grave: Allegro — Adagio — Allegro molto (um 1743)

   Günther Israel Goldschmidt, Martin Israel Keil

4. Lieder: a) Vittoria, mio core . . . . Giacomo Carissini
   (1604—1674)

   b) O cessate di piagarmi . . . . Alessandro Scarlatti
   (1659—1725)

   c) Lied der Bojaren . . . . Felix Mendelssohn-Bartholdy
   (1809—1847)

   d) La Cana . . . . }
   e) Bolero . . . . } Spanisches Volkslied

   Adelheid Sara Müller (Alt) und *Werner Israel Müller* (Violoncello)

Pause

5. Concerto für Oboe und Klavier . . . . Giovanni Battista Pergolese
   (1710—1736)
   Largo — Allegretto — Andantino — Allegro

   Kurt Israel Michaelis (Oboe), *Martin Israel Keil* (Klavier)

6. Sextett für Flöte, Oboe, Klarinette, Fagott, Horn und
   Klavier . . . . Ludwig Thuille
   (1861—1907)

   Allegretto moderato — Larghetto — Gavotte (Andante,
   quasi Allegretto) — Finale (Vivace)

   Günther Israel Goldschmidt, Kurt Israel Michaelis, Helmuth Israel Stiebel
   Fritz Israel Rheinhold, Alfred Israel Lehmann, Martin Israel Keil

The program from one of Günther's last appearances with the Kulturbund.

that they had just attended the very last concert in the eight-year history of the Kulturbund Orchestra.

Günther and Rosemarie did their best during those weeks to keep their great news to themselves, letting on to none of their colleagues that their years in Germany were coming to a close. But after the concert on May 15 they confided in their conductor. Rudolf Schwarz was very sad at the prospect of losing them, yet overjoyed at their good fortune. He immediately offered to write them each a letter of recommendation, fully assuming that they would try to find orchestra jobs in America.

In letters dated May 19, 1941, Schwarz spoke highly of their musical talents. Of Günther he wrote, "He is a high-spirited musician with special technical and artistic abilities. His tone is warm, full and very beautiful, his clean intonation and technical brilliance are striking, and his musical intelligence enables him to be flexible enough to understand and support all the conductor's intentions. We have the confident expectation that Herr Goldschmidt, with the extraordinary diligence and artistic ambition he has exhibited up until now, will continue to develop into a wind player of the first rank."

Schwarz was even more complimentary when it came to Rosemarie. "We possess in her," he wrote, "a noted instrumentalist who both musically and technically is equal to the demands of the orchestral literature. Her playing is tonally and rhythmically flawless, representative of the finest aspects of stringed intrument style, and it is a great joy for the conductor to hear. We are losing in Frau Goldschmidt one of our most valuable members."

It seems as if my parents had made quite an impression on their boss. It does a son proud!

The same Jewish relief organization that had secured their tickets on the *Mouzhino* also arranged for them to leave Berlin for Lisbon on Sunday morning, June 1. They would take a train via occupied Paris. Each was allowed to carry a single suitcase. The task of deciding what to take with them and what to leave behind was both agonizing and simple. Because they had very few objects of value aside from their instruments, most of what they chose were books and scores of music. On top of that, they brought a few favorite clothes and Julian's little wooden fiddler. That was all.

A customs official visited their apartment to inspect each item. He made it very clear that no gold or silver could leave the country and then inspected each book and every piece of music to ensure that Günther and Rosemarie were not smuggling secret documents to the United States. Before leaving he informed them coldly that they could each take no more than four dollars out of Germany and that the rest of their small savings would be confiscated by the Reich. The official then asked for their passports, looked them over, and told Günther with more than a touch of glee in his voice that they were incomplete: he would have to visit the headquarters of the Gestapo to obtain a final stamp of approval.

The next morning was chilly and rainy. Günther walked about a mile from Prinzenstrasse to the gleaming new Gestapo headquarters on Prince Albrechtstrasse. He stood outside for several minutes in the rain, working up the courage to enter. Once inside the building, he took a deep breath and stepped lightly across the white marble floor to a desk occupied by an officer with the death's head insignia of the SS emblazoned on his black uniform. Before Günther could speak, the officer did, at top volume: "*Verfluchtes Juden-Schwein! Mit Ihren nassen Dreckfüssen haben Sie ja nun den ganzen Boden verschmutzt!*" ("Cursed Jew-Pig! With your dirty wet feet you've soiled the whole floor!")

Günther turned pale and his heart stood still. Had he just forfeited his chance at freedom? Without a word, he reached into his pocket, slowly pulled out the passports, and as gently as he could laid them on the officer's desk. Not daring to meet the other's eyes, he gazed down at the "soiled" floor.

"So you want to leave the Fatherland, do you?" sneered the officer. "Well, good. Good riddance, I say, to you, to your little whore, and all the rest of your tribe."

With that, he reached into a drawer, pulled out a rubber stamp, and with four vicious motions of his right arm, as if he were grandly imagining his fist striking the face of one of his chosen victims instead of sitting at a desk with two documents and an ink pad, the Gestapo officer rendered my parents' passports legal.

He flung them at Günther, exclaiming, "Now get your dirty feet out of here!" Günther did not have to be told twice; he rushed out of the building and into the rain, deeply grateful that nothing truly bad had happened. But it was an incident that never left him; years later, he confessed that the image of that unknown man in uniform had always made it difficult for him to approach a policeman, even to ask for directions on an unfamiliar highway.

And now, with only a few days remaining until their departure, came the last meeting with their colleagues in the Kulturbund. The 1940–1941 orchestral season was over, but Rudolf Schwarz summoned his musicians for a final rehearsal, to read through the piece with which he intended to open the new season in the fall: the Symphony No. 4 by Danish composer Carl Nielsen.

Nielsen came from a musical household. His father, a housepainter by trade, played the violin at home and the cornet in his village band. Young Carl contributed to the family's income by herding geese, but he also found time to take piano lessons and learn fiddle playing from his father. At fourteen he became a regimental bugler in the 16th battalion of the Royal Danish Army. Five years later, in 1884, he entered the music conservatory in Copenhagen, beginning a career that produced some of the most fascinating and deeply felt music of his time.

The outbreak of World War I horrified him. "The whole world seems to be disintegrating," he wrote to a friend. "National feeling, which up to now was regarded as something lofty and beautiful, has instead become like a spiritual syphilis that has destroyed the brains, and it grins out through the empty eye sockets with moronic hate." Nielsen found his personal antidote to Europe's sickness in his deep belief in the power and beauty of music, which led him to begin work, in the fateful summer of 1914, on his Fourth Symphony.

He proclaimed that in his symphony he would "endeavor to indicate what music alone is capable of expressing to the full: the elemental will of life. In case all the world were to be devastated by fire, flood, and volcanoes, and all things were destroyed and dead, then nature would still begin to breed new life again. Soon the plants would begin to multiply again, the breeding and screaming of birds would be seen and heard, the aspiration and yearning of human beings would be felt."

"This," insisted the composer, "is music's own territory. Music *is* Life, and like Life, inextinguishable." From the day of its premiere, in 1916, Carl Nielsen's Fourth has been known as the *Inextinguishable* Symphony.

All this Rudolf Schwarz told his musicians when they gathered for a special rehearsal on a Thursday afternoon in late May of 1941.

"This is music," he said, "that speaks directly to our situation and that of our listeners. All of us—musicians, electricians, tailors, grocers, mothers, and fathers—need to be reminded that life is paramount. Even where it is stamped out, it eventually returns. Where there is life, there is spirit. And where there is spirit, where there is even one human soul, there is music. We are proof of that. We have suffered, yet we have endured. And we have made music."

Schwarz paused, cleared his throat and went on.

"And that is why I have asked you here this afternoon, to play through this symphony with me and to keep it in your hearts until we meet again to perform it for our public in the fall. Some of you, I know, will not be with us then. But wherever you are, a part of you will always be here. And you will have this music, this inextinguishable music, to remind you of us, always."

With that, Schwarz took up his baton and began the rehearsal.

The *Inextinguishable* Symphony begins aggressively, almost violently, as if reflecting the "syphilitic" condition of its origins. But less than two minutes in, a calm settles over the orchestra and the clarinets announce a sweet little melody that will recur several times throughout the next forty minutes. Nielsen describes a great struggle, suggesting the guns of war with a volley of blows hammered out by two sets of kettledrums on opposite sides of the stage. But through it all, the sweet melody persists, eventually taking on a defiant note of triumph in the symphony's final measures. It is a particularly moving and yet ambiguous triumph; the melody has a downward rather than an upward arc, as if Nielsen is emphasizing both the victory and the forces of destruction that must always be overcome.

Günther and Rosemarie had never heard or played music quite like this before. At the end they both had tears in their eyes, moved beyond words by the force of Nielsen's conviction and the success of his inspiration. Schwarz led the orchestra through the complete symphony once only, and then sat back while he and his musicians caught their breath.

"Thank you, ladies and gentlemen, for indulging my wishes. You see what an extraordinary piece this is. Go now, and have a lovely summer. We will see each other again in late September, when we will begin to work on this symphony in earnest. I believe that it will have a powerful effect on our audience."

Günther and Rosemarie slowly packed up their instruments and prepared to leave the theater for what they knew would be the last time. On their way to the street they knocked on Rudolf Schwarz's dressing room to say goodbye. He enveloped them both in a long embrace.

"How does that song go?" he asked Günther with a sad smile. "'Give my regards to Broadway?' Please, children," he continued softly, "be careful. And be happy. And remember us who are staying."

"How can we ever forget? Thank you," said Günther, "thank you a thousand times."

"For everything," added Rosemarie. "Including introducing us to that symphony today. As I was playing, I heard our story in its pages."

"Yes," said Schwarz. "It's the story of all of us, isn't it? 'Music is Life . . .' Well, goodbye. I'm playing at the synagogue this weekend and have to run to another rehearsal."

Günther and Rosemarie took a long last look at the maze of corridors and dressing rooms that had been their home away from home for more than two and a half years. Then they trudged out into Kommandantenstrasse, the descending theme of Nielsen's Fourth sounding silently in their hearts.

Only hours remained of their lives in Germany. On Saturday night, May 31, they visited the little house on Manfred von Richthofenstrasse to say farewell to their mothers and Eva. It was chilly and rainy, and a mist of sorrow hung over the house. Adding to the gloom were the dim lights and shuttered windows mandated by the blackout. There were occasional lighthearted references to the day when the family would be reunited in America, and Toni reminded the children several times that they should do what they could to help the family once they arrived at their destination. But my father remembers his conviction that this would be the last time they would ever meet. He and Rosemarie had brought along a gift of fancy writing paper to ensure a steady stream of letters across the ocean, and everyone chattered gaily about how often they would write: three times a week, five times a week, every day! Toni presented the departing children with a precious memento: a dozen little silver-plated knives and forks, each of them only six inches long, that had belonged to her mother. Günther knew it was illegal to take this silverware out of Germany, but he was determined to smuggle it out anyway.

At last there seemed nothing more to say and Eva turned away to weep. Noticing his sister's tears, Günther stood up and declared, with mock severity, "I have a new regulation to announce. Tonight, in bed, exactly ten minutes of sadness will be permitted under each blanket. But no more. After ten minutes, the household is ordered to consider only happy thoughts. Failure to comply with this edict will result in the most dire punishment. Am I completely understood?"

Toni and Else nodded solemnly and Eva smiled and wiped her eyes. After a long and weighty moment, everyone rose and walked out to the garden. Rain fell lightly into the enforced darkness. Drops of water coursed down the five faces as they exchanged their goodbyes. When my father hugged his mother for the last time, she whispered to him words that have never left him: "*Seid gut zu einander!*" ("Be good to each other!")

Holding each other by the hand, their eyes on the dark, damp ground, Günther and Rosemarie walked slowly away. As he had been on the wind-swept pier in Hamburg, Günther was painfully conscious of the irrevocable parting of the generations of his family.

Decades later, I recognize in this scene the source of the hole in my heart that nothing, not even the greatest happiness, has quite been able to fill. Within the garden gate stand three women, abandoned by husbands and father and now by children and brother, as a yet more horrible fate slouches towards them. Walking sadly away, like Adam and Eve banished from another garden, a burning guilt kindled within them, go my parents, embarking on a journey they would never have chosen in normal times. Trying hard not to think of either the past or the future, they steel themselves for the present, for an ordeal both frightening and liberating. And I, having never known anything but safety, can only contemplate their actions with awe.

At the appointed hour the next morning, Günther and Rosemarie reported to the Berlin Zoo railroad station with their suitcases and their instruments. Günther had wrapped his mother's miniature silverware in two pieces of soft cloth and hidden them in the lining of his pants. The organizers of the relief organization saw to it that all went like clockwork. The train cars were stifling and filled to capacity and their windows were painted black so that no one could see either in or out, but the locomotive pulled out of the station precisely on time. And how fortunate my parents were that they left Berlin on a train headed west instead of east!

Before reaching the French border, the train made brief stops in Merseburg, Erfurt, and Kaiserslautern, and each time Günther and Rosemarie stole a few moments to send a postcard back home to Richthofenstrasse. After a few hours Rosemarie managed to take a brief nap, but Günther stayed wide awake, kept from sleep by the hot, crowded conditions and by his own teeming excitement. Everything he saw seemed unreal, and several times he had to shake his head vigorously to reassure himself that he wasn't dreaming, that he really was on his way to freedom in America.

The passengers were not permitted to use the toilets on the train, but as it neared Paris the authorities announced that there would be a long rest stop. Everyone longed to catch a glimpse of the beautiful city; the paint on the windows, however, rendered that impossible. In the underground station, the passengers who wished to use the toilets were required to file through a double line of German soldiers stationed there to prevent anyone's attempting an escape into town—as if anyone wanted to! On their way back to the train, Günther paused for a moment to speak to Rosemarie and immediately one of the guards screamed at them to keep moving and to remain silent.

As the train rolled west through occupied France, Günther's thoughts flew south, to his father and brother in their camp at Rivesaltes. How close they now seemed, and yet how much more in danger of falling into the clutches of the forces who held Paris! As he and Rosemarie approached their longed-for freedom, he was more conscious of the frightful vulnerability of his family.

At the border with Spain, Günther and Rosemarie saw German forces for the last time. They feared another encounter with SS or SA troops but were pleasantly surprised to find instead regular soldiers stationed at the border to check, once more, each item being taken out of the country. The young man who inspected their luggage stopped when he discovered their music and began to page through it.

Günther, fully conscious of the forbidden silverware he was hiding in his pants, summoned the courage to ask, "Do you read music?"

The soldier smiled. "Oh yes," he exclaimed eagerly. "Back home I played the organ in church. I hoped one day to study seriously, but . . ." He shrugged and hefted his rifle. "I play a different instrument now."

"And where is home?" Günther prodded, encouraged by the young man's manner.

"Leipzig," replied the soldier proudly. "Where Bach played for so many years."

"I hear it's a beautiful city," said Günther. He paused. "Now I suppose I'll never know."

"No, I suppose not." The young man stared at Günther for a moment. Then he placed the music carefully back into the suitcase, closed it, and handed it back.

"I'm sorry," he said softly. "Good luck to both of you."

"And to you, too," Günther and Rosemarie responded together. For years afterward, my father thought of the polite young soldier and wondered if he survived the war, and if he ever again played the organ in the city of Johann Sebastian Bach.

Now that they had crossed the border into Spain, the travelers were out of German jurisdiction at last. Sighs of relief were audible up and down the station platform where they waited for a new train that would take them the rest of the way to Lisbon. Strangers clapped each other on the back and smiled at their good fortune. One man spat surreptitiously back in the direction of the Fatherland and cursed it under his breath. My parents contented themselves with a kiss and a long embrace.

When the Spanish train pulled into the station, everyone was shocked by its appearance. Its cars were dilapidated, its seats sagging and covered with filth. The civil war that had wracked the country so recently had drained it of much of its wealth and ruined its infrastructure. The poverty the war had caused was personified by hordes of homeless children who lined the rails as the train chugged slowly westward. They spent their days and nights begging for bread, even from those who were fleeing for their lives. Their dark, hungry eyes haunted Günther for days, and he wrote of them to his mother and sister.

On Tuesday, June 3, their train limped into Lisbon, and the first part of their long journey was over. The agency had arranged for all the passengers to be taken to a hotel, and my parents fell into bed and slept for the better part of twenty-four hours. It was their first chance to relax for many months and they took full advantage. For the next several days they walked through the streets of the beautiful city, marveling at the warm weather and vivid colors. In a narrow street near the harbor, as they walked arm in arm, Günther and Rosemarie were solicited by three prostitutes who hung out an open window inviting them to sample their wares, which they boasted were the pride of Portugal. Rosemarie laughed; Günther felt scandalized.

In no time, a week had pleasantly passed and it was time to board the *Mouzinho*, a nine-thousand-ton freighter of the Portuguese merchant fleet captained by Paulo da Conceicao Baptista. The ship was equipped to carry about three hundred passengers on a normal voyage, but for this trip across the Atlantic nearly nine hundred souls, many of them refugees, had booked passage. Women and children were assigned cabins on the upper decks and men down below, but the berths were so small and the air so foul that Günther and Rosemarie decided to spend a quarter of their fortunes—a dollar each—to rent steamer chairs. In this way they passed the voyage, on deck, out in the open air.

On Tuesday, June 10, the S.S. *Mouzhino* pulled out of Lisbon for what turned out to be the second-to-last voyage to leave Portugal with Jewish refugees. My parents had secured passage just in time.

During the next eleven days, as their ship glided by the green Canary Islands and the occasional German U-boat, as they contended with bouts of seasickness and the ever-present smell of olive oil wafting up from the galley, and as they passed the nights on their steamer chairs, holding hands and looking up at the dancing stars, Günther and Rosemarie had many hours to contemplate their future and to begin to contend with their past. They were two young people, aged twenty-seven and twenty-four, who had been forced to endure the legal restrictions and personal enmity of National Socialism all their mature lives. Owing to their own skills and the dedication of the men and women who had founded and maintained the Jüdische Kulturbund, they had managed to spend their time making music and raising the spirits of thousands of people who had been subjected to the same danger and misery. The Kulturbund had provided them with protection from forced labor. Their salary, meager though it was, had formed the basis for their ability to purchase their tickets out. They were profoundly grateful for the opportunity the Kubu had offered, fully aware that without it they would most likely not be sailing to America and a new, free life.

They were also deeply aware of those whom they were leaving behind. Alex and Helmut. Their mothers and Eva. Their friends and colleagues in the orchestra and their chamber music circle. Rudolf Schwarz. Adolf Cohen. The merchants and shopkeepers in the neighborhood around Prinzenstrasse. What would become of them?

If my parents had possessed the slightest inkling of the depths of the dark answer to that question, how could they have endured their peaceful voyage, how could they have made their excited plans for a new life in music in the United States, how could they have looked to the future with optimism and hope?

Like people everywhere, Günther and Rosemarie thought that the biggest challenge that faced the world that June was the defeat of the German Army as it prepared to launch its epic invasion of the Soviet Union. Their encounter with the heart of darkness that would cast its long shadow over all the globe for many years to come was still ahead of them. The massive tree that would shade their lives had been planted, but it had not yet begun to sprout.

So as dawn broke on the morning of June 21, 1941, the emerging light of the longest day fell warmly on their faces as they stood on the deck of the *Mouzhino* and caught their first glimpse of the Statue of Liberty. Günther had roused Rosemarie shortly after four that morning so that they would not miss the gleam from Liberty's torch. When they saw her, they felt as though her lamp was shining especially for them. Their hopes were boundless. They felt reborn. And in their hearts they heard the melody of an inextinguishable symphony.

23

"Crying Like Dogs"

SHORTLY BEFORE NOON, Günther and Rosemarie walked down the gangplank of the *Mouzhino* and set foot on U.S. soil. That first day of summer was stifling, and the two young people felt uncomfortably hot in the woolen clothes they had packed in the cool spring of Berlin. But they didn't mind their discomfort; they were finally free.

Their former colleagues in the Kulturbund spent the summer of 1941 (in the memorable words Martin Luther King Jr. would utter more than twenty years later) "sweltering from the heat of oppression." But they also continued to perform. Two days after the *Mouzhino* sailed from Lisbon, Berthold Sander conducted the orchestra and members of the opera company in a program of favorite scenes from Verdi operas, beginning with the overture to *La Forza del Destino* and concluding with the Triumphal March from *Aïda*. On August 9, the actors offered a play by Franz Molnar called *Spiel im Schloss,* or "Game in the Castle," directed by Ben Spanier. It would prove to be the final production in the history of the Jüdische Kulturbund.

On September 11, a week before the next scheduled rehearsal of Carl Nielsen's Fourth Symphony, the Gestapo delivered a letter to Moritz Henschel, the deputy chairman of the Kubu board. Signed "on behalf of" a certain Dr. Kunz, the letter invoked the so-called Decree for the Protection of the People and the State of February 28, 1933, and announced that the Jüdische Kulturbund was hereby dissolved. The letter went on to forbid "all activity that attempts a continuation or re-establishment of any organization that appears to embody the same or similar goals" as the Kulturbund. The next day brought a follow-up telephone call ordering that all instruments belonging to Kulturbund musicians immediately be delivered into the custody of the Reich.

It was all over. With the stroke of a pen, the Nazis had terminated eight years of music, drama, lectures, and films—eight years in which the Jews of Germany had tried to help themselves rise from the depths of hopelessness and unhappiness into which their tormentors were determined to sink them. From its first days, the Kulturbund had always operated at the pleasure of the Nazis. Now, at last, that pleasure had run its course.

Why now? After eight years, the Nazis had concluded that interim solutions to the "Jewish problem"—humiliation, segregation, enforced emigration—had proved inadequate. Now an *Endlösung*, a Final Solution, had been devised: the extermination of the Jews from Europe. Ten days before the order to dissolve the Kulturbund was issued—on September 1, 1941—a new law had revived the medieval practice of forcing Jews to wear a yellow star in public. The next month brought three more blows in rapid succession: on October 10, Jews were forbidden to leave their homes without police permission; on October 18, the deportations of Jews from Berlin to the ghettos and killing centers of the East began; on October 23, the country's borders were sealed and Jews were no longer allowed to leave Germany.

For the Jews, the Kulturbund had served as a source of art, employment, and community. For the Nazis, however, the association had been nothing more then a useful tool. First, it contributed to the segregation of Jews from Germany's "Aryan" population. Second, it was an important element in the Nazi propaganda machine that was designed to fool the community of nations into believing that Germany's Jews were being well treated. The Final Solution rendered more minor attempts at social segregation obsolete, and, with Germany at war with the world, there was no need to maintain the smokescreen. Against this developing backdrop, the Nazis concluded that further Jewish performances, whatever their subject matter, could only qualify as farce. The Kulturbund was no longer useful, and the curtain was rung down.

With no theater to shield them, the artists and employees of the Kulturbund suddenly found themselves at great risk. At the beginning of June 1941, as Günther and Rosemarie Goldschmidt began their journey to the United States, approximately one hundred people were employed by the Kulturbund, including actors, musicians, stagehands, electricians, box office workers, and clerical staff. A researcher at Berlin's Akademie der Künste, which mounted a major exhibition about the Kulturbund in 1992 and continues to maintain the single largest collection of Kubu documents, told me that without combing through thousands of lists of names it is impossible to know exactly how many of those one hundred souls survived the Holocaust. We can be sure, however, that virtually all of them were sent to the death camps that, in September 1941, were being readied for their unspeakable operations.

Many of the principal players in the story of the Kulturbund, because of their talents, their resourcefulness, and their sheer good luck, managed to escape Germany. Most of them established successful careers on foreign soil:

Hans Wilhelm Steinberg, conductor of the Kulturbund Orchestra of Frankfurt, moved to Palestine in 1936, where he conducted the newly formed Palestine Symphony. In 1938, he emigrated to the United States to become assistant conductor to Arturo Toscanini at the NBC Symphony. As William Steinberg he served as music director of the Buffalo Philharmonic, the Pittsburgh Symphony, and the Boston Symphony. He died in 1978.

Julius Prüwer, who succeeded Steinberg in Frankfurt and also conducted the Berlin Kubu Orchestra, emigrated to New York in 1939. He died there of natural causes in 1943, at age sixty-nine.

Ernst Drucker, concertmaster of the Frankfurt Kulturbund Orchestra, emigrated to the United States in 1938. He performed with the Adolf Busch String Quartet, the NBC Symphony, and the Metropolitan Opera Orchestra. He died in 1993.

Composer Max Kowalski survived his incarceration in Buchenwald following the November Pogrom. In 1939 he emigrated to London, where he died in 1956.

Kurt Baumann, who came up with the orginal plan for the Kulturbund, emigrated to the United States in 1939. From 1946 to 1972 he was a librarian at Cornell University in Ithaca, New York. He died there in 1983.

Julius Bab, who hired the Kulturbund's acting company, left Germany for France in 1939 and later that year emigrated to the United States. He died in 1955.

Rabbi Leo Baeck, one of the founders of the Kulturbund, was deported to the Theresienstadt concentration camp in 1943. He survived and emigrated to England. He died in London in 1956.

Fritz Wisten, the longtime Kulturbund actor and director who served as Kubu artistic director during its last years, was married to a non-Jewish woman and thus was able to go into hiding in Berlin from late 1941 until 1945. After the war he was a major figure in the theaters of East Berlin. One of the first plays he directed, in 1946, was Lessing's *Nathan the Wise*. He died in 1961.

Rudolf Schwarz, who conducted the Berlin Kulturbund Orchestra from 1936 to its dissolution in 1941, was deported in 1943 to Bergen-Belsen and later to Auschwitz. He survived both ordeals, emigrated first to Sweden and then to England, and became the conductor of, successively, the Bournemouth Symphony Orchestra, the City of Birmingham Symphony Orchestra, the BBC Symphony, and the Northern Sinfonia. For his services to music, he was made a Knight Commander of the British Empire in 1973. Sir Rudolf Schwarz died in 1994 at the age of eighty-eight.

Not all of the Kulturbund leaders were so fortunate, however.

Werner Levie, administrative director of the Kulturbund and artistic director for a year after the November Pogrom, left Germany for his native Holland in 1939. After the Nazi takeover of his country in 1940, he established a Dutch version of the Kulturbund. In 1943, Levie was deported to the Bergen-Belsen concentration camp. He died there one month after the camp's liberation.

Kurt Singer, the Kulturbund's flamboyant artistic director, stayed in Amsterdam after the November Pogrom, giving music lessons to children. He, too, was taken prisoner after the German defeat of Holland in 1940. In 1943 he was sent to the concentration camp at Terezin, or Theresienstadt, a facility called by the Nazis a "model resettlement center" because of the number of artists confined there. Self-important even then, he wrote to a friend from Terezin that he had been specially assigned to that camp "in recognition for my contributions to art." He eagerly threw himself into the cultural activities that were permitted at the camp to impress foreign observers, such as the International Red Cross. Singer helped prepare the Terezin premiere of *Brundibar*, a children's opera by Czech composer Hans Krasa, himself a prisoner at Terezin, on September 23, 1943. In January 1944, weakened by cold and malnutrition, Kurt Singer died at the camp. He was fifty-eight years old.

All of these people, as significant as their contributions to the Kulturbund were, have remained mere names to me, historical figures who have come alive only as I read about them or heard about them from others who had actually known them. But I have also been privileged to meet a few of the thousands of German Jews who performed during the Kulturbund era or were witnesses to its activities. Without exception, they were kind and welcoming, more than willing to share what they could of the memories and documents of their youths.

Hannah Kroner, a dancer with the Kulturbund, emigrated with her family to the United States in November 1939. In December 1999, she was living in Bayside, New York, where she had served as director of the Hannah Kroner School of Dance for more than fifty years.

Henry Bloch, who studied with Julius Prüwer in Berlin and played chamber music with my parents there, emigrated to America in May 1941. He played with orchestras in Baltimore, Houston, and Hartford, and with the orchestras of the New York City Ballet and the Metropolitan Opera. In December 1999, he was living in Manhattan.

Hilda Klestadt Jonas emigrated in 1938, first to Canada and then to the United States. She enjoyed a long career as a pianist and harpsichordist, having studied with the legendary Wanda Landowska. In December 1999, she was living in San Francisco.

Kurt Michaelis, who was the principal oboist of the Berlin Kulturbund Orchestra, left Germany in the summer of 1941 and traveled to the United States on a banana boat. He spent more than fifty years with C. F. Peters Music Publishing. In December 1999, he was living in Goshen, New York.

Gerti Totschek Colbert, who brightened many a Kulturbund concert and chamber music gathering in Berlin, saw her younger sister leave

Germany as part of the *Kindertransport* in 1939. In March 1941, she and her parents emigrated to America. In December 1999, she was living on Long Island.

Werner Golde, an electrician who helped illuminate the Kulturbund's theatrical productions, emigrated to the United States in 1938. He has spent much of the past twenty years assisting German-American Jews in their claims against the country of their birth. In December 1999 he was living in Queens, New York.

Since I was, obviously, only able to meet with former Kulturbund members who had survived, it has sometimes been hard for me to remember that these were the lucky ones. They possessed the right combination of courage, connections, foresight, and fortune to escape the fate of millions of other Jews who were no less deserving of a long life, but who found themselves trapped when the terrible trains began to roll eastward in the fall of 1941. Hannah Kroner told me about a conversation she had with someone who worked backstage at the Kulturbund when she told him of her family's plans to emigrate.

"You can't be serious," Hannah remembers him saying to her. "Why on earth would you ever leave? Well, all right, you can go, but I'm going to stay right here. And when you want to come back I will send you the affidavit you will need to return to Berlin."

"He did stay," says Hannah. "He stayed and he perished."

I was reminded again of the slim reed that separates the living from the dead when I flew to Cincinnati in February 1999 to speak with violinist Henry Meyer, the self-described "Benjamin" of the Berlin Kulturbund Orchestra.

Now a rotund man with a ready laugh, Meyer picked me up at the airport and escorted me to his neighborhood Chinese restaurant for lunch. The waiters all knew him and fussed over him, and they brought us big bowls of his favorite beef-and-noodle soup, which warmed us from the winter chill. I had known of his many years as a member of the famed LaSalle String Quartet. Now, as we sipped our soup, Meyer told me of his recent tenure as an adjunct professor at the Cincinnati College Conservatory of Music and of his frequent trips around the world, including yearly visits back to Berlin. After lunch he took me to his apartment, a bright and cheerful place adorned with many photographs documenting his life in music and his many friends. But then we sat down, I turned on my tape recorder, and the gloom of February seemed to force its way inside as he told me his story.

When the Kulturbund was shut down in September 1941, Henry Meyer was ordered to report to the labor office. He was assigned to work in a factory that manufactured what were euphemistically called "sanitary articles"—condoms. Meyer recalls that he was embarrassed about working with condoms, so when he was asked about it he would say that he worked "in menswear." When he was pressed about what kind of menswear, he would say "overalls."

Shortly thereafter, his parents were deported to the concentration camp in Riga, and he and his younger brother were sent to Dresden to work in a factory that made time bombs. Work began every morning at six. Since they were not allowed to ride the city's streetcars, they rose at four-thirty and walked more than four miles from their home to the factory.

In early 1943, Henry Meyer and his brother were transported by cattle car to Auschwitz. His brother died within a month; he got diarrhea, couldn't get out of bed one morning, and when Henry returned from his day of work, "my brother was gone." Soon, Meyer began to realize what was happening: "I saw the fires of the crematorium and smelled the stench, which was always present. I got up the courage to ask one of the guards and he said, 'Your people are burning there.'"

Soon, "I was in a state where I couldn't go on. I was brought to the hospital, and then selected to be gassed the next morning. In the night, a prison doctor came by and started a conversation. I said, 'Look, I know what happens tomorrow.' The guy then asked me what I did before and I said I was a musician, a violinist. I asked what he did and he said he was already a doctor, living in Breslau. 'In Breslau,' I said, 'in Breslau I played with the Kulturbund Orchestra.' He said, 'The Tartini Concerto?' 'Yes,' I said. 'I was at that concert,' he said. So then he went away for a few minutes, came back, went away again for a few minutes, then came back with a corpse over his shoulder. He plunked the body down next to me, picked me up, put me over his shoulder and took me to the next barracks. He exchanged me with that dead prisoner, exchanged our file cards with our numbers, and I was newly born."

The doctor got Meyer a good job at the SS pharmacy, and his strength gradually came back. One day another guard, having heard from the doctor that Meyer was a musician, yelled at him, "You! Number 104994! Report for instructions!" He was ordered to play in the band at the neighboring extermination camp of Birkenau, playing marches as the prisoners left the camp for work in the morning and again when they came back in the evening. Of course, Meyer had played the violin, not a band instrument, so when he saw a pair of cymbals leaning against the wall he told the SS commander that he was a real virtuoso on the cymbals. So that's what he played in the band at Birkenau, long enough to save his life. In fact, he became very popular with the guards because they would occasionally throw pebbles at him and he would "field" them with his cymbals. This would make a loud noise, "which the Germans loved."

When Russian soldiers approached Auschwitz from the east in the early months of 1945, Meyer was moved to Buchenwald, from where he was liberated. He made his way to New York and began his new life. In 1947 he attended a performance by the New York Philharmonic with his old friend Gerti Totschek. Bruno Walter, who had left Germany in 1933, conducted Gustav Mahler's *Resurrection* Symphony. It was the first time that Henry and Gerti had heard the music since the Kulturbund's memorable performance of February 1941. There had been so much misery and so much death in the intervening years. "Within two minutes," remembers Henry Meyer, "we were crying like dogs."

AFTER 1945, SS-Brigadeführer Hans Hinkel had nothing to turn to. He had been a devoted Nazi for twenty-four years and possessed no skills to offer Germany in the postwar period. He died in 1960.

And in the final analysis, what can we say of the organization Hinkel had overseen, the Jüdische Kulturbund? The perspective of six decades casts the Kulturbund in a fascinating, ambiguous light. In the end, what did it provide its artists and audiences? And what did it cost them?

There is no question that, at least until the time of the accelerated emigration of the mid-1930s, the Kulturbund employed a number of first-rate artists who had been expelled from mainstream German theaters. Its roster of actors included such stars as Jenny Bernstein and Alfred Berliner. There were eight former concertmasters of major German orchestras in the violin section of the Berlin Kulturbund Orchestra alone. After the war, Kubu alumni found prominent positions with orchestras, opera companies, and string quartets around the world. Hannah Kroner recalls, "We had the cream of the crop. It was as if the stars of the Metropolitan Opera, Lincoln Center, Carnegie Hall, and all the big New York theaters were kicked out of those organizations and reconvened in one place. *That* was the Kulturbund."

Those stars provided their audiences with memorable and moving performances that helped considerably to ease the pain of ever-uglier times for the Jews of Germany. Those performances also provided the artists with an important creative outlet—an opportunity afforded them nowhere else—as well as an income that would prove vital when they eventually sought to flee the country.

But was there a dark side to the Kulturbund? As the son of artists and as someone who works with musicians on a daily basis, I believe deeply in the power of art to make people whole. So I think what the Kulturbund provided its audiences was vitally important, particularly in light of what was going on outside the theater. But how great was the cost of the Kubu as it strove daily to make life more bearable? Was it so intent on enriching lives that it wasn't alert to the danger of losing lives?

Some observers think the answer is yes, including a few members of the organization itself, who found its combination of pride and naïveté in the face of its Nazi keepers alternately baffling and maddening. Early on, Julius Bab wrote to a colleague, "It is a ghetto operation, but we want to do so well that the Germans will feel ashamed"—as if proficiency in art was something that would somehow impress the Nazis and prompt them to ease their restrictions on Jews. The Kubu songwriter Kurt Tucholsky, writing from exile in Sweden, was even more caustic: "You imprison them, you pen them up in a Jewish theater and they only have one ambition: 'Now we'll show you that our theater is better!'"

But charges worse than hubris have been laid at the door of the Kulturbund. By allowing the Nazis to use the organization as a propaganda tool, did the Kulturbund lend a much-needed aura of legitimacy to that gangster regime? And worse still, by providing music, theater, films, lectures—above all, a sense of community—did the Kulturbund foster an atmosphere of normalcy that discouraged emigration until it became too late to consider such action? Had there been no Kulturbund, would thousands of German Jews have recognized the Nazi threat more quickly and taken the necessary steps to save themselves? Had there been no Jewish Kulturbund, would there have been fewer Jewish deaths?

Alan Steinweis, an associate professor of history and Judaic studies at the University of Nebraska who has written extensively about Hans Hinkel, thinks so. "The Kulturbund served as a mechanism for psychological accommodation to Jewish cultural disenfranchisement," he writes. "By providing Jewish artists and audiences with an outlet for creative expression, the Kulturbund rendered Jewish existence in National Socialist Germany somewhat less desperate than it otherwise might have been, thereby lulling German Jews into a tragically false sense of security about the future."

Journalist Henryk Broder, co-author of a German book about the Kulturbund, calls the association "a calamitous misunderstanding" in which the Jews were used by the Nazis as props in their own theater—Joseph Goebbels's theater of propaganda.

Former members of the Kulturbund are divided in their opinions. The harshest critic was actor Bert Bernd, who appeared with the Kulturbund from 1934 until his emigration in December 1938. In an interview with Henryk Broder in the late 1980s, he called the Kubu "a sick idea, a devilish plan," and criticized the common sense of Kurt Singer and Werner Levie. "I think that people like Singer and Levie were deceiving themselves. Singer was the best example of this form of self-deception. He was in the U.S.A. and came back! But all these leaders had no idea what was really going on. They talked themselves into believing that they were building the great Jewish theater. They believed only in their art and not in what turned out to be reality. So many people could have left, but didn't. The Kulturbund's function was quite simply to display to foreign visitors what a wonderfully thriving cultural life Jews had in Germany. We were little figures on the Nazi chessboard, figures moved around to create illusions. The whole thing was a lie from beginning to end."

But other former members of the Kulturbund disagree. Hannah Kroner can't bring herself to believe that the Kubu contributed to the deaths of any of its audience members. She thinks that "only a few optimists who would have stayed anyway stayed in Berlin because of the Kulturbund." Furthermore, she says, the Kubu brought joy to the lives of so many. "Our audience was my parents' generation, the people who had gone regularly to the opera and the theater and the Philharmonie, and they were very glad to have this opportunity. I'm sure they didn't think it was mere propaganda. This, after all, was the sole means of entertainment. There was no TV and the radio was all real propaganda broadcasting. You didn't dare tune into foreign broadcasts because if a neighbor heard you, you might be denounced and taken God knows where. The Kulturbund was it for all these people who'd grown accustomed to having the performing arts in their lives."

Henry Meyer thinks the argument that the Kubu contributed to the deaths of some of the association's members is "lots of nonsense." Meyer asserts that it wasn't the Jews who underestimated the Nazis, it was the other way around. "Where the Nazis made their big mistake was, they didn't expect that the Kulturbund would be so important, both to musicians and to audiences. If you let a full-blooded musician or any artist practice his profession, even under the force of the Gestapo, he comes alive, and that's what we did. For the people who came to the concerts, it was a great success. For those who played, it was something very special—after all, there was nothing else available. We were born to perform and when we did that we really lived."

Kubu actor Martin Brandt goes even further: "The Kulturbund was my spiritual salvation, my door to freedom. It saved us; it was our light. Yes, we had blinders on, because if we had known what was going on around us, we probably would've ended up in the loony bin."

Oboist Kurt Michaelis also appreciated the Kulturbund as a means to keep his sanity. "It was pounded into us all the time all the things we were not allowed to do," he says, "And the Kulturbund was something that we *could* do. It was restricted to us but we could do it. It was a safeguard and something to get us away from daily life. We knew that at night a knock could come on the door and someone could grab you and take you away. But somehow we stuck to our music and that helped keep us going. You would think that we would want to throw everything away and creep into a corner and not make music with our lives at stake, but it wasn't like that at all. We just played. And you cannot explain that to anybody because they wouldn't believe you. How could we give such wonderful performances as the Mahler Second Symphony, performances that moved you right through your whole body? It is still hard for me to understand how I could sit there and practice and make reeds and prepare for the next performance and concentrate on it as if there was nothing else in life that was important. But that's what it was. It's one of the miracles of life how you can go through it even when it's not so easy."

Violinist Eugene Drucker, son of Ernst Drucker, recognizes the inherent ambiguities in the Kulturbund but concludes that it was a good experience for his father. "The idea that this curious dualism could exist, which seems so surprising to us now, knowing as we do what was going to happen to the Jews—the fact that they were allowed to have this cultural life and this togetherness, I guess it has a sinister undertone. But if Jews had a choice in the mid-thirties and they could take part in this cultural life—even though they were forced to go through the Kulturbund—were they really supposed to turn it down? Even if it did give them a false sense of security and may have led to a few (or many) Jews working a little less hard to get out because of the sense of normalcy the Kubu fashioned. Were they to boycott the Kulturbund in the hope that its absence would have hastened the decision of the Jews to leave? After all, it wasn't that easy to emigrate. Certainly a lot of the musicians in the orchestra got out because musicians were probably better connected than some other people, people who had fewer means or less money. At any rate, I'm thankful that my father was able to play great music."

The actress Ruth Anselm concluded, "It was a ghetto theater but the audience loved it and came every night. And when the lights came up, we acted. The stage was our world. We didn't think about other things, we just performed. After all, artists are strange people to begin with, and we were able to do what we live to do."

My father agrees that the Kulturbund contributed to a sense of normalcy in Germany. He points out that he left the country for Sweden in 1936 and would have stayed in Stockholm were it not for the two attractions of love for Rosemarie and a steady job as a musician. The prospect of making music in a professional atmosphere made it possible for him to set aside his rational conclusion that Germany was no longer a suitable place to live. Later, living in Berlin, it was always more pleasant for Günther and Rosemarie to think about the next rehearsal or concert than it was to reflect on the latest edict that had been passed against them. "What was true for us must have been true for the people who came to hear our concerts," he says. "And of course nobody could see for sure what was coming. So if there is the opportunity to hear some good music, maybe you go listen tonight and think about your future next morning."

After thinking through all this "testimony," it's hard to arrive at a definitive conclusion about the role of this most complex institution. Given my personal connection to the Kubu, I'm drawn to Gene Drucker's line of reasoning. Certainly Günther and Rosemarie profited by their experiences in the Kulturbund, particularly when they first came to the United States and were able to get jobs as musicians. And as someone who has left plays and concerts walking on air, deeply moved and inspired by live performances, I can only imagine how important the Kubu was to people sorely in need of a little happiness.

But with the benefit of hindsight, so much of the Kulturbund story defies belief, particularly as that story is embodied in the personality of Kurt Singer. He was obviously an amazingly talented and dedicated man, willing and able to work incredible hours on behalf of his beloved organization. It seems equally obvious, however, that as time went by, the man approached megalomania, obsessed with his extravagant ideas and convinced of his own powers to reason with the Nazis. His need to perform and his belief in the importance of art led him to accept without protest the rules imposed upon him by Hans Hinkel and the Propaganda Ministry. Any compromise was acceptable, as long as it allowed the show to go on. Kurt Singer willingly entered into a devil's bargain.

It bears repeating that neither Singer nor anyone else could see the approaching horror for what it was. As it is nearly impossible for us, years after the fact, to grasp the enormity of the Nazis' crimes, how can we expect anyone to have been able to predict them? That said, and from the safe perspective of the present, I shake my head in wonderment at some aspects of Dr. Singer's conduct and personality: his naive insistence on transforming each new Nazi decree into the virtue of exploring and renewing Jewish traditions, even when the Kubu's audiences were not particularly interested in exploring those traditions; his opposition to the emigration of his artists, when their decisions meant life or death for themselves and their families; above all, his seemingly unshakeable faith that the Nazi boors recognized and cared about his talents as conductor, director, artist, and organizer. Kurt Singer dreamed a great dream, that beauty could overcome the beast. I wonder if, as he lay dying in the cold of Terezin, he ever awoke from his dream to face the bitter truth that beauty outlasts, but doesn't always win.

But even after Dr. Singer relinquished his duties as director of the Kulturbund, its new leaders kept renewing the bargain. In the shocking days after the November Pogrom, when Joseph Goebbels ordered the Kulturbund back to work, a few of its board members raised their voices in protest: how can we simply go back on stage, knowing what has happened to so many of our people? At that point, the bargain might have been broken, the decision made to do business with tyrants no longer. But in the one moment when they enjoyed some leverage, the leaders of the Kulturbund chose to compromise for the very worthy goal of getting two hundred of their colleagues released from concentration camps. For nearly three more years, the Kubu soldiered on, fulfilling its mission to provide employment for its artists and joy for its audiences. Its members did what they knew how to do, and they did their best. What were the Nazis going to do, anyway, kill them all?

In the end, there is something very, well, *Jewish* about the Kulturbund. It reminds me of a bitter joke: A new flood is foretold and nothing can be done to prevent it. In three days, the rising floodwaters will wipe out the world. A Muslim leader appears on television and pleads with humankind to convert to Islam; that way, they will at least find salvation in heaven. The Pope goes on TV and delivers a similar message: "It is still not too late to accept Jesus." The Chief Rabbi of Israel then takes to the airwaves to declare, "We have three days to learn how to live under water."

The gravelike Kulturbund Memorial on Kommandanten-
strasse. When I last visited it, in November 1999,
someone had left a rose on its horizontal bronze slab.

Today, nothing remains of the grand theater on Kommandanten-strasse where so many performances took place for the benefit—and perhaps for the pacification—of Berlin's Jews. But there is a simple memorial, erected in 1990, standing where the theater's entrance once was. It looks very much like a grave, with a granite headstone and a horizontal slab of bronze, on which are fashioned these words, in German:

> Here the Jewish Kulturbund was located from 1935 to 1941. Excluded from professional life, the Jews in Germany founded this self-help organization with its own orchestra and ensembles for opera, operetta, and theater. The Nazi authorities misused the Kulturbund for surveillance of Jewish artists and their audiences, which could consist only of Jews. In 1941 it was prohibited. Almost all of those who worked here were murdered in concentration camps.

24

"It Will Be on Your Conscience"

THE STORY of Günther and Rosemarie's first months in America could fill another book.

Lotte Breger, the schoolteacher who had thrown the party in Chinatown to raise money for their passage, met them at Ellis Island. First by ferry to Manhattan and then through the New York subways, she brought them to her apartment on West 86th Street for their first taste of American life. Mrs. Breger's daughter Nina had arranged for some of her friends to come over and welcome the new arrivals. My father remembers the relaxed and carefree atmosphere of the party: young men sitting backwards on chairs, their arms folded over the backrests, munching potato chips, drinking Cokes and beers out of frosty bottles, listening to a ball game on the radio in the kitchen. Laughter burst forth loudly and often. No one seemed afraid, or inhibited, or spoke guardedly for fear of being overheard by the wrong ears. It was during that hot and lazy afternoon, so different from his life in Berlin, that Günther began to understand the extent of the freedom he and his wife had attained at the end of their desperate flight.

The next afternoon they altered their identities. Mrs. Breger ("our second mother," my father calls her) took them down to the Immigration and Naturalization Service to sign their important "First Papers," documents indicating their intention to become American citizens as early as the law permitted. In the course of the afternoon they filled in forms that changed their names; Rosemarie dropped the "ie" in favor of a simpler "y," while Günther Ludwig Goldschmidt underwent a more significant transformation. He dropped the "Ludwig" and the umlaut in "Günther"; as "Gunther" it served as his new middle name. For his new first name he chose that of the first president of his new country, George Washington. The heavily German-sounding "Goldschmidt" became the more mellifluous "Goldsmith." At the close of business, Lotte Breger went home with two new people: George Gunther Goldsmith and Rosemary Goldsmith.

Within a few days, with the help of an employment agency that specialized in assisting newly arrived immigrants, George and Rosemary found jobs. My mother was a maid, cleaning and cooking for twelve dollars a week. My father spent forty hours a week cutting zippers out of discarded pants and polishing them on a wheel, reconditioning them so that they could serve again in the flies of new trousers. For his efforts he earned a weekly salary of fourteen dollars. It wasn't much, but with their twenty-six dollars a week George and Rosemary were able to afford their own apartment on 103rd Street near Columbus Avenue.

Their income was bolstered by two incidents in the next few weeks. George realized that he needed a silver flute to replace the wooden one he had brought with him from Germany. If he wanted to compete with American flutists he would need to play an instrument with the more brilliant sound favored by American listeners. But where would he find the money? Part of the answer was supplied by the widow of a doctor they had known in Berlin. She was a friend of Albert Einstein, who, she knew, was interested in worthy causes. She visited the great physicist, explained the situation, and within days George received a personal note from Einstein wishing him well. The envelope also contained a crisp ten-dollar bill.

(That note from Albert Einstein was the source of a much larger amount of money when, years later, George sold it to a New York autograph dealer for four hundred and fifty dollars. Today, of course, I wish my father had kept the letter.)

The next incident proved to be more lucrative but also more painful. Coming home from the zipper factory one afternoon, George noticed a display of oranges outside a grocer's on Columbus Avenue. He stood there a few moments admiring the fruit, not noticing that he was standing on the metal doors that covered the store's cellar. All of a sudden the doors gave way, and he plummeted twelve feet down onto a concrete floor, hitting his head as he fell.

A few minutes later, bruised and woozy, George learned his first bit of American slang. A policeman peered down at him from the street and, after ascertaining that the young man was basically all right, told him to "take it easy." George tried to translate the phrase literally and looked around for what the officer expected him to take.

An ambulance arrived shortly thereafter and rushed him to a nearby hospital, where his head was stitched and bandaged. The ambulance then drove him home and Rosemary, shocked at his white-swathed head, helped him to bed. Within minutes there came a knock at the door and in walked a Mr. Fensterstock, an attorney who said he would be delighted to help George recover damages from the careless grocer. The ambulance-chaser produced a document that promised him 40 percent of the take. Still somewhat shaken, George signed the agreement and Mr. Fensterstock hurried off.

Ten days later, the mailman delivered a check made out to George Goldsmith in the amount of one hundred twenty dollars. Fensterstock had settled with the grocer for two hundred dollars and kept eighty for himself. Still, the check was equal to what Rosemary made in ten weeks, and George concluded ruefully that his fall had been worth it.

All this time the two young musicians had been earning their small salaries in decidedly nonmusical ways. But toward the end of summer they learned about a traveling orchestra with headquarters in Chicago that was looking for new recruits. The ensemble's founder and conductor, a Czech-born artist named Bohumir Kryl, was to hold auditions in New York for a tour of the Midwest and South that was scheduled to last from mid-September until shortly before Christmas.

George and Rosemary eagerly made appointments to audition for Mr. Kryl in his hotel room. Rosemary played first and was immediately hired for the tour at twenty-five dollars a week. Then George went in. The conductor, shrewdly realizing that George wanted very much to join his wife, announced that, although he already had all the flutists he needed, he would be willing to take on both of them for forty-five dollars per week. Thus, at bargain prices, but immensely happy to have secured their first jobs as musicians in America, my parents signed on for the tour.

My father remembers Bohumir Kryl as a tall, very stout man in his sixties, who often conducted by wiggling around on the podium with his hands folded across his ample stomach. Most of the members of the orchestra were young people fresh out of college or recent immigrants like George and Rosemary, eager for work. The repertory included such concert favorites as Dvořák's *New World* Symphony, Schubert's *Unfinished* Symphony, Wagner's *Meistersinger* Overture (my parents' first opportunity to perform music by that Teutonic titan), some Strauss waltzes, and *Country Gardens,* a piece by Australian composer Percy Grainger that often served as an encore.

After a week of rehearsals—during which the musicians were not paid, since there were no concerts to generate income—the Kryl tour commenced on September 15. The players rode in an old converted school bus, a rattletrap machine that frequently stalled when confronted by steep inclines. At such times everyone was expected to get out and push. Everyone, that is, except Maestro Kryl, who rode ahead of the bus in a large automobile driven by the woman who was both the conductor's harpist and his mistress.

Many years ago my mother showed me a diary she had kept during that tour, with entries listing the cities they played, a diary long since lost. There were references to Springfield, Ohio; Springfield, Illinois; and Springfield, Missouri; Terre Haute and Evansville, Indiana; Lexington and Paducah, Kentucky; Knoxville and Nashville, Tennessee; Little Rock and Jonesboro, Arkansas; Monroe and Shreveport, Louisiana; and many towns in Texas: Lubbock and Amarillo, Waco and Austin, Beaumont and Galveston and San Antonio. The days were long and tiring, the meals came irregularly and were generally eaten on the run, and the concert schedule seemed never-ending. But George and Rosemary, only months removed from the terrors of Berlin, enjoyed themselves immensely. They were seeing fascinating corners of their huge new country, they were making music together, and they were earning forty-five dollars a week. They were not aware that just days before they had left on their tour, their Kulturbund colleagues had found themselves out of a job and facing disaster. But my father remembers thinking that the long and dusty American roads he and my mother traveled that autumn of 1941 were truly paved with gold.

On Sunday morning, December 7, they awoke in the Blue Bonnet Hotel in Corpus Christi, Texas. And there, just before boarding the bus for Brownsville, they and the other members of the orchestra learned of the Japanese attack on the United States naval base at Pearl Harbor. The musicians had a feeling that the day would not proceed normally, and they were right. As the bus rolled into Brownsville on U.S. Highway 77, federal police ordered it to halt and the passengers to identify themselves. George and Rosemary still had their German passports with them, documents that prominently displayed the sign of the swastika. The two were immediately taken into custody, and the police phoned Washington to determine whether they had just nabbed a couple of German spies posing as musicians. It wasn't until the following morning that the Immigration Office was able to cable Brownsville and clear their names.

After that evening's concert, Bohumir Kryl announced that he had run out of money and the rest of the tour was canceled. Furthermore, he said, the bus was staying with him and the musicians were all responsible for finding their own ways back north. George and Rosemary, not wanting to spend their recent savings on transportation, decided to hitchhike home. With their instruments under their arms and their thumbs in the air, they stood by the side of those gold-paved roads and, thanks to the kindness of strangers, covered the two thousand miles between south Texas and New York City in time to return to their little apartment on 103rd Street a few days before Christmas, their first Christmas in the New World.

Their new lives had begun, and George and Rosemary set about the task of establishing more solid careers. In the spring of 1942 they were offered positions—their first union jobs—with a music festival in Columbia, South Carolina. They played their first full season as orchestra musicians in America in 1942–1943 as members of the New Orleans Symphony. They spent the following season apart, as George performed with the Baltimore Symphony and Rosemary began a two-year association with the Pittsburgh Symphony and its renowned music director Fritz Reiner.

During their months in New Orleans they had met another German-born couple who now lived in Philadelphia, Eric and Leni Jackson. At the end of their time in the South, George and Rosemary decided to join the Jacksons in Pennsylvania. So during the summers of 1943, 1944, and 1945 they lived in a small studio apartment on Mermaid Lane in suburban Philadelphia, within a short bus ride of the rolling countryside. They had a small but affectionate circle of friends with whom they frequently enjoyed weekend outings and chamber music evenings, doing their best to recreate the most pleasurable elements of their former lives. They had established a savings account and could now afford new furniture and the occasional restaurant meal. As George and Rosemary they had escaped the terrors that Nazi Germany had planned for Günther and Rosemarie.

Those whom they had left behind, however, were not to be so lucky.

WHEN I BEGAN work on this book, my father sent me a packet of letters that he had been saving in a lower desk drawer for many years. The collection included twenty-four letters that his mother had sent him and Rosemary between June and November 1941 from Berlin, and six letters from his father and brother that had been mailed from their French internment camps between June 1941 and June 1942. Those letters have provided me a glimpse into the increasingly desperate lives of my relatives. They've also allowed me to recognize and understand more fully the heavy burden of guilt my parents had to endure during the time they were establishing their lives in the New World and during all the years thereafter.

While Günther and Rosemarie were still en route to America, Toni Goldschmidt wrote of her hope and wonder at the prospect of the children's reaching safety. After their arrival, and after they had written detailed descriptions of what they had seen on their journey and their first impressions of New York, Toni continued to write frequently, commenting on their adventures and telling them a few details of her life, and Eva's and "Mother Else's," on Richthofenstrasse. Eva's health, never robust, remained delicate, and she endured frequent visits to doctors who were incompetent, indifferent, or both. Eventually she recovered sufficiently to take a job at a big Siemens munitions plant, work for which she was required to leave the house at six-fifteen in the morning six days a week. There were increasing tensions between Toni and Else, as the two families struggled to become one. Grandmother Behrens, who was living alone in Bremen, remained hale and alert at age seventy-seven, but expected at any moment to be sent on "the big journey," code words for deportment.

A recurring theme of all Toni's letters, however, was her deep concern for her husband and younger son, her frustration that she knew so little of their condition, and her abiding hope that her children who were already safe in America would be able to free the whole family. The intensity of her expression causes me to think that this was a topic that came up more frequently in the days before the children left Berlin than my father remembers today. In letter after letter she writes, "We still haven't heard anything from Father and Helmut." When she does hear from them at last, her mood is only slightly lightened, as she writes, "I have the feeling that they must get out of there as soon as possible if they want to stay healthy. It seems that Father is suffering because of the wind that's been blowing steadily for six weeks. If only they would have some good luck at last! Then—and I can hardly believe this—you could pick them up at the pier. O my children, will something so wonderful still come to pass for us?!?!"

Some of her letters fairly burst with hope, as when she writes, "The thought that perhaps you will be able to welcome the two Odysseuses in a few weeks is almost too beautiful to be real!" Or when she enthuses, "It would be wonderful, wonderful if you could put them up in your apartment!" or "Maybe they could even be in your beautiful country by Christmas!" And then, "Once they have happily arrived in the U.S.A., Father and Helmut should make every effort to expedite *our* emigration so that everything is ready." For George's birthday on November 17, 1941, Toni writes, "I wonder if there is a tiny possibility that we'll be together next November 17th? Right now, it doesn't look as though it will come to pass. In spite of that I keep hoping!"

Over and over and over, she reminds her children of their responsibility: that they must do everything in their power to free Alex and Helmut from their incarceration in France. "I must ask you again:

Remember, you must not rest until Father and Helmut have joined you there! In their letters it is touching to read that they place all their trust and hopes in you!"

But in their letters to America, Alex and Helmut reveal not only trust and hope but, increasingly, anger and resentment as their years of captivity continue.

They had arrived in France in June of 1939, two of the 224 passengers of the *St. Louis* who had been arbitrarily selected to disembark in that country. The following May, when France was quickly defeated by the German Army, Alex and Helmut were sent to Rivesaltes, a camp in the Pyrenees mountains just across the border from Spain. It was one of hundreds of camps in France set aside for the internment of foreign Jews, camps euphemistically called *centres d'hébergement,* or "lodging centers." Author Susan Zuccotti calls them "uncomfortable, neglected, shameful creations of an antiforeign and anti-Semitic regime." Rivesaltes held more than three thousand prisoners in terrible conditions. Zuccotti writes that it was located "in one of the most mosquito-infested regions of France." A contemporary social worker described Rivesaltes in even starker terms:

> The entire length of the barracks, on both sides, two levels of bunks separated by old blankets, compartments where whole families milled about—father, mother, children, sometimes grandparents—in an indescribable promiscuity. It was dark, cold and humid and there was no heating. And seizing you by the throat upon entering, a bitter odor of human sweat which floats in this den which is never aired out.

On June 19, 1941, two days before Günther and Rosemarie spotted the Statue of Liberty from the deck of the *Mouzhino,* Alex and Helmut had spent more than a year in Rivesaltes. On that day, Alex mailed this letter:

Dear Children:

I hope that you will soon have completed your journey across the big pond and that it will have been, in spite of everything, relaxing and beautiful for you after all the strenuous see-saw days of your emigration. I wish you, with all my heart, a full measure of happiness and may all your hopes and plans be fulfilled.

I must tell you that we don't have anything to wear with the exception of a casual suit, not even underwear or shoes. Even though I assume that before we emigrate—unless it does not happen at all because of some overwhelming event—we shall each receive a suit, a pair of shoes, and a set of underwear, what we have now is completely useless. No tramp would consider our suit and shoes worth taking along, and it is urgently necessary if one wants to get a job or a profession over there to have some basic things. The latter worries me a lot. With my meager knowledge of the language, to become completely dependent on my children would be dreadful.

I know it would be a crime, after what we have gone through in the last 22 months, to await the end of the war here if there is any alternative. If necessary I could easily feed myself at Mother's domicile, of that I am sure. But since one mustn't gamble with the fate of one's family and one's own, the most intensive efforts must be made to get us over there as quickly as possible. I hope to be my old self again in a few months provided it all doesn't take too long. I am *sure* that you two are doing *everything* in your power to get affidavits for Mother and Eva *as quickly as possible,* so that I can hope to see you all once more in the not-too-distant future. It is this thought that keeps me going and will continue to keep me going.

When we sailed off on May 13, 1939, on the 'St. Louis' and you waved to us for such a long time from the dock, we could not have had an inkling that our voluntary separation would become such a long and involuntary one. With many good wishes and loving regards,

Yours,
Father

Günther and Rosemarie's arrival in America brought immediate benefits to Alex and Helmut. Because they now had documented relatives living in the United States, the prisoners were transferred to

Camp Les Milles, about twenty kilometers northwest of Marseilles, a camp that contained many people who only awaited visas for their own journey to freedom. Les Milles represented a marginal improvement over Rivesaltes—it was farther from the high mountains and less subject to the Mistral winds—and yet was still a wretched place to live. Again, Susan Zuccotti:

> At Les Milles, a former brick factory and one of the more bearable camps, internees washed in water from one long outside pipe pierced with twenty holes. The water was not potable and froze solid in winter. In good weather, the men ate in the open air near the latrines. The Mistral blew toilet paper through the dining area, but the food was adequate and there was little disease. Men slept on the floor inside the factory, which was immensely dusty from its former service and filled with fleas and vermin.

On September 22, 1941, the Jewish New Year, as George and Rosemary were beginning their tour with Bohumir Kryl, Alex wrote them again.

Dear Children:

I hope you haven't been worried about us because you haven't heard from us for some time now. But I work all day long cleaning vegetables in the kitchen and in the evening I'm dead tired and Helmut's time is completely occupied with various courses. There is a meager amount of pay for the work we do; weekly it amounts to perhaps 3/4 of the cost of shoe soles and heels. In addition to that you get a second helping of food at noon and in the evening. If one gets up every morning at 6 o'clock, by noon one isn't in the mood for writing. On this New Year's morning I'm sitting on my bed, using my blanket as a desk.

There are about 1300 people here, most of whom want to go to the U.S. There are repeated delaying tactics, and the moment the U.S. enters the war everything will come to a stop.

You can imagine that we are facing our third winter in France with quite a bit of horror. The food here is probably better than it was in Rivesaltes, but it's very unbalanced and contains little fat. Nevertheless, we have gained some weight. Helmut, who went from 127 pounds down to 94 pounds in Rivesaltes, is now up to 113 pounds, and my weight, which went from 136 pounds to 104, is now 112. Sad to say, scarcely any of the packages were forwarded to us from Rivesaltes, in spite of the repeated claims we filed. Last week two packages containing chocolate arrived and one containing 3 cans of sardines ordered by you. Thank you very, very much.

You don't need to worry about us two, although we are very concerned about Mother and Eva, and the worst thing is that one is completely helpless and cannot do anything for them. Unfortunately one can't tell anything from Mother's letters (she always sounds very confident) about how the two of them are doing physically. It's high time that both of them, like your Mother, dear Rosemarie, move to a less dangerous place. I think the worst of the horror is still to come, unless quite unexpected things were to happen. One must not think about it, and so work is the best medicine. I am deeply worried, in case we don't get away from here before the winter begins, about where we will get underwear and socks.

I know that you are doing everything possible to get us over there. Might personal appearances in Washington be possible? It also might be good, if everything works out all right, to think of making ship reservations. . . .

I hope to hear from you shortly. Many good wishes and love.

Yours,
Father

By the time of the Christian New Year, a little more than three months later, Alex's mood had darkened considerably. He and Helmut were no closer to being released from Les Milles, severe winter weather had closed in, and, worst of all, he had heard very little from America. In a letter dated January 2, 1942, one day after his sixty-third birthday, Alex took out all his frustrations on his son, berating him fiercely and repeatedly.

Dear Günther,

The day before yesterday I, at last, received your long-awaited letter. Thank you for your good wishes for my birthday; I send them back to you as 1942 New Year's wishes. I am very glad that you are doing well. I would have written you long ago, that is after the 7th of November when my last letter was mailed, if only I had received a *single* line from you since the 5th of September. About 4 weeks ago I thought it was ridiculous, as I told Helmut that I probably would not hear from you until my birthday. Unfortunately, however, it turned out I was right.

Look, dear Günther, you write us at best one page saying that you understand our lot and implore us (literally) not to despair. If after 2 1/2 years of internment we would indeed be on the point of despairing, which is in itself quite possible after all this disheartening, bleak time, then your nice words would change nothing. I see nothing but words, nice words, suitable for a magazine that among other things thinks it's giving its reader encouragement. They are the same words—only turned around—one heard when one came home on furlough, spoken by those who had not heard the whistle of bullets during the First World War. But that you believe you have to give us that kind of lecture really appalled me, so after thinking about it for hours the last two nights, I came to the conclusion that you haven't the slightest inkling of our situation.

In June, the last month we were in Rivesaltes, after we each had lost about 1/3 of our weight, we were at a point where I thought we would not live to see the winter. Helmut was working in the hospital barracks then, first as an assistant then as a medical orderly. Part of his job was to transfer the dead—sometimes 2 or 3 a day—and carry the bodies out. These were men who, had they had some degree of nourishment, would not have died. And we saw people literally dying of hunger before our eyes.

Then came our transfer to Les Milles. For 4 months I worked from early till late at night as assistant in or outside the kitchen, mostly in the broiling sun, the oldest among 25 people, until I got an infection on my right hand that lasted 6 weeks. It was not only painful but handicapped me considerably. Since the work is still done outside—the temperature has on occasion been between 10 and 15 degrees F in the mornings—and with the meager pay of 45 fr a week, for which one cannot even buy *one* loaf of bread, I decided not to go back to work there after my hand healed. Recently, although the food here has become wretched, I have recuperated so that I now weigh about 120 pounds, still 15–20 pounds less than in the old days. Helmut also has regained a good part of the weight he lost, but unfortunately since our departure from Germany he has had 10 throat infections, the last one 14 days ago. Sometime this week his tonsils are supposed to be surgically removed; then he will presumably be less prone to infection. We wouldn't have decided to do this if the newly arrived specialist had not recommended it as absolutely imperative.

The worst thing is that we haven't any underwear or coats. When our underwear is being washed, we actually have to go to bed since we don't have a change of underwear. What was previously called de-lousing is very problematical since the disinfection cars are so old—they probably date back to World War I so the young breed of vermin isn't even killed.

We live from one mail delivery to the next; the mail is distributed at 2 p.m. If you receive nothing one day, then you hope for something the next day. So when I realized that you hadn't sent us any news between September 5th and now, you can understand why I was *very* sad about that. Nor can I understand that part of your letter in which you say it has so far been impossible for you to help us. I know from Mother's letters that you get $45 a week and that you are saving up for a new flute and to join the musicians' union. You didn't trust me enough to write me about that—your birthday letter could have been written by any stranger since there is no personal information about you in it except for telling me what states you played in! Helmut is just as sad about all this as I am. It is the first but very serious disappointment I have experienced in one of my children.

Yesterday morning Helmut, who is still my best comrade as he has been from the start, gave me for my birthday half a day's ration, ca. 110 grams of bread, an orange, and a fountain pen bought with the pay he just received for work performed in the spring in Rivesaltes as a medical assistant. The pen is very simple, no golden penpoint, but it will last a few years. He was very dear and made the day really festive. On January 1st, 1941, we slept on wooden cots without straw; in 1940, with the temperature −15 degrees F, we slept in a large room on stones and litter; this year we sleep in the drying room of an old brick factory. Still, it's better than the two previous years!

On the whole the climate here is good—whereas in Rivesaltes in the nearly endless Pyrenees there were storms; the Mistral virtually saps your strength. I will bless the day that brings us freedom again. At my age, every month spent under the current conditions shortens one's life; and it is time that the portals to freedom be opened for us, so that we're not all used up before it finally comes to pass. Therefore, do everything you can to get us out.

For you, all good wishes and love.

Yours,
Father

Try as I might, I cannot imagine what my father must have thought and felt when he opened that letter in his cozy apartment in New York. What lacerations of guilt and fear and pity must have scarred his soul! To have his own father, trapped in unspeakable surroundings, level such accusations of indifference and selfishness at him must have been unbearable.

The worst of it was that George *had* written to France on several occasions in the autumn of 1941, only to have his letters either returned to him or disappear into the maw of the German censors. Nonetheless, there may be truth in Alex's charge that George did not possess "the slightest inkling" of what his father and brother were going through and had expended more of his energy on his own situation and that of his wife as they began their new lives in America. Yet how could George and Rosemary have known—really known—the extent of the crimes being committed in Europe, or anticipated the even more hideous crimes that were still to come?

George immediately sent a return letter to France that included the sum of twenty-five dollars. By this time, the Kryl tour having long since finished, he was back at his job in the zipper factory earning fourteen dollars a week. This letter got through, although not until the middle of March. In return, about a month later, letters from both Alex and Helmut arrived in which they thanked George for the money and told him, in Helmut's words, that they were "relieved that you, dear Günther, understood what we were saying in our last letter."

Helmut went on to assure his brother that contrary to George's assumption, he and their father were deeply interested in all aspects of George and Rosemary's lives, no matter how mundane those details might seem. Helmut also revealed that his tonsillectomy had been put off until warmer weather arrived, and wrote of the many ways he had been "making use of the time of my imprisonment. I am taking part in various courses, language courses (Spanish among others), an electro course, a bookbinding course. In addition I attend various lecture series—one about the development of European Intellectual History called 'From Homer to Goethe,' one about U.S. history, etc. At the moment I'm also reading Shakespeare plays. After having read Othello and Macbeth I am now reading King Lear, and also, with growing admiration, Tolstoy's 'War and Peace.'"

In the same envelope was a letter from Alex in which he voiced some optimism because he had learned that in the last few days, visas for German citizens who wished to emigrate to America were once more being issued in Marseilles. But he also expressed his deep concern for the three women who were still living on Manfred von Richthofenstrasse in Berlin. Toni's weight was down to ninety-four pounds and Eva's to eighty-five. But they, at least, still enjoyed a certain amount of protection from the authorities because of Eva's work at the Siemens plant. Alex feared, however, that Rosemary's mother, Else, was in danger and went on to say that the women's neighbors, "Hans and his wife and Else Speier and family, have had to set out on the long trip"—in other words, had been deported to somewhere in the East. He was increasingly aware that time was running out for all of them.

Indeed, the next letter to arrive from France, dated May 9, 1942, from Helmut, read, in part:

Dear Rosemarie, dear Günther:

Many thanks for your kind and interesting letter dated March 26th. When it arrived I was lying in the infirmary, silent as a fish. A very capable young specialist from here removed my tonsils on April 24th. For a couple of days I was not allowed to speak or to eat anything except ice. But in the meantime I've recovered quite well. I am very glad that it's finally been done!

After not hearing anything for weeks, we are now getting mail from Mother more regularly. The last letters we received were dated March 30 and April 6. Unfortunately there was no good news: On the morning of March 30th your mother, dear Rosemarie, had to depart. Her spirit, when she said goodbye, was admirable! I'm sure I don't have to tell you how very sorry I am! So far we don't know where she was taken. But we hope to find out soon.

In fact, Else Katzenstein Gumpert was deported to Trawniki, a labor camp established in what had once been a sugar factory southeast of Lublin, Poland. She was sixty-three years old. According to the *Encyclopedia of the Holocaust*, "In the spring of 1942, Jews from Germany, Austria and Czechoslovakia were brought to Trawniki. Many of them died of starvation and disease, were deported to the Belzec extermination camp, or were shot in the nearby forest."

Those details my father did not learn for many years. In May of 1942, as they traveled to South Carolina to play in the music festival, he and Rosemary only knew that her mother had been "taken away." Their journey took them through Washington, D.C., where fateful decisions about visas were being made every day. But they stayed on the train to fulfill their contractual obligations, rather than wander the corridors of Capitol Hill in search of a sympathetic ear. In Columbia they sent Alex and Helmut fifty dollars.

A month later, at the end of the festival, they returned to New York. Almost immediately, George wrote to Washington, requesting a meeting with an immigration official to discuss the case of his relatives in France. Within ten days he received a reply, informing him that an appointment had been arranged for the second week in November. The next mail delivery brought an envelope from Les Milles that contained letters from both Alex and Helmut, dated June 9.

Dear Günther and Rosemarie,

Your description of the city of Columbia, its landscape and people, interested me very much. It reminded me somewhat of the novel 'Gone With the Wind,' which of course takes place for the most part in and around Atlanta (Georgia). Fortunately, I can report to you that we are both well. Helmut has recovered from his tonsil operation and has recuperated. For about 4 weeks now he has been working 5 days a week in the Quaker kitchen which was recently set up for about 1/3 of the camp inmates. His bonus, on top of the basic portion of food, benefits me too. For about the same time I have been on barrack room duty for about 60 people living in our room, for which I get a small payment with which I can buy about 1 kilogram of dried peas a week: I pick up and distribute meals and bread (more than 38 stops) and receive a food bonus, although in many cases it's scarcely worthwhile but still does make a difference. After having been so worn down at the beginning of spring, I now feel better and weigh, dressed, about 120 pounds. That's still far too little but I hope to be able to catch up again. If I can't gain more weight, I don't think I will be able to live through a fourth winter.

About 8 days ago we received 2150 Francs through the Quaker office in Marseille, without any indication of who the sender was. Since I assume that you are responsible, I thank you *very, very much.* With the money we bought, because it was urgently necessary, a suitcase, a pair of used shoes for Helmut, and a hat for me—for I haven't had one for two years.

Dear Günther, I don't wish to sound ungrateful for this gift, but it occurs to me again that if you really knew our situation you would have helped us even more long ago. You had decent engagements for months, and if you had put away 50 cents for us every day during that time, it would have helped us immensely. You surely want us to come over; but if I am no longer able to support Mother and myself because of ill health and lack of strength, then I don't want to become a burden to my children. You have seen to it that we received a third affidavit, for which we are grateful. But if you had personally gone to the State Department Immigration Office on your way through Washington in May, we would probably have had our visas long ago and perhaps we'd be in the same position as others on whose behalf personal efforts were made.

I have described our situation for you several times. This will be the last time. If you don't move heaven and earth to help us, that's up to you, but it will be on your conscience. It won't be long before Helmut, who is still growing, will no longer be able to exist under the present conditions without permanent damage—this is a fact, and no words need be wasted on it. I find it very touching: often he has literally divided his last piece of bread with me. I have been very frank today, and I would regret it if you were angry with me, but an honest word can also be binding rather than divisive.

In the last few days we have had hot weather here; the vermin plague, in particular fleas and bedbugs, has become very severe. Helmut, undaunted, continues to work at the big cooking kettles in spite of the heat. Today he had a day off; slept almost all afternoon after going to his book-binding course in the morning. It has been reliably reported that those over 60

will be released if 9,000 francs are deposited for their livelihood. But I want to stay with Helmut in the hope that the hour
of freedom will ring for us in the not-too-distant future. For
today, many loving regards and good wishes.

Yours,
Father

On the back of the first sheet of Alex's letter were these lines from
Helmut:

Dear Rosemarie and dear Günther,

Since Father has already reported to you in detail, I just
want to add my warm regards and good wishes. I'm sure we'll
get a letter from you in the next few days; we're eagerly waiting
for it! Perhaps we shall receive the long awaited Visa! Father is
counting on it. Oh, what stories we could tell you then!! I'm
sure I don't have to emphasize that Father and I help each other
out wherever we can and on the whole we are good friends.

That's all for today. Next time I'll write more!

Yours,
Helmut

If everything suddenly works out, we would arrive at *your*
place a few weeks after this letter reaches you!

It would be the last letter from his father and brother that my
father would receive.

In early August 1942, the Vichy government of France delivered
about ten thousand foreign Jews into the hands of the Nazis. On
August 5, the secretary general of the French police sent a confidential
memo to all local authorities in the unoccupied zone in which he outlined detailed instructions for that delivery. The dispatch forbade the
deportation of elderly Jews of more than sixty years of age.

Nevertheless, on the afternoon of Monday, August 10, both Alex
and Helmut were among more than 270 Jews—whose last names began

with the letters *A* through *G*—ordered to assemble under the hot sun in the courtyard of Les Milles. That evening Alex experienced a final humiliating march, as once more he found himself herded through a city in full public view. He, his son, and their fellow prisoners were marched to the railroad station and loaded into boxcars. An eyewitness reported, "They were cattle cars, strewn with bunches of straw. In each car, a jug of water and a bucket to serve as a toilet."

The cars' doors were sealed tight, but the train remained in the station all night in the stifling August heat. The next morning, August 11, the train rolled north to—in the words of author Susan Zuccotti—"a camp in a town on the outskirts of Paris that was soon to become a familiar and dreaded word in Jewish households: Drancy." So close to the City of Lights that prisoners could see its skyline on clear days, Drancy was a transit camp surrounded by a double row of barbed wire.

Three days later, on Friday, August 14, Alex and Helmut Goldschmidt were among 1,015 Jews loaded onto another train and shipped from Drancy to Auschwitz. When they arrived, at least 875 people were immediately gassed, my grandfather among them. He was sixty-three years old. My uncle was selected for work duty, assigned a barracks, and tattooed with the number 59305. Less than two months later, on October 9, at 9:20 in the morning, Helmut died. The cause of death was listed as typhoid fever. He was twenty-one.

Of all the terrible images of my family's story, imagining my grandfather and uncle, those two "good friends" who had endured so much together in the previous forty months, being separated by the wave of a Nazi doctor's hand on the teeming siding of Auschwitz is by far the worst. Did they know what was about to happen to Alex, as father was sent off to the left while son was sent to the right? Did they have a final moment together, a clasp of hands, an embrace, a long last look? How in God's name did Helmut survive those next two months amid the unspeakable brutality and with the awful knowledge of his father's death resounding in his being with every beat of his heart?

"Your people are burning there."

The end came quickly for the other endangered members of the family. Jeanette Rosenbaum Behrens, my father's prim and proper grandmother, had been sent to the Theresienstadt concentration camp on July 24 and died there on September 25. She was seventy-nine.

On October 19, ten days after Helmut's death, Toni and Eva Gold-schmidt were both deported to the Jewish ghetto that had been established in Riga, the capital of Latvia. The exact date of their deaths is unknown. They were, respectively, fifty-five and twenty-two years old.

25

Coda

ONLY MANY YEARS later, in 1995, from the Holocaust and War Victims Tracing and Information Center of the American Red Cross, did my father learn definitively what had happened to our family. Not until the summer of 1999, with the help of Scott Miller of the United States Holocaust Memorial Museum, did I find out the details of the fate of my uncle Helmut. With the end of the war in Europe in May 1945, and the gruesome photographs and newsreels that accompanied the coming of peace, George and Rosemary simply assumed the worst and made little effort to track down the facts. The immense tree in the house was in full leaf, and they quickly learned how to ignore it.

They also had to come to terms with another death. In January 1946, with Rosemary in the ninth month of her first pregnancy, she developed toxemia. Late in the month her baby, a son, was delivered by cesarean section. Four days later, on January 30, the infant died.

Rosemary was inconsolable for months, telling George over and over that she had lost interest in life, in music, and that she would never play her instrument again. To try to lift her spirits, George arranged for her to audition for the viola section of the St. Louis Symphony Orchestra. She unwillingly boarded the train to New York, where she played for Vladimir Golschmann, the St. Louis Symphony's music director. Rosemary was immediately offered a contract with the orchestra, commencing with the 1946–1947 season. In September 1946, George and Rosemary moved to St. Louis, a city they would call home for the next twenty-one years.

A year later, on September 26, 1947, they took their oaths as new citizens of the United States at the Old Court House in downtown

St. Louis. In the summer of 1949, their son Peter was born, and three years later I came along. Peter was given the middle name of Alexander, after his paternal grandfather, and I was named Martin Julian, after Rosemary's father.

Throughout the 1950s and 1960s my mother was a central figure of the musical life of St. Louis. She eventually became the symphony's assistant principal violist, she played with the city's summer opera orchestra, she gave recitals, she played regularly with a string quartet. In 1967, at the invitation of the great and formidable conductor George Szell, my mother joined the Cleveland Orchestra. She remained a member of that renowned institution for fourteen years, until her retirement in 1981. She continued to give expression to her love of chamber music, marking the Beethoven Bicentennial in 1970 with a complete cycle of his string quartets with the Severance Quartet, an ensemble she had helped to form. At the time of her death from cancer in 1984, she had settled into the music community of Tucson, Arizona, where she had established another string quartet. My mother had come a long way from the dangers of her life in Germany and the uncertainties of her early life in America, fashioning a significant career for herself as a musician.

My father, on the other hand, abandoned his flute for the world of retail sales. He first sold books at the downtown St. Louis branch of the Doubleday Book Shop and then joined the Famous-Barr department store as a furniture and home decorating salesman. He eventually rose to department manager and, upon moving to Cleveland and landing a position with a related company, to divisional merchandise manager.

But my father was never happy in the world of commerce. He recalls hating the sales meetings, the pep talks, the misleading advertisements, the backstabbing and betrayal that too often mark the corporate environment. "It was a life full of frustrations year after year after year," he says. Why then did he give up his life as a musician?

By way of explanation today, he points to the fact that in the 1940s and 1950s, American symphony orchestras did not enjoy the fifty-two-week seasons that many of them do now. It was therefore important for him to earn a year-round salary to support his growing family. By bringing in a paycheck week after week, he says, he enabled

After twenty-one years in the St. Louis Symphony and fourteen years
as a member of the Cleveland Orchestra, my mother retired to Tucson,
Arizona, in 1981. But she remained an active musician. This is her
last professional photograph, for a string quartet recital at the University
of Arizona in September 1982.

my mother—who he insists was more talented than he was—to establish her career, an act of self-denial that brought him a great deal of
satisfaction. Through her life as a working musician, my father was able
to enjoy a vicarious musical life of his own.

It all makes perfect sense. And it's probably true. My father is a
generous man and is fully capable of denying himself so that others
around him, those he feels close to, can thrive and prosper.

But what if that is not the whole story? My father admits that he deeply regrets not maintaining his career as a musician, and that he regrets not going back to school once he had found safety in the United States. In 1945 a government official told him that he would have to go to school for only one year in order to obtain an advanced degree that would enable him to teach or to find employment commensurate with his skills and interests. And yet he chose not to.

"I had certain understandings of music history and perceptions of the interrelationship of music, drama, and life that might have brought added understanding to students in the classroom and added pleasure and dimensions to listeners on radio or in the concert hall," he says today, "if I had found a way to bring my talents to fruition—if I had gone back to school. I did not do such a thing, a nondecision that never—even to this day—has stopped haunting me."

Why, then, did he accept the painful terms of that "nondecision"? It was the practical thing to do, of course—a guaranteed income is a seductive option for a young man with dreams of a family. But nine years earlier he had rejected the practical choice of a safe life in Sweden in favor of a risky return to Nazi Germany in pursuit of love and music. The George Goldsmith of 1945 possessed the same romantic soul and artistic yearnings of the Günther Goldschmidt of 1936.

But the summer of 1945 brought with it the hideous news of mass murder and the awful realization that those desperate letters from France in 1941 and 1942 had been a warning, an ominous message that he had not heeded. His father and brother had told him to do everything in his power to help them, to get them out, to *save their lives*—and he had failed. Never mind that he was a poor immigrant, struggling to make ends meet by polishing zippers for fourteen dollars a week. No excuse could possibly exonerate him when set against those nightmarish images of living skeletons in the liberated yards of Buchenwald and Dachau, or, worse still, the bulldozed bodies within the walls of Auschwitz and Birkenau. "It will be on your conscience," Alex had vowed, and Alex was right.

"The unanswered question which disturbs me most profoundly and which I shall carry to my own death," my father now says, "is whether through an enormous last-minute effort I could have saved my father and brother from their horrible end."

Guilt takes many forms. Sometimes it acts as prosecutor, judge, and jury. In the year that followed the end of the Second World War, my father learned of the probable violent deaths of his family and made a choice to abandon his flute. I believe that those two facts are not coincidental. I believe that my father, as penance for the deaths in his family, unconsciously sentenced himself to an unhappy professional life, one far removed from the realms of art and music that he deeply loved.

I should hasten to point out that my father rejects this analysis. With all the love and compassion I can muster, I stand by it.

Am I saying that my mother had no conscience? Of course not. She too suffered the guilts of the survivor. But she also possessed a drive and a confidence instilled in her by *her* father, not to mention an enormous talent. And she was fortunate to have by her side a man who supported her ambitions, who wrote the letter that got her the job in St. Louis and who gladly moved to Cleveland with her twenty-one years later. George was immensely proud to be the husband of a member of the Cleveland Orchestra and took great pleasure in Rosemary's accomplishments. But he could never fully accept the manner in which he made his living. To this day, when someone asks him what he did before his retirement he replies, "I was a musician."

An element of his past that he also finds hard to accept is his Jewishness. As I have already observed, my brother and I were raised with virtually no religious instruction. We therefore had no sense of ourselves as Jews. I always understood that my parents had come from "a Jewish background," but I was also aware of the Christmas trees in the homes my parents grew up in. My father never went any further in his religious identification than to occasionally refer to himself as a "so-called Jew."

In March of 1999, during one of my visits to Oldenburg to conduct research for this book, I visited the city's archives. With the help of two of the staff archivists, I learned a number of valuable bits of information concerning the family business, the addresses of their various

My father and mother in their backyard in Cleveland in 1980 with some of the products of Rosemary's green thumb.

homes, and so on. In the midst of conveying these interesting but routine facts, one of the archivists brought me a bombshell: the rabbinical records of the Oldenburg synagogue for the autumn of 1926, the year my father turned thirteen. There I found the record of Günther Ludwig Goldschmidt's bar mitzvah!

I was thunderstruck, no more surprised than had I discovered that my father had actually played third base for the Tigers. My father, the so-called Jew, had been bar mitzvahed? So how Jewish was he, really? And, for that matter, how Jewish was I?

When I returned to the States and visited him at his home in Tucson, I tried to learn more about his coming-of-age ceremony. But he steadfastly insisted that he remembered nothing about it, not even that it took place. In the same conversation I asked him if he thought of himself as a Jew.

"No," he replied instantly.

"But you were bar mitzvahed," I said. "You played in an all-Jewish orchestra."

"Adolf Hitler thought I was Jewish, so I had no choice."

"Both your parents were Jewish. Doesn't that make you a Jew?"

"I don't consider myself a Jew."

On we went, round and round the mulberry bush. He could not bring himself to say, "I am a Jew."

We are all free to believe what we choose to believe, of course, and my father's opinion is that organized religion has contributed more than its share to human strife and unhappiness over the years. He says he is most comfortable considering himself a tolerant man of the world, aligning himself with no religion. It's a position that has been espoused by many contented people, and it makes perfect logical sense to me that my father should be among them.

But again—what if that's not the whole story?

I think it's at least plausible to consider that my father says that he is not a Jew because the association is too painful. Adolf Hitler called him a Jew, and forced him to add "Israel" to his name, and killed his parents and siblings, and would have killed him as well were it not for some fortunate circumstances—all because of this unseen aspect of his identity. I think it's possible that my father got into the habit of spurning that part of his identity while it threatened him, during his years in Germany. Once in America he found it easy to maintain the habit. Why should he be a Jew when to be a Jew brings so much pain?

My father also says that he remembers very little of his younger brother, Helmut. I wonder how much of that amnesia is self-inflicted. To remember details of a life so cruelly lost, especially one he feels responsible for, must be unbearable. As T. S. Eliot has observed, "Human kind cannot bear very much reality."

Both my parents contributed to the sense of unreality that permeated our house while my brother and I were growing up—by making no mention of the immense tree that grew up through the roof and cast its shadow on our lives. My brother and I never heard the story of our family, the story of cruelty, humiliation, and undeserved death. It must have been too painful for my mother and father to even think about what had happened, much less talk about it. I'm sure, as well, that they must have wanted to protect Peter and me from the truth, for fear that we would have trouble sleeping at night or developing a sense of trust. How little they suspected that, even without words, we could feel and absorb the unspoken pain that circulated like dust in the air of our home, and how much we were aware of the darkness, the enormous unknown, but deeply felt, presence that blocked a clear view of the sun.

My awareness of this presence in my life has taken several forms. Early on I developed the family talent for pretending that something that so obviously *was* there wasn't there; this ability to pretend helped me, I think, to cultivate my skills as an actor. I am also aware of a part of my life I keep hidden away, a repository of unspoken grief I think of as the basement. I go down there infrequently, afraid of the ghosts that lurk in the unfriendly darkness. But I know that the basement is always there, never more keenly than when my lovely wife, who feels my fears, whispers to me, "You're safe now."

I share my father's distaste for our age's embrace of victimhood. He, who suffered so much, is uncomfortable with the designation "Holocaust survivor," because, unlike his father and mother and sister and brother, he never spent time in a camp and he emerged physically unscarred from that horrible era. But I know that he carries emotional scars that will never heal, as did my mother until her death, and as his sister Bertha did until her death in 1998, just days before her eighty-ninth birthday. My father respects the direct victims of the Nazis too much to claim that distinction for himself.

And I, who grew up safe and sheltered, surrounded by beautiful music, how can I possibly assume the role of victim without desecrating the memorials to those who died, and diminishing the honor due those who walk among us with faded blue numbers on their arms? I cannot. I must simply embrace the responsibility that has fallen to my generation: we must do our best to understand those eldest still with us, those who have "borne most"; to talk to them, and love them, and bear witness.

WEDNESDAY, NOVEMBER 10, 1999. A cloudy, chilly afternoon in Oldenburg. So much time during the preparation of this book I have spent living in what British historian G. M. Trevelyan called "that land of mystery which we call the past." Today, as the century nears its end, the mystery reaches forward to embrace the present. Sixty-one years after Grandfather Alex marched through these streets at the point of a gun, the citizens of Oldenburg have gathered to retrace his steps.

For more than a decade a group of Oldenburgers has come together every year to commemorate the anniversary of that most shameful moment in their city's 650-year history. The march, which follows the exact route taken by the captive Jews and their Nazi guards, is Oldenburg's way of atoning for the sins of its forebears, its dramatically declared ritual of remembrance.

My brother Peter and I have come to honor our father and grandparents by taking part in the march. We have been welcomed warmly, in particular by Oldenburg's mayor, Hiltrud Neidhardt, and her husband, Roland; by Ali Zahedi, an Iranian-born writer and filmmaker; and by a young Lutheran pastor named Dietgard Demetriades. They are pleased that we have come all this way to join them. We are overwhelmed by their kindness and hospitality.

At three o'clock that afternoon, about three hundred people have gathered in the Pferdemarkt, the market square where Alex and his forty-two fellow prisoners began their ordeal. After a few solemn words by one of this year's organizers, we begin to walk. The line of people stretches for more than a hundred yards: old folks, schoolchildren, mothers with baby carriages, young men pushing bicycles, a woman in a wheelchair. Two marchers carry a banner that reads, "November 10, 1938: Nothing is forgotten. No one is forgotten."

In the whirl of emotions and sensations, I am struck by two things. Policemen, so unlike the police sixty-one years ago, assist us in our effort, stopping traffic at intersections and easing our way. And the silence. Three hundred people walk almost noiselessly through the streets. Pedestrians cease their conversations as we approach. Drivers in automobiles that have been stopped to let us pass wait silently, patiently enduring the traffic. It seems as if the entire city is taking part.

We walk the cobblestone streets of the old city, pass within a block of the site of the Haus der Mode, emerge onto Elisabethstrasse where it borders the Schlossgarten. Suddenly, the clouds part and the late afternoon sun pours its benediction upon us through the golden trees. It is like a peaceful dream.

But then we turn left, and the dream is over. The grim and ugly prison, its dirty red walls topped by razor wire, stands waiting today as it did for my grandfather. Its squat, unarguable presence is a shock, an almost palpable blow. The prison's heavy iron gate has been drawn back, its courtyard stands open. I am painfully aware that I am about to cross its threshold, to recreate that awful step when Alex Goldschmidt's life essentially ended. No.

I notice that Pastor Demetriades is at my side. She has sensed my discomfort. She touches my arm and softly asks my grandfather's name.

"His name was Alex," I say, grateful for the interruption. She nods, and moves off. When we walk into the prison courtyard, I am still deeply aware of the significance of the moment, but my agitation has eased.

Two brief speeches. Two teenage girls sing a Jewish folk song. The march is ended.

My heart numb, I turn to find Peter. But there again is Pastor Demetriades. She takes my hands and looks unblinkingly into my eyes.

"When Cain slew Abel," she says to me, "God marked him with his brother's name so that all could see it. That mark has kept Abel's name alive across the generations. Those whom Germany killed have had their names kept alive by the mark with which God has touched my country."

She smiles sadly and continues, ever so softly.

"And that's the case with Alex—his name shall live forever."

The pastor hugs me then and I sob on her shoulder, crying for those poor people in their unmarked graves, the relatives I never knew and miss so much.

Before I leave the city that cast out my grandfather and has now welcomed me back, I revisit the Oldenburg archives, a modern glass-and-steel building no more than half a mile from the prison. The archivists show me a roster of Oldenburg's citizens. I direct them to the page marked Goldschmidt and inform them that Günther, son of Alex, has a son named Martin who was married in October 1999. They eagerly write down names, addresses, dates of birth. Our family is not extinguished.

ACKNOWLEDGMENTS

In September 1997 I was invited by the Baltimore Museum of Art to introduce the brilliant film called *Thirty-Two Short Films About Glenn Gould.* Before the movie began, I met with the director of the museum's film series, Mark Crispin Miller, who asked me a few questions about my musical background so that he could introduce me. Very briefly, I told him that my parents had played in an all-Jewish orchestra in Nazi Germany, that my father had actually left Germany for safety in Sweden but returned to his homeland to be by the side of the woman who was to become his wife, and that they had managed to get out of Germany just in time, in June 1941.

When I'd finished my tale Professor Miller looked at me a moment and then said, "That's some story. You oughta write a book."

So my list of acknowledgments begins with Professor Miller, who has since joined the faculty at New York University, for casually uttering the comment that directed me to the beginning of the path that has led to the volume you hold in your hands. But the journey would not have been possible without the assistance and encouragement of many other people.

My friend Ted Libbey recommended his agent as a man who would get the necessary job done in a low-key and effective manner, and he was right. My thanks to the man who is now my agent as well, Bob Silverstein. He in turn led me to my sensitive and caring editor at Wiley, Hana Lane, whose critical judgment seems not to be adversely affected in the least by her misguided passion for the Yankees.

My journey in Germany was greatly aided by some wonderful people who opened many doors for me. They include the mayor of Oldenburg, Hiltrud Neidhardt, and her husband, Roland, who have become dear friends. Dr. Friedrich Wissmann of Oldenburg University was immensely helpful during my first visit to my father's city, as was Dr. Udo Elerd of the Oldenburg Stadtmuseum. Thanks also to Rudolf Wyrsch and Hans Raykowski at the Oldenburg Archives. Filmmaker Farschid Ali Zahedi and Pastor Dietgard Demetriades made me feel welcome in ways too deep for words.

My research in Berlin proved fruitful thanks to the assistance of Jürgen Wittneben and Hansjoerg Schirmbeck at the Akademie der Künste and Irene

Runge of the *Jüdische Gemeinde*. And many thanks for assistance both musical and culinary to ex-pat extraordinaire Paul Moor.

In Düsseldorf I learned what I could about my mother and Grandfather Julian thanks to the extraordinary efforts of Angela Genger and Hildegard Jakobs of the Mahn- und Gedenkstätte. Thanks also to Kurt and Barbara Suchy for information and hospitality.

And in Frankfurt, Joachim Martini and Judith Freise proved to be invaluable sources, superb musicians, and wonderful new friends. *Vielen Dank!*

Here in America, my thanks begin with Aaron Kornblum, reference archivist at the United States Holocaust Memorial Museum, for his tireless efforts and bracing humor. Many thanks also to his USHMM colleagues Scott Miller and Susan Snyder.

Steve Robinson of Nebraska Public Radio lent a sympathetic ear and introduced me to Professor Alan Steinweis, the world's foremost authority on Hans Hinkel. Professor Steinweis then introduced me to the deeply knowledgeable Sybil Milton, who in turn introduced me to Angela Genger in Düsseldorf, thus proving once again that one thing leads to another.

At National Public Radio, my friends Laura Bertran and Penny Hain read early drafts of the manuscript and offered a number of helpful suggestions, while Kee Malesky cast her eagle eyes over the full manuscript and made many critical saves. And a special cartographical thank-you to Andy Trudeau.

Thank you to Michael Dirda, senior editor of the *Washington Post Book World*, for tracking down that Faulkner quotation. And my deepest thanks for superb translations and warm friendship to Alice Kelly and Margot Dembo.

Special thanks to seven marvelous people who lived the experiences I have tried to describe in this book and who generously shared their memories with me: Henry Bloch, Gerti Totschek Colbert, Werner Golde, Hilda Klestadt Jonas, Hannah Kroner, Henry Meyer, and Kurt Michaelis.

I do not know how to thank the man who shared the most, my father, George Goldsmith. I can only say, "I love you."

Thanks and love also to my father's life partner of more than a decade, Emily Erwin. Thanks to my brother, Peter, for sharing the final stages of the journey. And thank you to my in-laws, Fred and Shirley Roach, for providing that cozy upstairs room for those final pages.

Finally, heartfelt thanks to some wonderful friends who lent their constant encouragement and support: Miles and Susan Hoffman, Susan Schilperoort and Christopher Kendall, and Glen and Lauren Howard.

And thanks always and forever, till salmon sing in the street, to my wife, Amy.

BIBLIOGRAPHY

Akademie der Künste, ed. *Geschlossene Vorstellung: Der Jüdische Kulturbund in Deutschland, 1933–1941.* Berlin: Edition Hentrich, 1992.

Bullock, Alan. *Hitler: A Study in Tyranny.* New York: Harper & Row, 1964.

Dawidowicz, Lucy S. *The War Against the Jews, 1933–1945.* New York: Bantam, 1975.

Faust, Anselm. *Die Kristallnacht im Rheinland.* Düsseldorf: Schwann, 1987.

Felstiner, Mary Lowenthal. *To Paint Her Life: Charlotte Salomon in the Nazi Era.* Berkeley: University of California Press, 1997.

Fleming, Gerald. *Hitler and the Final Solution.* Berkeley: University of California Press, 1982.

Freise, Judith, and Joachim Martini. *Jüdische Musikerinnen und Musiker in Frankfurt, 1933–1942: Musik als Form geistigen Widerstandes.* Frankfurt: Verlag Dr. Otto Lembeck, 1990.

Friedlaender, Saul. *Nazi Germany and the Jews, Vol. 1: The Years of Persecution, 1933–1939.* New York: HarperCollins, 1997.

Geisel, Eike, and Henryk Broder, eds. *Premiere und Pogrom: Der Jüdische Kulturbund, 1933–1941, Texte und Bilder.* Berlin: Siedler, 1992.

Genger, Angela, and Kerstin Griese, eds. *Aspekte Jüdischen Lebens.* Düsseldorf: Mahn- und Gedenkstätte, 1997.

Gilbert, Martin. *The Holocaust: A History of the Jews of Europe During the Second World War.* New York: Henry Holt, 1985.

Goertz, Dieter. *Juden in Oldenburg, 1930–1938.* Oldenburg: Isensee Verlag, 1988.

Gutman, Israel, ed. *Encyclopedia of the Holocaust.* New York: Macmillan, 1995.

Kater, Michael H. *The Twisted Muse: Musicians and Their Music in the Third Reich.* New York: Oxford University Press, 1997.

Levi, Erik. *Music in the Third Reich.* London: Macmillan, 1994.

Richarz, Monika, ed. *Jewish Life in Germany: Memoirs from Three Centuries.* Trans. S. Rosenfeld. Bloomington: Indiana University Press, 1991.

Roth, Andrew, and Michael Frajman. *Jewish Berlin.* Berlin: Goldapple Publishing, 1998.

Rovit, Rebecca, and Alvin Goldfarb, eds. *Theatrical Performance During the Holocaust.* Baltimore: The Johns Hopkins University Press, 1999.

Schaap, Klaus. "Der Novemberpogrom von 1938." In *Die Geschichte der Oldenburger Juden und ihrer Vernichtung*, ed. Udo Elerd and Ewald Gaessler. Oldenburg: Isensee Verlag, 1988.

Shirer, William L. *The Rise and Fall of the Third Reich: A History of Nazi Germany.* New York: Simon & Schuster, 1959.

Steinweis, Alan E. *Art, Ideology, and Economics in Nazi Germany: The Reich Chambers of Music, Theater, and the Visual Arts.* Chapel Hill: University of North Carolina Press, 1993.

Thomas, Gordon, and Max Morgan Witts. *Voyage of the Damned.* New York: Amereon, Ltd., 1974.

United States Holocaust Memorial Museum. *Voyage of the St. Louis.* Washington: USHMM, 1999.

Zuccotti, Susan. *The Holocaust, the French, and the Jews.* Lincoln: University of Nebraska Press, 1999.

INDEX